The Eclipse of Counci

Council housing is widely criticised, rejected by government and is the object of waning public support. Yet at one time direct state provision accounted for one-third of the nation's housing stock. How did this decline come about? Ian Cole and Robert Furbey trace the emergence, rise and decline of council housing and explore its fluctuating status within the welfare state.

The authors ask whether council tenure was misconceived from the start and whether it should now be seen as a suitable case for reform, or for total abolition. They examine why, of all welfare sectors, public housing has been subjected to the most intense attack by the Conservatives since 1979, and consider why it has proved so vulnerable. Their detailed analysis charts the development of policies towards council housing and the long-term retreat into a residual tenure. A distinctive aspect of the account is its analysis of the quality of housing offered by local authorities, and the responsiveness, democracy and efficiency of housing management. Particular emphasis is given to the deal which users have received from local authorities and their varying responses to that deal. The authors also review New Right arguments for the final eclipse of state housing while at the same time discussing initiatives to reform it.

The Eclipse of Council Housing presents a lucid study of a key social policy issue which is central to the current housing crisis, and challenges the view that council housing should be consigned to the scrapheap. It will be invaluable to all students and lecturers in social policy, housing, town planning and urbolicy and housing professionals.

Ian Cole is Head o**Furbey** is Principal Lecturer in the Housing Division, School of Urban and Regional Studies, Sheffield Hallam University.

The State of Welfare
Edited by Mary Langan

Nearly half a century after its post-war consolidation, the British welfare state is once again at the centre of political controversy. After a decade in which the role of the state in the provision of welfare was steadily reduced in favour of the private, voluntary and informal sectors, with relatively little public debate or resistance, the further extension of the new mixed economy of welfare in the spheres of health and education became a major political issue in the early 1990s. At the same time the impact of deepening recession has begun to expose some of the deficiencies of market forces in areas, such as housing and income maintenance, where their role had expanded dramatically during the 1980s. *The State of Welfare* provides a forum for continuing the debate about the services we need in the 1990s.

Titles of related interest also in *The State of Welfare Series*

The Dynamics of British Health Policy
Stephen Harrison, David Hunter and Christopher Pollitt

Radical Social Work Today
Edited by Mary Langan and Phil Lee

Taking Child Abuse Seriously
The Violence Against Children Study Group

Ideologies of Welfare: from Dreams to Disillusion
John Clarke, Ian Cochrane and Carol Smart

Women, Oppression and Social Work
Edited by Mary Langan and Lesley Day

Managing Poverty: the Limits of Social Assistance
Carol Walker

The Eclipse of Council Housing

Ian Cole and Robert Furbey

London and New York

First published 1994
by Routledge
11 New Fetter Lane, London EC4P 4EE

Simultaneously published in the USA and Canada
by Routledge
29 West 35th Street, New York, NY 10001

© 1994 Ian Cole and Robert Furbey

Typeset in Times by LaserScript, Mitcham, Surrey
Printed and bound in Great Britain by
T.J. Press (Padstow) Ltd, Padstow, Cornwall

British Library Cataloguing in Publication Data
A catalogue record for this book is available from the British Library

Library of Congress Cataloging in Publication Data
Cole, Ian, 1952–
   The eclipse of council housing/Ian Cole and Robert Furbey.
   p. cm. – (The State of Welfare)
   Includes bibliographical references and index.
   1. Public housing – Great Britain. I. Furbey, Robert, II. Title.
   III. Series.
   HD7288.78.G7C64   1993
363.5′85′0941 – dc20   93-15487
                                                       CIP

ISBN 0–415–09899–8
     0–415–09900–5 (pbk)

'You can make your home the base for your adventures,
but it is absurd to make the base itself an adventure.'

Aneurin Bevan, *In Place of Fear*, 1952

Contents

Acknowledgements

The government is 'delighted', apparently, by the response of academic institutions in enabling more people to pass through the doors of British higher education. Well, that's good to know anyway. But spiralling staff–student ratios and heightened demands to secure research grants and to engage in other exercises in 'income generation' can certainly play havoc with uncosted activities such as writing a book.

Looking back, our timetable for completing this book was not attuned to the increasing and inescapable other claims upon our time and energy. And so, as our progress slowed, we were fortunate indeed to have in Mary Langan a series editor who offered just the right combination of encouragement, tolerance and constructive criticism needed to keep us on course during the more dispiriting times.

We have been able to draw also on a particularly supportive group of friends and colleagues for their comments on draft material and for their wider companionship. Particular thanks are due to Peter Arnold, Jane Darke, Christine Davies, Colin Foster, Barry Goodchild, Rob Sykes and Helen Ward. And, when all grumbles concerning staff–student ratios are over, we gladly record our debt to the stimulus and dialogue provided by the students with whom we have shared ideas in recent years as they worked for their BA Housing Studies, Postgraduate Diploma in Housing Administration or BA Urban Studies. In the end, of course, responsibility for the final manuscript is ours.

Vera Day has provided a wonderfully accurate and fast typing service. Her patience and good humour are all the more remarkable, as she has been working with two authors who are often flying around on different orbits and who insist on using different word-processing systems.

And our final thanks are to those closest of all to us who have lived with us through the whole project. Without them, this might have been completed more quickly – but it would not have been worth doing at all.

Ian Cole and Robert Furbey

Series editor's preface

'Nobody is noticing how we are dismantling the old welfare state of Clement Attlee and completely rebuilding.'

Kenneth Clarke, Home Secretary, *Guardian*, 2 April 1993

Mr Clarke, formerly minister of both health and education, was concerned that gloom over the recession and controversy over Britain's relations with the European Community were distracting public attention away from the government's welfare reforms. Yet, as the *Guardian* commented, 'we're noticing the first bit alright, it's the rebuilding that's a wee bit harder to spot' (*Guardian*, 2 April 1993).

For the duration of Margaret Thatcher's government, from 1979 to 1990, despite all the anti-welfare rhetoric, the welfare state remained largely intact. However, there could be little doubt that, since John Major took over the Tory leadership, and particularly since his surprise election victory in April 1992, the process of 'dismantling' the welfare state rapidly has gathered momentum.

The introduction of the 'internal market' into the national health service, and the emergence of 'trust hospitals' and GP 'budget holders' marked a fundamental change in the system established by Clement Attlee's Health Minister, Aneurin Bevan, in 1948. Parallel changes in the education system have effectively dismantled the framework of local authority control introduced in the 1944 Act, even before Attlee came to power. Proposals for an end to the universal character of Child Benefit and state pensions to curb the burgeoning social security bill would abandon a key feature of Beveridge's celebrated 1942 report.

The community care reforms, which came into effect on the very day that Clarke made his speech about 'dismantling' and 'rebuilding', symbolise the state of welfare in Britain in 1993. Though these reforms were presented in the rhetoric of user empowerment and consumer choice, it was clear that the government's central concern was to reduce social security spending on institutional care by handing responsibility – and a substantial funding shortfall – over to local authorities. On the eve of the introduction of the new arrangements a survey of local authorities revealed plans for cuts of more than £500 million, leading to the closure of old people's homes, day centres and nurseries, and higher charges for home helps, meals on wheels, etc. (*Guardian*, 30 March 1993). The government's cynicism was further exposed in guidelines to councils on how to avoid being sued by individuals who were assessed as needing a service the council was unable to provide.

Although Mr Clarke feared nobody was noticing the restructuring of welfare because of current controversies over the budget and the Maastricht Treaty, there is a more substantial reason for the lack of public debate or resistance to these trends. In part 'nobody is noticing' the destruction of the welfare state, because hardly anybody now defends the system introduced by Attlee and his colleagues in the post-war Labour government. The views expressed by key contributors to Labour's National Commission on Social Justice confirm the trend of the main opposition party to move towards the abandonment of the principles of universalism and state welfare, in favour of selectivity and market forces. When even the official opposition has lost confidence in the welfare state it is not surprising that its structures can be dismantled without causing too much public fuss.

The new consensus in favour of a radical restructuring of the post-war welfare state has transformed the terms of the debate about social policy. For half a century an anti-welfare, pro-market Right confronted a powerful social democratic consensus in support of a comprehensive state welfare system and made little headway. Now the tables are turned as radical confidence in state intervention in welfare, as in industry, has collapsed. Thus even though critics expose the damaging consequences of the market in welfare – hospitals that run out of money for operations before the end of the financial year, councils that lack the resources to support carers in the community – the absence of any conviction that there is an alternative means that protests are muted and resistance minimal.

The changing terms of the debate about the future of the post-war welfare state have influenced *The State of Welfare* series since our first book, *Ideologies of Welfare*, by John Clarke, Allan Cochrane and Carol Smart, was published in 1987. For much of this period the direction of policy remained uncertain as the government proceeded tentatively against powerful vested interests and pressure groups in key areas of welfare. Yet it is striking that it was in the sphere of housing, the subject of this latest book, that the agenda of the New Right was first and most successfully advanced. The close association between the social democratic tradition and the unpopular tower blocks and council estates of the 1960s put it on the defensive from the start. In this book – *The Eclipse of Council Housing* – Ian Cole and Robert Furbey examine the far-reaching changes in the role of council housing in the wider context of the restructuring of the British welfare state. We have much to learn from their discussions and conclusions.

Mary Langan
April 1993

Introduction

Council housing is facing extinction. Since the advent of industrialisation, Britain has followed a unique path among developed capitalist countries by launching mass building programmes in the public sector, with dwellings owned, managed and maintained by local authorities. However, by the year 2000, council housing may have become a historical relic. It is conceivable that three-quarters of the population will be living in owner-occupied dwellings, with rented housing for the remaining 25 per cent of households being provided by a mixture of private landlords, housing associations, trusts and tenant co-operatives. In many local housing markets this tenure configuration is already emerging. Direct state provision to meet housing need is rapidly on the wane.

The scale and recency of this change is, by any standards, remarkable. When the first Thatcher government was elected in 1979, over 30 per cent of the population lived in housing provided by the state. Only eight years later, a government White Paper was explicit about ending the role of local authorities as providers of new housing: 'there will no longer be the presumption that the local authority should take direct action to meet new or increasing demands' (HMSO 1987: 6). This position has been reinforced by a commitment to transfer the ownership and control of the existing stock – whether through direct sales, transfers to other landlords or policies such as turning rent payments into mortgages. This sharp reduction in direct state provision in the housing market is a major political and social transformation which demands a fully articulated critical evaluation. Yet the sheer pace of policy change – in financial subsidy and control, in redefining the role of housing associations and local authorities, in expanding owner-occupation and reshaping patterns of housing investment – has often seemed to inhibit a longer range perspective.

In this book, we suggest that the emergence and consequences of this strategy can best be understood by a historical analysis of state housing set in the wider context of the restructuring of the British welfare state. The processes affecting council housing are not unique. In the past fifteen years, the state's role in providing a range of public services has come under sustained attack. The Thatcher governments in particular left few stones unturned in a bid to transform assumptions and expectations about the role of the public sector. Policies such as the opting out provision for state schools and NHS hospitals, and greater selectivity in income maintenance, have come to represent the most comprehensive overhaul of the post-war welfare state since its inception. Yet the claims of achieving a 'welfare revolution' have often been stronger on rhetoric than impact. Public support for the principle of state-provided education and health services has, for example, proved stubbornly persistent.

Housing has been different. During the 1980s, the government was able to translate its ideology into a decisive policy programme. How can we account for this success in 'breaking the spell' (Anderson 1981) of state provision in housing? How has the government been able to achieve the aim of amputating the housing arm of the welfare state? What has been the political and consumer response to this process? Is the demise of state housing irreversible or is there a way back for public provision? To what extent does the strategy foreshadow a similar process in health or education? This book attempts to answer such questions from a historical standpoint, and speculates on likely problems and challenges for housing policies in the future.

Our basic purpose in writing this book is to develop an understanding of the changing role of council housing in the wider process of the restructuring of the British welfare state. Our analysis is based on three major propositions. First, we argue that, of all state services, council housing has always been the most vulnerable component of the package of ideas, services and institutions collectively known as the welfare state. The insecure and uncertain status of the state's intervention in the housing market has thus made it particularly susceptible to a sustained ideological and financial attack. Second, we suggest that working-class support for the principle and practice of state housing has always been rather fragmented and equivocal, especially in comparison to other aspects of the welfare state. It has not been difficult for governments to capitalise on long-standing divisions in the working class while undermining council housing and to exploit the negative experience of many tenants about the design, management and maintenance of this sector. A third theme is the extent to which the state's role in the housing market is being restructured and transformed rather than abandoned altogether. This process carries social, political and economic risks which are currently giving rise to serious problems in the British housing market. Paradoxically, this may yet create the opportunity for a new and more popular public sector role in housing provision.

We will expand on each of these themes by way of introduction.

THE RESTRICTED SCOPE OF STATE HOUSING

It is undeniable that housing policies since 1979 have transformed the nature of the housing market through such measures as the reduction of subsidies to state housing, the transfer and sale of public housing stock, and the vigorous promotion of owner-occupation. However, the state's role in the British housing market has been hedged with contradiction, inconsistency and ambiguity from the outset. Government strategy since 1979 has simply made this more transparent, through a quickening of pace rather than any startling shift of focus. The demise of council housing may now be on the cards, but the tenure was in a critical condition well before Margaret Thatcher became Prime Minister.

As we explore the origins of council housing in Chapters 2 and 3, we develop the argument that housing has never been accorded an equivalent status or legitimacy to state health, income maintenance or education services. The dictates of private property landlord/tenant relations, the influence of private finance and land ownership, the balance of political forces and changing economic priorities by successive governments, have ensured that the dominant definition of housing is as a commodity rather than a social right. Changes in the state's intervention in the housing market have been reflected in the type, tenure and quantity of dwellings built at different stages over the century – but state provision has throughout been the handmaiden to private market processes.

In Part I, we argue that state housing has not so much failed as been denied the chance to succeed in the first place, as another review of the history of council housing has pointed out.

> Despite the five million dwellings that have been built by 'social landlords' since 1890 the sober story to be told is often one of lost opportunities, wrong turnings, and above all of a continuous battle to establish the legitimacy of social renting as part of the solution to the nation's housing needs.
>
> (Lowe and Hughes 1991: 2)

Our historical overview in Part One seeks to show that policies towards state housing were not simply 'lost opportunities' prompted by casual government neglect, nor incompetent local authority investment or management procedures. Rather, they illustrate a longer-term process which marginalised the sector – outside times of immediate post-war crisis and shortage – and promoted owner-occupation as the most desirable tenure form for the majority of households.

We suggest that the working class as a whole never formulated an unequivocal demand for the development of local authority housing as the solution to the failure of the private market. Working-class demands ranged from better standards to rent control, from new building to more amenities, from improved conditions to state subsidies (Wilding 1972; Byrne and Damer 1980, Swenarton 1981). Yet the essential point is that these did not coalesce simply into pressure for municipal landlordism *per se*.

While we would accept that the failure of the private market to provide affordable housing and reduce the contradiction between rent levels and wages, coupled with growing working-class power, cleared the way for state intervention and subsidy, this need not have taken the specific form of new housing built, managed and allocated by local authorities. The 170,000 council dwellings built between 1919 and 1923 were, then, the result of a particular form of subsidy and government policy, and specific historical contingencies rather than the inevitable outcome of a mass working-class campaign for local government intervention.

Neither should we assume that, once provided, municipal housing was accepted as an indisputable bonus. In many cases, local authorities – controlled by land and property owners and various petty bourgeois interests – were far from ideal landlords. High rents were also a deterrent to semi-skilled and unskilled working-class private tenants and many continued to seek an improvement in their housing situation through the private sector (Bowley 1945). In comparison with more universal services which subsequently formed the welfare state, access to council housing was highly restricted and dependent on levels of household income.

The historical perspective in Part I suggests that council housing was viewed from the start as a flawed, expensive and selective service, pitted with constraints and clearly subservient to private market logic and interests. For many working-class households municipal landlords remained an irrelevance or an imposition, rather than a guaranteed means of securing decent rented housing at a reasonable cost. Furthermore, the steady retreat from council properties built to high standards in the 1920s turned to a headlong rush by the mid-1930s. Similarly, in the post-war era, the high water mark of Bevan housing in the late 1940s soon gave way to inferior design, standards and materials.

Of course, housing policies are far more than the result of parliamentary legislation. They hinge on the shifting balance between dominant economic and political forces and countervailing class or community pressures. The development of state services has often owed more to working-class political action and labour movement pressure than the enlightened (or cunning) benevolence of dominant economic interests. A direct assault on public services runs a risk of provoking widespread resistance and collective action to defend hard-won gains. However, insistent attacks on council housing have often prompted little more than a murmur of protest or dissent.

Some of the reasons for this response may be outlined here. Council tenants are becoming a powerless minority as the social composition of housing tenure changes. The development of state housing on a large scale was primarily a response to the political threat posed by demands from organised labour, and the skilled working class comprised many of the original beneficiaries. The residualisation of council housing has been a two-fold process over the past fifty or sixty years (Malpass and Murie 1990). First, many traditional council tenants have now been attracted into home ownership, either directly or through buying their property under the Right to Buy scheme. Second, public housing has increasingly provided for those without the economic power to move into home ownership – the poor, elderly and unemployed – and without the political power to demand a better service. This process of residualisation and polarisation has resulted in the most marginalised, rather than most powerful, section of the popu- lation living in state housing.

We will, however, suggest that any account of the eclipse of state housing must go beyond reference to changing subsidy regimes, or the impact of macro-economic forces in different periods. Housing is more than an expensive, physical product provided through a distinctive kind of market. It affects the quality of people's lives in personal and complex ways. A fully developed analysis of council housing in Britain must there- fore embrace an evaluation of the actual *experience* of tenants in the sector – paying their rent, improving their homes, receiving management and maintenance services from the council and, occasionally, acting on their collective concerns to advance their interests.

THE EXPERIENCE OF STATE HOUSING

Growing levels of disenchantment with state housing in Britain have em- erged from the actual experience of living on council estates. We argue in Part II that the popularity of housing tenure reflects more than its status as an economic commodity. The consumer response to housing hinges on qualitative aspects, as well as quantitative peaks and troughs in production or subsidy level. We think it is crucial to convey a sense of state housing as a lived experience for millions of people and not just a historical artefact. Housing is an object for use, a source of status and identity, the locus of domestic labour and a framework in which class, gender or ethnic divisions may be changed or reinforced.

This focus turns our attention to the use-value of public housing in terms of changing design and amenity standards, the underlying assumptions about gender roles, family relations and cultural differences, the quality of housing management as a service, and the collective response by tenants to such issues.

Compared with other welfare professions, housing management has developed in a distinctive (and largely unexplored) manner. The ambiguous status of public housing – a stillborn social service lodged within a capital- ist dynamic of property relations – is crystallised in the contradictory pressures on housing management. Housing management has not acquired an integrated sense of professional identity to the same extent as other welfare services, such as social work. The vulnerable status of council housing in the British welfare state has been matched by an equal vul- nerability in the professional status of housing management. The local authority housing service has been infused with a strong element of control and containment, structured around the landlord–tenant relationship. The power relationship between service provider and consumer, between pro- fessional and client, has been more explicit than in other public services. The ethos of housing management has often made it difficult for council tenants to see state housing as 'their' service. The negative consumer experience of state housing is not wholly due to crumbling bricks and mortar, high rents or insensitive design. It has often been compounded by the impact of paternalistic and unresponsive housing management, forever reminding tenants that decent housing was a commodity which came at a price rather than as a basic social right.

In many accounts of housing policy, the individual and collective re- sponses of users are often marginal. Yet we feel that this perspective should be integral to *any* analysis confirming the experiential aspect of state housing provision, rather than its purely fiscal or physical attributes. The views and actions of council tenants themselves demand attention. In Part II, we examine and seek to interpret the apparent quiescence of most tenants confronted with the marginalisation of council housing. We suggest that the residualisation of council housing initially exposed the fragmentation of the tenants' movement as a collective force, with some local exceptions, and this process eased the way for an intensified attack on the values and practice of public housing. Ironically, the process to force through the transfer of council housing to other landlords, following the 1988 Housing Act, has had the effect of re-collectivising the experience of living in council housing and has prompted a renaissance of the tenants' movement.

COUNCIL HOUSING AND THE RESTRUCTURING OF THE WELFARE STATE

To what extent do changing government policies and popular assumptions about the declining role of council housing mirror wider doubts and criti- cisms about state welfare services?

It is widely acknowledged that economic recession, the rise of unemployment, demographic change and the political ascendancy of the New Right during the 1980s led to a process of restructuring in the British welfare state (Wicks 1987; McCarthy 1989). It is important to note the uneven impact and pace of this process in different public services. The first two Thatcher governments, for example, did not launch an attack along the entire frontier of state welfare services; rather, a series of sporadic incursions was made, targeted at its weakest points of defence. This selective approach proved more effective, and was certainly more insidious than an all-out challenge to the core principles of state welfare. In this process, the vulnerability of council housing as an insecure foundation of the welfare state – in terms of its origins, limited coverage, cost and exposure to market processes – was clearly demonstrated.

In Part III, we show that housing bore the brunt of the Conservative government attack on the welfare state during the 1980s; and council housing conveniently served as a symbol of the negative features of the public sector – inefficient, bureaucratic, remote, mismanaged and wasteful. It was a good place to begin a long-term process of structural transformation without provoking intense public resistance.

At the beginning of the government's third consecutive term of office in 1987, a more ambitious welfare strategy emerged as a sign of the increasing self-confidence of the Thatcherite project. In particular, state education and health were to be given a dose of the medicine meted out to council housing. Certain features can be discerned as preconditions of this process – an uncertain level of public support, the strains of consumer discontent, a perceived expenditure crisis and a concern with declining standards.

The strategy to restructure health and education services was intended to follow a similar path to policies towards public housing in the 1980s. The first step involves a reorientation of central–local relations, through greater central control of capital and current expenditure, targeted funding, the launch of demonstration projects circumventing local authority involvement, and the creation of new organisational structures. A second feature is an emphasis on different management styles, involving the introduction of performance targets and assessment, the espousal of a 'business' orientation, an attack on the influence of state professionals, and the development of new means of monitoring and control. A third stage invokes the rhetoric of consumer choice, providing alternatives to monopoly state provision through the creation, as a first step, of 'quasi-markets' (Le Grand 1990). This is often coupled with the introduction of material incentives for private provision to encourage con-sumers to exercise their choice in a particular manner, thereby marginalising the remaining users of state services. All these elements were present in the Conservatives' housing strategy in the 1980s and they became increasingly prominent in their health and education policies as well.

Our analysis in Part III does not imply that there was a detailed blueprint which was initially applied to council housing and then pursued by health, education and social security ministers. However, the experience of the politically successful assault on state housing in the early 1980s undoubtedly provided important lessons and clues to the government's welfare programme. At the same time, both the strong populist motif of Thatcherism and the less overt ideological tendencies of John Major's subsequent strategy demanded a certain flexibility, in which programmes could be fashioned to meet the changing requirements of economic prospects, real or manufactured public moods, media reaction and political gain. In practice, the form, content and pace of the strategy for the residualisation of state health, education, income maintenance and social services have varied considerably.

The process of residualising state housing has been deep-rooted and decisive, but it has yet to culminate in the total collapse of the sector which seemed likely in the mid-1980s. The transformation of council housing has met with intermittent resistance from local authorities, pressure groups and tenants themselves. The criticisms from the Right about the management, design and funding of public sector housing have been countered by ideas aiming in various ways to improve the service. Proposals have ranged from a redirection of overall central government priorities to different funding mechanisms for investment and maintenance, a new emphasis on management skills and organisational structures and processes and a fresh commitment to greater tenant involvement.

In Part III, we consider various initiatives to revitalise council housing which originated at the local level during the 1980s, through programmes for decentralisation, tenant participation and customer care. They barely amounted to an alternative blueprint for a national housing policy for Britain in the 1990s. Nevertheless, these strategies merit consideration because they provide pointers for a renewal of a public housing sector under different political and economic conditions. Our analysis therefore concludes by reflecting on the form that a more responsive and popular public housing service might take in the future.

The need to assess the prospects for reforming the socially rented sector in the housing market has become more pressing in recent years. It is prompted by the growing evidence of the failings in the majority housing tenure, as the long-standing success story of owner-occupation started to turn sour. In the early 1990s, the combination of high interest rates, economic recession, falling house prices and rising mortgage repossessions all emphasised the importance of sustaining a range of housing options – not least through a viable and responsive social housing sector. This theme is taken up in the Conclusion to the book.

HOUSING AND THE STATE

At the heart of our overall analysis lies a conception of the changing role of the state – both in general welfare provision and in the housing market as a whole. It is misleading to assume that the decline of council housing somehow signals that the state's role and significance is being correspondingly reduced. The process is more complex. An understanding is needed of the roots of state intervention in the British housing market, the continuing dominance of private property rights, and the extent to which public housing has been consistently marginalised. A broadly historical perspective is required to place recent policies towards council housing in their proper context.

Before we begin to trace through pressures leading to state intervention in housing, however, we need to establish more clearly ourselves what we mean by the state. There is a vast and often arcane theoretical literature on the function of the state in modern capitalist societies. This can only be presented in outline if it is not to deflect us from the central themes in this book. Yet a broad indication of our approach to the state is an essential first step if we are to develop our thoughts on how changes in the housing market are suggestive of a broader restructuring in the role and function of the state, shifting in a complex way the boundaries between the public and the private sectors. This is the focus of Chapter 1.

1 Interpreting the role of the state

RATIONAL MODELS OF STATE WELFARE

In the Introduction we acknowledged that council housing has been a constitutive, if rather peripheral, element of the British welfare state. Our subsequent account of state housing policy and provision therefore needs to be situated first in the context of conceptual explanations about the state. For most of the twentieth century the dominant explanation of the growth of state welfare activities has involved an understanding of such developments as a response by an essentially neutral state instrument to emerging 'problems' as perceived by the electorate, by 'reformers', or by experts within the state machine itself. According to this view, policy is directed by a 'rational planning model' comprising three stages: surveying the facts of the problem; identifying the best solution; and implementing the necessary policy to remedy the problem (Pickvance 1982: 19). Hence, as the negative corollaries of the nineteenth-century urbanisation became clear, so the state responded to the agitation of reformers and the findings of its own Royal Commissions by introducing, first, limited 'permissive' legislation, but later more wide-ranging powers culminating in the complex housing and planning system of the period since 1945.

According to this view, in expanding its activities of housing regulation and direct production the state is performing a necessary function which permits the resolution of dilemmas posed by the coming of industrial society. Such a system 'had' to emerge if society was not to be threatened by rising crime, disease, illiteracy and political dissent. The state is benevolent, able to identify the 'reasonable' solution to identified problems, and to act in the interests of society as a whole by enacting reform to permit peaceful progress into the future. In Tawney's words, 'the causes of the movement are not obscure. It is the natural consequence of the simultaneous development of an industrial civilisation and of political democracy' (quoted in George and Wilding 1985: 85).

The attractions of such an account of the state's activities for the state itself and its personnel are fairly clear. State policy is identified as responsive, functionally necessary, far-sighted, and reflecting the interests not of a sectional group but of society as a whole. It is a view of state welfare which may be equated with a 'Whig interpretation of history' in which historical change

> is preconceived as 'progress', and *accounted for* as a movement closer toward the present . . . . Such history – in the more specific context of urban studies – traces a continuous process of 'onward and upward' policy development and improvement in the chaos of Victorian urbanisation, through successive stages of legislative innovation, to the present-day system.
>
> (Rees and Lambert 1985: 8–9, emphasis in original)

It is, therefore, an account which bestows legitimacy upon the role of state bureaucrats and professionals who can convince others (and possibly themselves) that their work constitutes a rational technical route to the good life.

The last two decades, however, have seen a growing disillusionment with this rationalist model of the state as a neutral instrument for meeting the essentially agreed functional needs of a changing society. In part, the critique of this conventional view was prompted by the events and changed economic circumstances after 1973. The growth of state expenditure permitted by the 'long boom' of the post-war years sustained a growth in welfare services which could be financed without any social group experiencing a real decline in material living standards. With the onset of recession, however, the welfare state came under fierce attack by a resurgent New Right and cuts in services were implemented, notwithstanding the persistence of the problems which welfare provisions were supposed to ameliorate. In this context, the legitimacy of welfare professionals has been threatened and state personnel have been obliged to recognise that the services which they administer cannot be regarded as part of a rational and irreversible progress towards a reformed society. Rather, the welfare state must be understood as existing within a society characterised by a changing balance of political power instead of an enduring, apolitical rationality (Rees and Lambert 1985: 12).

Our analysis of council housing is clearly linked to its role as one aspect of the British welfare state; but this was rarely subject to detailed theoretical analysis until the 1970s. The unique British academic discipline of social administration, for example, developed out of a set of commonly held ideas and assumptions about social welfare. The analysis of the welfare state, and the role of council housing within it, was lodged in a pragmatic and empiricist idiom, devoted to incremental reform and focused on administrative detail. The intervention of the central and local state into areas of social need was viewed as unquestionably beneficent; the collection of adequate research data on issues such as low income, educational opportunity and poor housing was the passport towards improving conditions and securing social justice. The discipline of social administration seemed beyond theory, beyond dogma and beyond reproach – its essence was an intellectual infused process of 'do-gooding'.

As the canons of social administration came under increasing scrutiny during the 1970s, the overt assumptions of the perspective were exposed, and its debt to Fabianism made more clear. For Fabians, change was to be promoted through incremental reform, rather than revolution, instigated by administrators, professionals and elected representatives blessed with knowledge and ideas provided by social scientists. The state intervened to promote individual welfare through the evolutionary development of enlightened social policies.

Fabian ideas were evident in the Minority Report of the 1908 Poor Law Commission and were increasingly incorporated into the Labour Party's programmes in the inter-war period. The triumph of Fabian values, however, had to wait until 1945.

> The construction of the welfare state in the wake of Labour's election victory in 1945 seemed to bring the translation of the Fabian dream into an only slightly flawed reality. It promised a new society based on a philosophy of gradualism and collectivist solutions organised through the state and backed by the rational analysis of social science experts.
>
> (Clarke *et al.* 1987: 89)

Post-war Britain, it seemed, was secure in its settled world of Keynesian economic management and 'cradle to the grave' welfare provision. The Butskellite consensus of the 1950s and 1960s ensured that arguments about the scale and character of state intervention were only played out in a minor key. Fabianism had initially gained prominence by debunking the apparent pretensions and dogmas of Marxist and *laissez-faire* theorists. Bland empiricism did not always prevail, as the incisive contributions of writers such as Richard Titmuss and T.H. Marshall testify (Abel-Smith and Titmuss 1987; Rees 1985). However, the core theoretical assumptions of Fabianism remained largely unexplored, as any conceptual uncertainties were obscured by relentless 'radical earnestness'. The key task for Fabianism was not to specify the structural contradictions of capitalism, or to check out its own epistemological foundations as a philosophy. Rather, its role was to resolve an array of residual social problems through gaining the ear of government ministers and devising efficient social welfare programmes. The rationalist model of policy-making was assumed by Fabian analysis, in which governments achieved their objectives by relying on expert knowledge, professional judgement and applied research. Fabians 'tended to appoint themselves to the role of intelligence officers of the welfare state with the task of consolidating its achievements and guiding its future development' (Lee and Raban 1988: 25).

The fragility of the Fabian analysis of the state became more evident once the period of sustained post-war economic growth came to an end in the 1970s. Critics from Right and Left uncovered the blind spots and weaknesses in the approach – its reliance on an expanding tax base to finance welfare reform, its failure to recognise the tenacity of market mechanisms, its assumption that the boom–slump economic cycle was over for good, its neglect of class forces and interests. Above all, the Fabian view was challenged on the basis that the welfare state had failed to achieve its objectives of social justice and greater equality. The fallibilities of the Fabian perspective left it open to the ideological and political critique of the New Right, which set itself against the view that government 'must be the chief architect of welfare provision' (Taylor-Gooby 1991: 3). We will examine the nature and impact of this attack on Fabianism in Chapter 7, as part of our review of Thatcherite policies. An equally fundamental conceptual challenge to Fabian philosophy, however, was posed by Marxist explanations of the state. The Marxist model provided a diametrically opposed account to that of the New Right in detailing the irreconcilability of capitalist and welfare state imperatives, but they shared much in common in their critique of Fabianism. Marxist perspectives take many different forms, but they share a caustic view towards the Fabian model of a benign and progressive welfare state meeting undifferentiated public needs. For Marxists, the needs served by social welfare are in fact quite specific – those of the ruling class, secured through the production and reproduction of labour power to ensure capitalist accumulation. As Pierson explains, 'the benefits of the welfare state to the working class are not generally denied, but they are seen to be largely the adventitious by-product of securing the interests of capital' (Pierson 1991: 51).

During the 1970s and 1980s Marxist writers insisted that state welfare policies could be comprehended only by reference to the wider structural constraints and social inequalities which characterise a capitalist society. In this society the state is not a neutral and external arbiter acting rationally to secure 'progress' as defined by social consensus. Instead, the state acts in a context of political conflict and social inequality, with the overall function of meeting the needs, not of 'society', but of specific sectional interests.

FUNCTIONALIST EXPLANATIONS OF STATE WELFARE

By locating state welfare policies in the context of the social, economic and political conflicts of wider society, Marxist analysis offered the prospect of a more penetrating account of the state's activities than complacent Fabian explanations which depicted the state as acting in a benevolent and rational manner to meet the challenges of new stages in social evolution. However, while the *detail* of Fabian and Marxist theories of the welfare state differs sharply, the *form* of explanation advanced is often essentially the same, for both are characterised by a similar and problematic functionalist logic.

Swenarton (1981: 194) points to the ironic similarity between the old liberal view of housing policy as a response to 'problems of overcrowding and housing shortage' as described by Bowley (1945) and the 'contradictions in the reproduction of labour power' identified by Castells (1977). There is a further, more general, similarity in these perspectives. Just as the earlier orthodoxy portrayed the state as acting to meet the functional needs of society as defined by rationality and broad political consensus, so many Marxist contributions have sought to locate state urban policies within a wider constellation of structures which comprise capitalist society and in terms of their contribution to the functional requirements of a dominant capitalist class (see, for example, Castells 1977). According to this framework, the requirements of capitalist interests are twofold: the need for the continuing accumulation of capital, met by state policies sustaining industrial and commercial profitability; and the need for social order, met by state policies bolstering the legitimacy of capitalist social relations and, where necessary, amounting to direct repression.

Within this general account, housing provision is seen as contributing to the fulfilment of both the accumulation and the legitimation functions for the capitalist class. At every stage in its development capitalism is characterised by the search for profit. Yet also crucial for the capitalist are the costs of securing the reproduction and the extended reproduction of the workforce; that is, of ensuring that the worker remains able physically to work, to rear the next generation of workers, and to be incorporated morally within the ideological parameters of capitalist culture. These costs rise as changes in the capitalist mode of production demand increasing expenditure on the health, education, mobility and housing of the workforce. There has been a tension, therefore, between the need to meet the demands in the sphere of consumption that labour be reproduced, and the need for profitability in the sphere of production. Success in the latter requires that costs in the former are minimised.

The massive increase in the scale and scope of the state's activities since the mid-nineteenth century is interpreted by Marxists as a response to this tension. By intervening to provide many services, the state reduces the direct cost to the capitalist class of meeting the cost of social reproduction. Moreover, the nature of these means of 'collective consumption' is such that the prevailing order of capitalist society can be maintained as these services are employed to legitimate the *status quo* and to discipline the employed and unemployed population. In this way, the rise of welfare services such as housing is explained in terms of the functions which they perform for the capitalist class.

Initially, Marxist functionalist accounts of the state welfare system, and of public intervention in the housing market, appear inviting, as they help to demystify apparently benign public policies. On closer inspection, however, some damaging criticisms can be made of this general mode of explanation. Problems in the logic of functionalist explanation are reflected in inadequacies in the ensuing substantive analysis.

Functionalist logic explains phenomena in terms of the effects which they produce. Hence, in the Marxist framework, the stability of capitalist society requires that the state supplies means of collective consumption, *so* these are produced. The fundamental problem here is one of logic. Can the identification of an *effect* (for example, the reproduction of labour through state provision of council housing) also be regarded as an adequate account of the *cause* of that development? Such a position is highly determinist, indicating either a complete commitment to a structuralist analysis in which system needs produce their own fulfilment unalloyed by human agency, or a view of a capitalist state as omniscient and omnipotent in identifying and promulgating the long-term interests of capital. By focusing upon effects, functionalist approaches give an inadequate account of causes. Writing himself from a Marxist perspective, Gough notes

> The *functions* of social policies must always be distinguished from their *origins*. Analysing the former can, strictly speaking, tell us nothing about why a particular policy was enacted, how it was administered, and so on.
> (Gough 1979: 54 emphases in original)

A functionalist account, as advanced for example in Manuel Castells' early work, may be suggestive of productive lines of inquiry in housing research. But, in common with other such approaches,

> The Marxist model of the state and its functions is best treated as a highly simplified one which may suggest certain tendencies in actual policies but which cannot be taken as a sufficient description of its actual activities.
> (Pickvance 1982: 22)

The move towards a more adequate understanding of why state housing policy takes a particular form, therefore, requires us to relinquish the certainties of Marxist functionalism in favour of an *historical* explanation; that is, one which explores how state intervention in housing originated and developed rather than one which commences from its 'necessary' functions and perceived present effects.

An empirical investigation of housing in Britain uncovers further deficiencies in this model of explanation of state policy. First, it is not clear that the function of reproducing labour and legitimating capitalist social relations *has* to be achieved through direct state provision in the form of council housing. Indeed, Britain is unique among industrial capitalist societies in resorting to this specific form of state housing support. Daunton, quoting the Milner Holland Report (Ministry of Housing and Local Government 1965a), reviews the wide range of alternative strategies:

> In Germany, for example, 'primary reliance was placed upon the encouragement of private investment in housing through the granting of low interest rate loans and tax incentives'. In the United States, public housing has not played a large role, and the 'encouragement of home ownership through improving the availability of long-term mortgage funds at low interest rates has been the foundation of . . . housing policy since the 1920s'. The Swedish government has used mortgage and interest-rate subsidies, capital grants and family housing allowances. In France, the government provided subsidies for the construction of new housing in the private sector, whilst public housing was supplied by specialist agencies rather than by local authorities.
>
> (Daunton 1983: 293)

A second problem with the Marxist functionalist model is that, even if at one historical moment a particular state housing policy does emerge as a response to the needs of capital, the *maintenance* of this policy over time still has to be explained. Although council housing initially may have had beneficial effects for capitalists, this does not itself ensure the continuation of the policy when political and economic conditions change.

Finally, Marxist functionalist explanations imply that state housing will be of consistently minimal quality, in keeping with its role in simply reproducing labour, and that public intervention, once instituted, will maintain a broadly level standard and form. Yet much council housing in Britain has hardly embodied the very basic level of provision implied by a structural role as a simple facilitator of capitalist accumulation, reproduction and legitimation. Hence

> The argument would seem to be grossly over-stated. It may be, for example, that capitalists 'need' their workers to be housed in reasonable accommodation . . . but the post-war welfare state in Britain would

seem in many respects to have exceeded these 'requirements'. It simply makes no sense, for example, to suggest that capital 'requires' its workers to be housed in centrally-heated council houses with garages . . . . There is an enormous gap between the level of provision which capitalists may deem 'necessary' for reproducing labour-power or ensuring legitimacy, and that which has actually been provided over the years.

(Dearlove and Saunders 1984: 317)

This observation is confirmed by the way in which policies identified as 'necessary' in the early 1970s were revealed as expendable in the 1980s with the privatisation of a large segment of British public housing and a restructuring of state housing support. When, as in the 1980s, a large segment of labour becomes redundant, then it needs no longer to be reproduced so much as controlled. In this way the apparently eternal truths of functionalist explanation are vulnerable to the consequences of historical change.

The functionalist Marxist analysis of housing policy, which relies on an examination of its effects rather than its historical causes, is thus riddled with both logical and substantive difficulties. We are therefore obliged to adopt the daunting (yet eventually more fruitful) course of unravelling the complex interplay of historical forces which combine to initiate, maintain and change housing policy. When so many potentially relevant factors present themselves we are confronted by a difficult task. Although we hope that our position will become apparent through the rest of this book, it is important to offer a brief outline of the principles which have guided our selection and interpretation of the empirical evidence on the development of housing policy in Britain.

Our critique of functionalist explanations of state welfare has focused primarily upon Marxist analyses. Yet in beginning to formulate a causal, historical analysis of the origins of state involvement in housing policy this perspective may still be used as a point of departure if we can retain the insights to be gained from the Marxist focus on the centrality of structures of capitalist investment, production, and consumption in social development while avoiding the logical and substantive pitfalls of functionalism. The Marxist notion of structure must constitute an indispensable element in the explanation of social events. Certainly social structures are created by people, yet these individuals and groups are obliged to act within a framework of structures produced, often by more powerful agents, in earlier times. A crucially important structural influence on human action framing state social policies such as housing in twentieth-century Britain has been Britain's status as a capitalist society. This is also the starting-point for Dickens and his colleagues, who observe that

> Capitalism is both an overarching social structure and an international economic system. This is fundamental to the way people conduct their everyday lives and build their societies. The provision of housing . . . is one part of everyday life and its social organisation. It is, therefore, quite possible to elaborate theories which explain how housing is provided by reference to the basic dynamics of capitalist society.
>
> (Dickens *et al.* 1985: 1)

This reassertion of the importance of structural determination in social affairs is essential if we are to avoid moving to the opposite pole to extreme structuralism and enter what the same authors term the 'fake world of voluntarism' (Dickens *et al.* 1985: 2). A structural emphasis can avoid the excesses of functionalism if the provisional nature of all social structures as human constructions, liable to change and mediation in particular circumstances, is understood.

On turning to identify those human practices which are both constituted by and constitute capitalism as a configuration of social structures, some Marxists have directed attention to the importance of class conflict. Hence,

> Marxist political economy has the merit over pluralist theories of social policy in situating the 'conflict' within an ongoing mode of production, and it has the merit over functionalist theories of social policy in relating the socio-economic 'system' (its structure and development through time) to the class conflict which is an integral feature of it.
>
> (Gough 1979: 56)

According to this view, class conflict and the power of non-capitalist interests have to be assigned much greater significance than allowed by many Marxist theories of the state. While the existence and power of capitalist social and economic structures exercise a crucial constraint upon public policy, the state and its policies should be regarded as the product of struggles over citizenship rights, property rights, working conditions and many other issues which affect the balance of power and distribution of life chances in society.

In these struggles the working class, from time to time, has wielded significant power and has succeeded in wringing not merely grudging 'concessions' but substantial material gains through innovations in state policy. We can accept that the precise scale of the redistribution of re- sources effected by the British welfare state is a matter of contention, and that capitalist interests may benefit from state housing provision. Yet it is also possible to argue that the growth of state welfare, including council housing, has brought substantial advantages to working-class people. As our analysis of the history of housing policy will show, the extent to which welfare rights have expanded at the expense of property rights has ebbed and flowed in broad relationship to the real or perceived power of labour, and, more recently, according to the shifting balance of advantage in renting or private ownership perceived by households. Furthermore, the extension of housing welfare rights has usually been opposed by capitalist interests. Certainly, examination of specific policies reveals that they often come to function as a support to capital, but this is only to underline the point that state policy, far from being functionally determined, is *contingent* on a changing balance of political and economic power. Working-class pressure may prompt the state to launch a housing initiative but capitalist interests will seek to limit the damage and to influence the extent and nature of the policy change. In Gough's terms,

> It is the threat of a powerful working-class movement which galvanises the ruling class to think more cohesively and strategically, and to restructure the state apparatus to this end . . . . It is in this context that periods of innovation and growth in welfare policies can be understood. Both of the major classes see these policies as in their interests, but for quite different reasons. The working class because any policy which mitigates hardship or which modifies the blind play of market forces is to be welcomed. The capitalist class because it reduces working-class discontent, provides an added means of integrating and controlling the working class, and offers economic and ideological benefits too. Because underneath it all the interests of capital and labour are opposed, so the apparent harmony of interests rapidly breaks down.
>
> (Gough 1979: 65–6)

The continuing conflict is over the nature of the service, the way it is administered, the level of the benefits provided or, notably in the case of housing, the size of the state sector in relation to private and voluntary provision.

Marxism, therefore, with its focus upon the structural parameters constraining social policy in a capitalist mode of production, and its emphasis upon the role of class conflict in prompting and shaping welfare initiatives, constitutes a valuable point of departure for an analysis of housing. However, if we are to look for an incisive account of public housing provision, traditional Marxist theory alone cannot suffice, even when its functionalist excesses are avoided.

DEVELOPING AN ANALYSIS OF STATE HOUSING POLICY

Marxist analyses tend to explain housing policy through recourse to general theories of state, economy and class relations on a national scale. Such approaches neglect the geographical dimension to human existence whereby natural variations in climate, resources and accessibility are amplified by capitalist economic processes to produce a 'spatial division of labour' and substantial unevenness and inequalities between regions and localities. The concept of 'locality' has become the focus of much attention (see, for example, Urry 1981; Massey 1984; Duncan and Goodwin 1988). The spatial unevenness of capitalist development creates distinctive *local* variations in economic life, class relations, and political processes and institutions. These variations may have a major impact on welfare provision, especially for a service such as public housing which has been mediated through local authorities. The research by Dickens *et al.* (1985, Chapter 5) has shown how particular localities have in the past pursued quite idiosyncratic housing programmes even within a framework of control established by the central state. As Cooke observes,

> The local state is not merely an agency of the central state but takes its specificity from the local social structure of the general spatial division of labour with all that this implies for local civil society, local class structure, and, most importantly, local class relations.
>
> (Cooke 1983: 14)

The centrality of a national 'working class' to conventional Marxist work is a convenient abstraction which does permit the exploration of crucial structural relationships. However, it *is* an abstraction and one which may be of limited utility in accounting for the subjective consciousness of individuals and their willingness to engage in political action. It is in the locality that people live together, share experiences, develop attachments and antagonisms, and devise strategies for coping with life and defending their interests. It is unlikely, therefore, that an exclusive emphasis upon a national capitalist system and class relations will yield an adequate understanding of housing policies and experiences which are shaped, sometimes very significantly, by the particular nature of specific localities.

This last criticism points beyond Marxism towards the value of further perspectives in interpreting state housing policy and the response which it evokes. Class is certainly one important factor structuring social relations both nationally and locally. However, the Marxist emphasis upon class tends to exclude other, non-class allegiances which characterise 'civil society'. Indeed, in determining both the objective housing circumstances and individuals' subjective consciousness of their conditions, these alternative bases of social identity may be of major significance. In Part II of this book, for example, the importance of inequalities of both gender and ethnicity as considerations in housing design, allocation and housing consumption will be identified. Further bases of inequality and political action may arise as the result of growing state activity and the consequent division of the population into 'consumption sectors' – notably the tenurial conflict of material interests between owner-occupiers and tenants which may cross-cut class differences (Saunders 1981: 274–5; 1984a and 1990; and Dunleavy 1979 and 1980: 70ff.).

Divisions such as gender, ethnicity, religion and tenure may achieve a salience in social affairs greater than that of class, a possibility which suggests that the *ideologies* surrounding housing (for example, the extent to which 'working-class' people are willing to rally in the defence of citizenship rights in housing rather than to have recourse to individualistic strategies involving the pursuit of private property rights) are not easily predicted upon the basis of a solely class-based analysis.

Marxism emphasises economic determination in the final instance, in its analysis of policy formulation and implementation. It has typically attributed relatively little importance to the *independent* effect of bureaucratic structures and professional power, certainly compared with Weberian perspectives. However, modern society is an immensely complex entity which is co-ordinated very imperfectly through the operation of a vast constellation of organisations and institutions, both public and private. As Williams argues, 'outcomes cannot simply be read off from structural inputs; in other words . . . processes operating *within* organisations may act to transform them' (Williams 1982: 98). Even if state housing policy initially reflected an attempted resolution of class conflict, the ensuing establishment of specialist bureaucracies and the growth of distinctive professional interests in housing are likely to produce new social divisions and new independent influences on housing production and consumption. These issues are explored further in Chapter 5.

It seems clear, therefore, that a causal, historical analysis of housing policy drawing purely upon Marxist analysis of capitalist structures and class conflicts will offer only a partial understanding. Manuel Castells, for example, recognised this in his later work, as the following extract illustrates:

> Although class relationships and class struggle are fundamental in urban conflict, they are not, by any means, the only primary source of urban social change. The autonomous role of the state, the gender relationships, the ethnic and national movements, and movements that define themselves as citizen, are among the alternative sources of urban social change.
>
> (Castells 1983: 291)

But the very length of this list reveals the problem. Adherence to a single perspective may lead to a blinkered view but at least it gives direction to study and a clear, limited agenda of questions. How are we to examine the origin and development of housing policy in the light of the many potential influences reviewed in the preceding paragraphs? And how are we to pay due recognition to the role of social structures in shaping individual attitudes, action and historical development, whilst avoiding a determinism which neglects the creative role of human consciousness and action?

One analytical approach to the historical complexity of housing provision is offered by Dickens *et al.* (1985, Chapter 7). These authors, adopting a realist epistemology, distinguish between *necessary generative mechanisms* and *contingent relations.* In realist terms, 'necessary generative mechanisms' refer to those essential properties of an object which give it an inherent tendency to behave in a particular way and to produce particular effects. Whether it will do so, however, depends upon its interaction with 'contingent factors', historically and spatially specific influences which bear the imprint of human consciousness and choice. For example, Marxists have suggested that the need to achieve accumulation of capital in capitalist society is a necessary mechanism with implications for housing. More recently, some sociologists (including, indeed, Dickens) have displayed a renewed interest in biological, ethological and psychological research which purports to indicate the necessary generative effect of innate 'biotic' drives in human affairs including housing (Dickens 1990). In a different vein, some radical feminist writers have identified gender relations as just as 'necessary' as class relations in determining the nature of advanced capitalist society. Such necessary mechanisms interact with specific historical contingent factors such as national, local or temporal variations in class, gender or ethnic relations or in political systems to produce concrete social outcomes.

This realist distinction between necessary and contingent structures and processes is itself controversial and open to attack (Saunders 1986: 206ff. and 352–62). A particular objection is that there are 'no obvious guidelines (other than the researcher's own value-conditioned interests) for determining what is necessary and what is contingent' (Saunders 1986: 357). In practice, much urban research has simply identified the necessary generative mechanisms latent in spheres such as housing as corresponding to the classic Marxist conflict between wage labour and capital and the activity of the state in capitalist society in seeking to resolve the tensions between capital accumulation and labour reproduction. We accept that mere force of assertion cannot establish these concepts as central in social inquiry (Dickens 1990: 172–3). We do not follow Dickens in seeking to construct what may be termed a 'super realism' in which the net is cast even more broadly to identify necessary mechanisms in a grand synthesis of physical, psychological and social processes. Instead, we shall utilise the necessary/ contingent distinction broadly as employed by Dickens and his colleagues in their earlier work (Dickens *et al.* 1985). This does not signal a rigid prior commitment to Marxist theory. It is simply a convenient heuristic device or model by which to organise our empirical analysis and over which we exert a light hold.

Our identification of the capital–wage relation as a potentially fruitful point of departure for interpreting the rise of council housing certainly reflects in some measure our interests and values or 'meta-theoretical assumptions'. But we shall be using non-Marxist analyses and evidence of the possible importance of various 'contingent' factors to produce an interpretation which draws upon Marxist analysis but which is also significantly at odds with the view held by many Marxists of the history and character of state housing in Britain. Indeed, we remain open to the possibility that phenomena identified initially as 'necessary' or 'contingent' will have to be reassessed as the result of our review of the evidence. Our account of council housing in Britain will therefore acknowledge the independent significance of factors such as gender, locality and professionalisation which are often sidelined in conventional Marxist analysis. We will be emphasising the importance of *historical* causes and the specificity of the state's role in British housing policy, rather than making assumptions about the functional effects of public housing in an abstract or universal manner. We will also give fuller consideration to Fabian and New Right perspectives on the welfare state and the role of council housing. The contribution of Fabianism to the post-war, social democratic welfare settlement is considered in Chapter 3, while our subsequent analysis of council housing in use reflects on Fabian influences in design (Chapter 4) and the development of the housing management profession (Chapter 5). The ideology of the New Right, and its incorporation into Thatcherite policies towards housing and state welfare, is considered in Chapter 7.

The success of the New Right in the 1980s underlined the vulnerability of state housing to political attack and financial retrenchment. An understanding of these recent developments, however, requires an examination of the changing context in which state intervention in housing first emerged and then developed. The purpose of the two chapters which comprise Part I of this book is, therefore, to explore the social, economic, political and ideological constraints and choices which have combined to determine the changing character and status of British public housing. This approach assists our interpretation of the more quantitative aspects of housing policy, such as developments in finance and subsidy arrangements and the relative size of public and private tenures. It is also essential to any subsequent understanding of the *quality* of state housing and its management as experienced by users, which is the subject of Part II, and the current crisis in council housing and the future development of housing policy examined in Part III.

Part I

The development of state housing policy

2 The origins of state involvement

In Chapters 2 and 3 we intend to cast light on the present crisis in council housing by reference to the past. Our account is not advanced as a comprehensive chronology of the history of state housing in Britain. Rather, the intention is to seek in the historical record – which is in some periods immensely rich but in others disappointingly sparse – the reasons for council housing's fragile status as an element of the modern welfare state. Only by reaching back can we fully understand why the restructuring of state provision has proceeded further in housing than in any other arena, and why privatisation and residualisation have made such an impact.

There is a clear danger in providing a synoptic review of housing policies in the past hundred years; a risk of oversimplifying a complex welter of structures, processes, personalities and events. Recent years have seen a substantial growth in the historical analysis of housing policy and the impressive and extended contributions of, for example, Dunleavy (1981a), Swenarton (1981) and Malpass (1990), each of whom focus upon a specific aspect of housing in a particular period and provide a clear indication of the perils confronting an attempt at a rapid voyage through housing history. However, if present policies and practices do indeed reflect the structures, conflicts and decisions of earlier times, some analysis of the historical development of housing policy must be offered and the attendant risks run.

Many of the virtues and deficiencies of British council housing in the late twentieth century can be traced to the circumstances and events surrounding the tenure's birth and early development in the years from the 1880s to 1939. In the origins of state housing provision we uncover evidence significant for our later interpretation and evaluation of current policy and our assessment of the future of council housing. 'The value of history lies in helping us to understand the nature of present structures; what imperatives lay behind their introduction? We may more usefully defend or criticise the "welfare state" if we understand more clearly why it came into being' (Thane 1982: 2). In this way an analysis of the origins of state involvement in housing provision can help to reveal whether a public housing sector is irretrievably flawed in principle, as claimed by many commentators of the New Right, or whether the shortcomings of this tenure are the product of specific processes which exert a less deterministic hold over future policy options.

WAGES, RENTS AND HOUSING – A NECESSARY CONTRADICTION?

This chapter will utilise the distinction made at the end of Chapter 1 between necessary generative mechanisms and contingent relations as a means of organising our examination and interpretation of the particularly rich historical research evidence on the origins of council housing. In this section we select as our point of departure the contention that the emergence of council housing in Britain was a necessary response to a deepening contradiction between the simultaneous needs of accumulation and social reproduction in a capitalist society.

Before 1919, over 90 per cent of households rented their dwellings from private landlords. A stimulus to state action on housing, identified both by modern commentators and by many observers in the late nineteenth and early twentieth centuries, was the gap between working-class wages and the rents necessary to secure housing of a reasonable standard:

> House rents rose continuously to 1914. Rent, however, absorbed an ever increasing share of earnings. At the beginning of the nineteenth century, house rent probably accounted for 5 per cent of GNP: in 1851 it contributed 8 per cent, and fifty years later 9 per cent. In the period 1880–1900 rents rose anything between 13 and 17 per cent, depending on the preferred method of calculation. The smaller the income the higher the proportion devoted to rent. The working class formed the higher-rented section of the community, and the poorest the highest. In Edwardian Britain rent swallowed up a third of the income of the very poor.
>
> (Englander 1983: 5–6)

The chronic shortage of adequate housing produced by this tension between wages and rents was a crucial context framing the state's gradual assumption of significant housing powers.

Even when real wages did rise, as in the 1870s and 1880s when falling prices gave an advantage to those remaining in employment, inelasticities in housing *supply* prevented a corresponding change in the wage/rent ratio (Burnett 1986: 151). For many workers, during the eighty years leading to the First World War wage rises were largely abolished by increases in housing costs.

Constraints on housing supply can be traced to several sources. First, the spatial unevenness of capitalist development generated intense demand for labour and a related population growth in a limited number of urban areas. Much of the work was of a casual nature and this, together with the low wages and limited transport technologies which prohibited lengthy commuting, obliged the poor to live close to potential workplaces and job opportunities which arose often at short notice. The inelasticity of land supply in such industrial and commercial centres constituted a major obstacle to the supply of additional dwellings at affordable rents. These shortages were compounded as large areas of working-class housing were demolished to permit street improvements, office and commercial developments, and the coming of the railways.

A second constraint in the supply of lettings for working-class households is found in the growing availability of alternative, more profitable and straightforward investment opportunities for private landlords. It is true that the decision to let private housing was not always governed by typical investment criteria. Most private landlords were small investors for whom the bricks and mortar of 'homes' had an emotive appeal as a safe haven for their savings. Nevertheless, the development of industrial capitalism did offer a broadening range of new investment opportunities both within Britain and overseas.

Opinion is divided as to the relative significance of the growth of overseas investment as a drain on domestic housing finance (Burnett 1986: 145; Melling 1980: 16–17). Yet Britain's imperial world pre-eminence in the nineteenth century and her related adherence to an economic policy of free trade did present to British investors an unusual choice of foreign opportunities. Furthermore, Britain's place in the world economy certainly constrained housing supply in another way, as periodic surges of funds overseas prompted the Bank of England to raise interest rates to protect the gold standard and stimulate inward investment. While this might encourage investment in mortgages, higher interest rates also reduced landlords' profits, so acting as a further disincentive to residential investment (Melling 1980: 20).

Third, housing supply is also influenced by building costs and their effect on builders' profits. Ball has argued that a major reason for the continuing high relative cost of housing in the twentieth century is the low labour productivity in housing compared with other industries (Ball 1978; and 1983 Ch. 6). In the nineteenth century, too, the dominance of the building trade by small, under-capitalised firms ensured that few cost-saving changes in manufacturing methods occurred. While the cost of building materials fluctuated between 1870 and 1914, they did not rise overall. However, labour costs rose markedly as building workers strengthened their market position, not only absolutely but also in relation to other trades (Gauldie 1974: 177–8). The proportion of wages in total costs, therefore, rose from about one-third in the middle of the nineteenth century to about one-half at the beginning of the twentieth century (Daunton 1983: 35). A steady rise in land costs, aided by restrictions placed upon the use of sites for working-class housing, was another factor which depressed the profitability of private housebuilding during these decades.

The weakness of effective demand for housing and the inelasticities in its supply were reflected in the well-documented physical and social conditions of Victorian Britain. Merrett (1979: 5–6) quotes contemporary descriptions of the filth, damp, overcrowding and absence of clean water, sanitation and fresh air in the lodging houses of London and the cellars and yards of Leeds. Poor housing was a major cause of the high morbidity and mortality of the Victorian and Edwardian eras. Infant mortality remained at about 150 per 1,000 live births throughout the period from 1838 to 1902, and it was only during the last decade of the nineteenth century that adult death rates fell below twenty per thousand (Hobsbawm 1969: 160).

The woeful physical state of large tracts of Britain's housing stock, together with what were seen as the attendant social problems of criminality, vice and drunkenness, confronted the Victorian middle class with what Dyos terms a 'twin-headed genie' (Dyos n.d. 1). Furthermore, Britain's economic and military efficiency were seen increasingly as threatened by the speed of uncontrolled urbanisation and the proliferation of the slums. The continuing low standards of living of many households, embodied most obviously in poor housing, came to be regarded as posing an internal political threat. Hence, the stability of an economic system which employed labour power to produce commodities for domestic and assiduously acquired foreign and imperial markets was being compromised by the failure to produce one of the commodities, housing, which was crucial to future capital accumulation. It is this contradiction between the productive and reproductive needs of British capitalism that has been seen as a necessary mechanism prompting the emergence of public housing policy. Certainly the failures of the housing market created pressure for state initiatives. But was it a compelling pressure, strong enough to ensure the eventual development of a major programme of municipal housebuilding?

A RELUCTANT STATE

Early housing policy cannot be viewed as having been directed simply by unalloyed humanitarian sentiment or far-sighted rational social planning.

Rather, the state's first limited essays in housing intervention have to be viewed as being prompted by immediate material and political dilemmas, by contradictions which overcame resistance to involvement. While the failure of the market can be regarded as perhaps a *necessary* mechanism goading the state into action, in this section we must consider whether the gap between the housing costs and incomes of poorer working-class households amounted to a *sufficient* condition for the emergence of a major programme of public housebuilding. The state's ability to withstand pressures for major involvement in housing provision for so long suggests that its eventual response was not the product of necessity in the stronger functionalist sense.

The reluctance with which the state began to infringe private property rights on the nineteenth-century housing market is reflected in both the timing and detail of early housing legislation. The powerful reports on the conditions in which many working-class people were compelled to live by observers such as James Kay (1832), Southwood Smith (1838), Edwin Chadwick (1842), and Henry Mayhew (1849) were met by only the most tardy and tentative of governmental commitments. While the initial legislation *empowered* local authorities to adopt housing and health measures, it *obliged* them to do very little and offered negligible central government support for local initiatives. For example, the 1868 Artisans' and Labourers' Dwellings Act (which was introduced not by the government but by a private member, McCullagh Torrens) enabled, but did not compel, local authorities with populations of over 10,000 inhabitants to force owners of insanitary dwellings to demolish or repair their property at their own expense. No obligation was placed on local authorities to rehouse the 'beneficiaries' of these earliest efforts at slum clearance. The Artisans' and Labourers' Dwellings Improvement (Cross) Act of 1875 did extend the scale and scope of these powers by empowering local authorities to purchase and clear areas of unfit dwellings, to draw up improvement schemes for the land and to rehouse displaced inhabitants on the original site. If the authority itself was to provide any new dwellings, however, capital had to be raised from the rates or by borrowing. Further, in calculating the rents no subsidy to the tenants was to be assumed, and the dwelling was to be sold to a private buyer within ten years.

The Housing of the Working Classes Act of 1890, although it in some ways weakened the original Torrens and Cross measures on unfitness, compensation, and rehousing, can be regarded as the major housing statute before 1914. Part III of the Act permitted local authorities for the first time to building working-class housing outside clearance areas and to manage them, charging 'reasonable rents', without obligation to dispose of them within ten years. This gave councils the discretion to subsidise their housing operations from their rate funds. Yet there remained no compulsion to build and no central government financial assistance was forthcoming.

Viewed nationally, such measures accomplished very little. Clearance without replacement merely intensified the problems elsewhere. Further measures such as the 1875 Public Health Act, which empowered local authorities to establish their own by-laws to control environmental and housing standards, have been seen by some as another disservice to lower-paid workers through their implications for building costs and rents (see Burnett 1986: 154ff.). Moreover, powers to rehouse without significant central government financial support were insufficient to stir most local authorities to action, given the high expense of bridging the gap between wages and the cost of new dwellings.

The intrinsic weakness of this early legislation was compounded by the unpromising political and administrative environment into which it was launched. The composition of most local councils hardly presaged a vigorous response to the housing question. Hence

> It was the small tradesman or shopkeeper who was most often attracted to town council service, men of the class most open to temptation, for whom there was the greatest advantage in wielding influence over, for instance, the granting of contracts or the appointing of officials. It was not a coincidence that they came from the same class to which the majority of investors in cheap housing also belonged . . . . So the wishes of town councillors, builders and owners of house property were often seen to have remarkable agreement.
>
> (Gauldie 1974: 124–5)

The property owners who controlled most councils therefore had a clear interest in minimising the loss of profit and the increased rates levy threatened by slum clearance and local authority building programmes.

In addition to the local political opposition confronting major public housing initiatives, existing administrative structures also constrained decisive action. Even after the Municipal Corporations Act of 1835, which established the basis for modern democratic local government in the major urban centres of England and Wales, and the broadly parallel 1833 Royal Burghs (Scotland) Act, the expanding public commitments to social policy were vested in a wide range of municipal, county and parish authorities together with a plethora of *ad hoc* bodies. Indeed, until the 1888 Local Government Act county areas in England and Wales remained unreformed and undemocratic. The 1888 Act was, in fact, an exercise in *decentralisation*, transferring certain functions from central departments of government to the county councils (Hampton 1987: 18). This climate of decentralisation helps to explain why the early housing legislation, faced also with a long-standing tradition of local autonomy, generally encouraged local action rather than compelled it. The Local Government Board (established as late as 1871 to give a national oversight to the growing functions of local authorities) possessed largely only advisory powers in relation to localities (Thane 1982: 46).

Beyond this legislative caution, the official concern to avoid major central government expenditure on housebuilding was also shown in a reliance upon other, more economically and ideologically congenial housing strategies. In particular, the second half of the nineteenth century saw energetic attempts by the 'five per cent philanthropists' to demonstrate that private housing of significantly improved standards *could* be provided for working-class households and still yield an adequate commercial return to the investor (see Tarn 1973). Generally, such housing schemes did meet their objective of securing a 4 to 5 per cent return, although not without some difficulty (Burnett 1986: 85) and in a market where, ideally, 7 or 8 per cent was deemed necessary to secure a ready flow of finance (Gauldie 1974: 226). Hence, the profits on these dwellings were insufficient to attract the funds necessary to build houses in the numbers required. Furthermore, to permit even a 4 or 5 per cent profit, rents had to be fixed at a level affordable by only the affluent artisan class, despite Octavia Hill's attempt to house the poor and achieve adequate returns by pioneering intensive management techniques.

Beyond these 'five per cent' schemes, another potential alternative to state intervention was found in the dwellings supplied by employers for their workers. Celebrated examples included those by Edward Akroyd at Copley and Akroydon near Halifax, Titus Salt's Saltaire at Shipley, and later W. H. Lever's Port Sunlight near Birkenhead, George Cadbury's Bournville, and Joseph Rowntree's New Earswick at York. Motivated by a complex and varying blend of religious faith, humanitarianism and hard business calculation, several such schemes gained widespread acceptance as 'model estates'. However, their celebrity underlines their exceptional status, as most employers rejected the financial commitment involved in attempting to oversee the reproduction of their own labour force (and indeed that of other local employers), feeling able to leave housing supply to the private property market. As with other philanthropic housing, the poorest did not benefit from employers' accommodation and this source of housing remained 'more important in educating public opinion, in influencing future town planning development than in housing the working class' (Gauldie 1974: 194).

In view of the combination of legislative weakness, municipal autonomy, local political resistance and central government reliance upon private alternatives, it is not surprising that the addition to the housing stock produced by municipal housebuilding by 1914 was only about 24,000 units (Merrett 1979: 26). Even after the enabling legislation of 1890, council houses constituted only about 1 per cent of total annual output. Public housebuilding in rural areas, where needs were identified as particularly acute (Wilding 1972: 4), was especially limited. While decades passed and housing conditions for poorer households remained dire, it appears that the clear environmental, political, social and even economic tensions produced by unfit housing did not amount to a 'necessary generative mechanism' rendering a major programme of council housebuilding inevitable. How was the state able to avoid the assumption of major housing responsibilities?

To answer this question it is helpful to follow Martin Daunton in looking again at the private housing market in Britain in the late nineteenth and early twentieth centuries. Examining the point at which, after years of non-intervention, the state finally committed itself to the direct supply of dwellings after the First World War, Daunton suggests that

> an understanding of the reasons for this massive intervention in the market for working-class housing is an important historical question. But it must not be allowed to obscure a different and equally important question: how did the private housing market operate? It might be that the tensions in the operation of the private market ultimately demanded public intervention. *However, such a possibility should be treated as a hypothesis to be tested, rather than taken as a proposition which is self-evidently correct.*
>
> (Daunton 1983: 194, emphasis added)

Certainly we can point to serious and intensifying problems in the private housing market prior to 1914, but it would be quite wrong to assume that no workers secured acceptable housing through the market, or that there existed some undifferentiated 'working-class' experience of private landlordism, housing costs and housing standards. To the extent that the market worked for some, the political pressure for state involvement was ameliorated and the emergence of council housing can be seen less as the inevitable, 'necessary' outcome of structural contradictions and more as the result of particular 'contingent' historical events. This is an issue which can be explored through the analysis of housing as an area of class conflict to which we now turn.

HOUSING AND CLASS – THE LIMITS TO CONFLICT

We have seen that class conflict as an agent of social change occupies an uneasy position within strictly functionalist Marxist accounts of state welfare provision. Hence, the degree and kind of working-class political mobilisation tends to be regarded simply as a barometer providing an indication of the maturity of social contradictions and the presence of 'necessary' mechanisms for change, with protest a predictable response to structural stimulus. If, however, we follow Dunleavy in remaining 'highly sceptical of any attempt to deduce explanations of urban politics from the structural features of the capitalist mode of production' and regard it as 'inherently unlikely that structural explanations alone can produce causally adequate or determinant accounts of social processes' (Dunleavy 1980: 54), then political conflict over housing provision assumes a heightened and more subtle significance. Working-class pressure for housing reform and the state's response become intelligible as a conflict between agents who are *active* in making sense of their circumstances, in making choices, and in developing strategies within structural limits (Dunleavy 1980: 54). Adopting an emphasis upon human agency rather than structural determinacy in the politics of housing encourages us to regard class conflict in this sphere as of central rather than derivative importance. It becomes of interest not simply as an indicator of 'necessary' economic contradictions between the productive and reproductive needs of capital, but more as a key aspect of those historically 'contingent relations' which make the development of state social policy less predictable. Such a perspective encourages greater attention to the *variations* in working-class perceptions and experience (influenced by differences in occupation, local variations in political culture and landlord–tenant relations, gender and other factors) which may fragment and limit, as well as promote, pressure for reform.

It is important not to understate the extent of working-class mobilisation on housing issues or to miss other signs of an unrest which can find no outlet in collective political action and the expression of a clear alternative housing agenda. Yet we must not exaggerate the extent of market failure and of the related protest and frustrated anger or, even in the presence of discontent, the enthusiasm for council housing as a policy remedy.

Many have written, often in exasperated tones, of the apparent inertia of working-class households in reacting against the appalling state of many nineteenth-century homes. However, as David Englander argues in one of the most comprehensive historical analyses of housing conflicts in the period preceding the First World War:

> Historians have often been too ready to step into the breach to pronounce upon 'working-class apathy and helplessness' or, having stumbled across evidence to the contrary, to respond in tones of barely concealed amazement . . . . The silence of the poor is deceptive. The non-realisation of ambition is not in itself evidence that none is possessed

. . . . The want of basic amenities – adequate drainage, proper sewerage
and paving, lavatories, a constant, or indeed any, supply of running
water – provoked a good deal of resentment . . . . The non-participation
of working people in the sanitary reform movement is not evidence of a
want of interest in such questions.

(Englander 1983: xiii-xv)

Therefore, even before the mid-1880s, the point at which housing histories
begin to register a significant working-class housing voice, it is possible to
uncover evidence of intense conflicts between tenants and their landlords. It is
true that in many cases protest often amounted to much less than a fully
elaborated agenda for housing reform. In the manner of industrial saboteurs at
the workplace, the rights of property in the domestic sphere were frequently
challenged by the poorest through acts of vandalism, notably in retaliation for
eviction. Before the point of eviction was even reached, the close knowledge
possessed by many tenants of the numerous obstacles confronting their
landlords in securing vacant possession was often used to good advantage. By
merely opposing an eviction order in the courts the process could be delayed
and the landlord's costs increased. Another strategy was to report the unfitness
of the landlord's property, again with the aim of deterring action by the
landlord through the threat of increased expense.

In the poorest areas of every city intimidation was employed on both
sides to either avoid paying rent or to secure it. In such districts, a common
tactic of tenants was to move on before the landlord could take action to
recover arrears. Many poorer working-class households harboured considerable resentment against landlords, particularly as regards the practice
of distraint, the common law right of landlords to seize the effects of a
tenant as compensation for the non-payment of rent. But they were too
weak and fragmented to offer an organised and coherent strategy. Their
actions reflected merely their immediate and pressing concern to 'get by'
and, on occasion, to satisfy their honour and acute sense of indignation.

For more 'respectable' households, however, the threat of eviction was
very infrequent. The central concern here was more confined to the threat
which the rise in rents relative to wages posed for living standards. It was
within this sector of labour that the first signs of a more organised housing
campaign can be discerned. This pressure, Englander argues, may in
general have been expressed in a spontaneous, fragmentary and episodic
form but it was not negligible or, indeed, devoid of success. For instance,
Disraeli's decision after the 1867 Reform Act to give the newly-enfranch-
ised section of the working population an interest in local financial 'pru-
dence' through ending the practice of 'compounding' (whereby landlords
paid the rates and levied a rent to cover the costs) bore down heavily upon

many tenants who found that landlords did not reduce rents in proportion to the previous rate element. The result was a major revolt by tenants. Mobilisation in east London was particularly marked, with 2,000 people attending a protest meeting in Bethnal Green convened by the newly formed Tenants' Mutual Protection Association, and a further 1,000 joining a torchlight demonstration in Hackney. Englander cites further examples of such collective action in Blackburn and Birmingham (Englander 1983: 88). Just two years later, through the 1869 Poor Rate Assessment and Collection Act, compounding was reintroduced and this retreat by the government qualifies as a significant achievement for working-class housing action and suggests significant latent class awareness in landlord–tenant relations.

In the last two decades of the nineteenth century the growing power and unionisation of labour, mirrored in the mounting strength of the Independent Labour Party and other socialist political groupings, offered the basis for a more far-reaching working-class agenda for housing. In part, this was reflected in a growing appetite and effectiveness in traditional disputes stemming from the existing housing system. During 1901, for example, a public meeting of the newly-formed Bermondsey Tenants' Protection League drew over 1,000 people to a protest meeting over a compounding dispute with landlords and the local authority in Southwark. Similar leagues formed in neighbouring districts of the capital (Englander 1983: 127ff.). Elsewhere in Britain the Edwardian years were marked by a significant growth in defensive struggles by tenants against the rents levied by their landlords, notably as the latter attempted to take advantage of industrial revival in 1913 to raise rents after the prolonged property slump coupled with spiralling rate charges of the preceding years. Englander documents the strong tenant response in several localities including Wolverhampton, Coventry, Birmingham, Leeds, Bradford, Liverpool and Edmonton.

Developing alongside these defensive struggles, however, was a demand for an altogether new housing system in which the state should intervene to control rents and, through the local authorities, itself underwrite the direct provision of working-class homes. In this development a notable role was played by the Workmen's National Housing Council, founded in 1898 by three members of the Social Democratic Federation which, from as early as 1885, had pressed for non-profit making municipal housing (Damer 1980: 78). The executive of the council was composed of trade unionists drawn from the skilled, 'respectable' households who formed the core of the many tenant protection leagues for which the Council became in some measure a co-ordinating forum.

The emerging Labour Party also sought to reflect the interests and attract the support of this relatively secure section of society. Given the

debates which have recently arisen concerning the appropriate response of the
Left to the sale of council houses, it is interesting to note that even as late as
1912 the Parliamentary Labour Party was not committed to a policy of state
subsidised housing (Englander 1983: 187 and 214). At local level, however,

> *Every* liberal and left-wing group, including trades councils all over the
> country, had the municipalisation of housing as a central issue through-
> out the last decade of the nineteenth century, and right up to the outbreak
> of the First World War.
>
> (Damer 1980: 78, emphasis in original)

In certain localities the organised workforce gained significant political
influence and this pressure for council housing led to tangible achievement.
Using the provisions of Part III of the 1890 Housing of the Working
Classes Act, councils in Sheffield, Liverpool, Manchester and, most
notably, the London County Council (Swenarton 1981: 29ff.) pioneered
estates of municipal suburban cottage dwellings.

It is clear, therefore, that through the unco-ordinated protests of the poor
against their immediate circumstances and the more organised, although
similarly shortlived and defensive, struggles of the not-so-poor, working-
class people did oppose the rights of their landlords and register, sometimes
with considerable effect, their moral outrage at the existing balance of
housing power. Moreover, the years leading to the First World War saw a
growing demand for an alternative, state subsidised mode of housing
provision articulated by the representatives of an increasingly organised
and powerful labour movement. There is, however, another side of this
story which must be considered if subsequent developments in the history
of state housing welfare are to be understood fully.

It is useful here to refer again to Daunton's suggestion that the popular
view, that it was intractable tensions in the private housing market which
ultimately demanded public intervention, is a hypothesis to be tested rather
than a proposition which is self-evidently correct. Indeed, it is Daunton's
argument that much writing on the history of working-class housing in
Britain is defective because 'it has concentrated on the pathological rather
than on the typical . . . the failure of the private housing market must not be
taken for granted' (Daunton 1983: 1–3). Englander too, his very different
theoretical orientation notwithstanding, notes that

> While slums remained, this should not obscure the real progress regis-
> tered during the nineteenth century, a period which experienced an
> overall improvement in standards of accommodation together with a
> marked reduction in overcrowding towards the end of Victoria's reign.
>
> (Englander 1983: xi)

If a minority, albeit a very large one, lived in slums, therefore, the majority did not, and considerable evidence exists to underline the success with which many households with modest but secure incomes met their housing needs through the private market. The extent of this success was one factor setting a limit to class conflict over the housing question and obviating, or at least delaying, the necessity for more radical state intervention.

We noted earlier that housing costs consumed an increasing proportion of working-class incomes during the late decades of the nineteenth century. However, this is explained partly by the fact that there was a decline in the price of other commodities. Also, Daunton notes that for many households the rise in rents reflected an improvement in the space standards and amenities of their dwellings. Average wages between 1880 and 1913 rose rather more than average rents so that real housing costs fell. To the extent that wage rises were partly absorbed by increased housing costs, it was because many were paying for an improved product (Daunton 1983: 35–6).

In some measure these improvements in housing standards were the result of the first tentative official responses to housing problems sketched above. Conditions were addressed by the gradual introduction of building controls in the nineteenth century. While the increase in rents arising from the improved street widths and layouts, room sizes and facilities of these new houses constituted a further disadvantage to the poor, for skilled workers with secure incomes these additions to the housing stock which soon covered large tracts of British cities in the late nineteenth century represented a major improvement in living standards. Other relatively prosperous working-class and lower middle-class households were able to take advantage of improved transport in the form of the train and the tram and, especially in the London area, the lower fares available through the Cheap Trains Act of 1883, to move to new suburban areas.

Beyond recognising these improving housing prospects for a significant proportion of working-class households, we should continue to resist the stereotype of powerless tenants obliged to accept occupancy purely on the landlord's terms. Crucial here was the state of the housing market, with the number of empty dwellings indicating the relative advantage of landlord and tenant (Kemp 1987: 13). In times and in localities of housing surplus a reliable, respectable tenant was a resource which a landlord could not lightly discard. Also, the predominance in England and Wales, unusual in Europe, of weekly lets, while it left tenants vulnerable to eviction at short notice, also offered mobility to households to seek employment or to adjust their housing costs in accordance with their current means.

Further limitations to class-based housing conflict are discovered in the composition of the landlord population and in the particular nature of landlord–tenant relations. The polarisation between landlords and tenants and the antagonism in their relationship should not be exaggerated unduly. As we have seen, even at the end of the nineteenth century much of the housing stock remained owned by the less affluent members of the middle class, shopkeepers, tradespeople, and indeed artisans who invested their savings in residential property. In a period before pension schemes and insurance policies, such investments offered people of modest means security and a potential avenue for social mobility (Elliott and McCrone 1982: 100). Many landlords were themselves tenants, notably in London where the leasehold system created numerous middlemen who bought up the remaining years of a lease and re-let their property, often in an over-crowded state, to realise their own profit (Burnett 1986: 152).

Also serving to blunt antagonism was the fact that these small landlords often lived close to their tenants with whom they developed very personal relationships. When conflicts did arise, both parties were often inclined to perceive them as particular, individual problems rather than as reflections of a universal crisis in landlord–tenant relations which required a collective response (Daunton 1983: 123).

It should be clear, therefore, that in the decades preceding major state housing intervention there was no single working-class housing experience. Considerable local variations in housing conditions, opportunities and landlord–tenant relations existed, with specific land, labour and capital markets producing major differences in the quality of accommodation available at a given rent. Nationally, the wage differentials between those in secure, well-paid employment and the casually employed poor, and the hierarchy of intermediate groups which separated them, were reflected, subject to local mediations, in a similar gradation of styles, space standards and furnishings in workers' homes (Burnett 1986: 171ff.).

A PRIVATE RESPONSE

The diversity of working-class housing experiences reviewed in the previous section was reflected in the varied strategies adopted by households to improve their housing circumstances. One option was to support the mounting campaign by many local labour organisations for a great expansion of municipal housing. However, the recourse by many workers to alternative avenues to better housing conditions adds weight to the view that the eventual emergence of a major state housebuilding programme owed as much to historically contingent factors as to necessary structural contradictions prompting a monolithic working-class opposition to existing property relations. In particular, it is important to draw attention to the growth in working-class home ownership even before the First World War.

While owner-occupation was unusual for all social groups prior to 1914, working-class home ownership did achieve significant levels in certain localities, notably in South Wales (Barlow 1987: 34) and in Sunderland where the shipbuilding industry offered relatively high wages and skilled occupations (Daunton 1983: 198). As Kemp shows, the full material advantages commonly associated with this tenure in the late twentieth century did not operate a hundred years earlier so that renting property was often preferred even by middle-class households (Kemp 1987: 5). Nevertheless, the level of working-class membership of friendly societies, building clubs and, later, permanent building societies in some districts testified to a desire among more secure working-class householders to improve their accommodation (and also their social status) through home ownership. Significant numbers of these working-class owner-occupiers were also landlords. For many working-class households, therefore, the private market offered important opportunities which operated as another limitation on mobilisation for an alternative structure of provision.

Although home ownership offered Victorian and Edwardian working-class households a means of distinguishing themselves in social status from other households (Saunders 1990: 19) and an economic investment through which to guard against later misfortune and infirmity, two further dimensions to this question are very relevant for the perspective of this book. First, the political meaning of owner-occupation and its psychological role in bolstering working-class subjective defences against the indignities and alienation inflicted by a capitalist labour market; and second, the wider ideology of private property rights which provided an important part of the context for the early search for home ownership.

Daunton suggests that the late nineteenth century brought two related changes at the workplace: on the one hand rising wages, improved job security and rising living standards; and on the other, an erosion of craft-based employment, an advance of factory-based production techniques, and a tightening of labour discipline. As a response, he argues that

> The working class turned away from dependence in their experience of work, towards a search for purpose in the life of the family and the home, which came to be seen as a source of assertive dignity. The reality of working-class life in the late nineteenth century was one of dependence at work and of deference in the community. The working-class institutions of self-help, and the creation of a home-based culture of domesticity, may be seen as a response to this experience. The outcome might be a conservative retreat from wider issues, but it might also be a mechanism to assert independence and identity within a setting of subordination. It was within such a setting that the use of housing was determined.
>
> (Daunton 1983: 266)

Variations on this theme of the growing importance of home and family as a shelter from the growing storm of public life have become common in sociology and town planning (for example, Sennett 1970; Goldthorpe and Lockwood 1968–9; Shorter 1977). Such a thesis should not be accepted uncritically. Thus, it can be argued that

> The male worker who returns at night to feed his tropical fish, and expects his wife to feed him, experiences a different cultural represent-ation of the relation between home and work from that of a woman worker who returns to the home and is faced with feeding husband and children and doing the rest of the housework before returning to work the next day.
>
> (Clarke 1979: 249)

Nevertheless, the growing care and attention lavished upon their homes by both men and women, the importance in more affluent households of keeping the 'parlour' as the best room, and the subtle differences in external finish and internal space and furnishings which acted as badges of status all suggest that housing came increasingly to perform this role in working-class identity. Through the home, distance could be placed be-tween the 'respectable' and the 'rough', and a free space within a generally constrained life created.

Working-class aspirations for home ownership were influenced also by the prevailing attitude to property rights in Victorian Britain. If, as Macpherson insists, property consists not in things but in *rights* in or to things (Macpherson 1978: 2), then it is clear that rights to other forms of welfare such as education, health and social security do indeed constitute property for those eligible. Yet, if we are seeking reasons why housing has never become more than a relatively short and fragile pillar of the modern welfare state, part of the explanation must surely lie in the specific form of property which it constitutes.

Education and health involve rights, either through citizenship or through purchase, to use a school or hospital the title to which rests with a public or private body. The rights in question are not to 'things' but rights to a service from others. Similarly, social security is a right to revenue rather than to a physical object. Education and health services, whether public or private, and social security, all incorporate rights *in personam*; that is, rights deriving from the legal relations which exist between the consumer and the supplier of the service (Reeve 1986: 15–16). Housing, however (although the distinction is blurred), bears rights *in rem*; that is, rights deriving from the owner's relationship to a thing, the dwelling and the land on which it is built. In law, housing constitutes real property as opposed to personal property, characterised by its attachment to the land with the tangibility, geographical fixity and relative security which this implies (Reeve 1986: 82).

Real property in land has long been accorded particular importance in structuring social relations and conferring more general social rights. Reeve quotes Hannah Arendt on the understanding held by the Greek and Roman civilisations that 'man could limit himself from necessity only through power over other men, and he could be free only if he owned a place, a home in the world' (Arendt 1961: 148). This implies that liberty is only secured through the possession of *private* property in land with relatively absolute rights over use and disposal. Such a notion of property is far from universal, and in pre-capitalist Europe it was normal for a number of individuals to have varying rights over the same plot of land. But by the nineteenth century, most land and housing had become part of a commodity market with the rights of ownership greatly enhanced. Property was synonymous increasingly with private property involving very full rights of use and disposal, to the point where ownership came to be regarded as of the object itself rather than of rights to the use of the object. In this context freedom and status were sought increasingly through the ownership of real property. Certainly, many working-class households were inclined to make their way within the existing framework of property relations and according to the ideologies which supported them.

To summarise, an alternative housing system in which the state, acting through the local authorities, intervened to redefine the rights of real property would imply a much more radical innovation than a redrawing of the rights of service producers and consumers in spheres such as education and health. Such a prospect was not immediately attractive to all working-class people. As we have seen, many affluent working-class householders were landlords who had an interest in a continuation of a broadly unregulated market. Rooted in an oppositional, mutual tradition, owner-occupation had become, for a minority of workers, a defensive response to the alienation and disempowerment of industrial capitalism and a basis for personal autonomy and self-esteem. Moreover, poor and comfortable alike risked losses as well as gains from a municipal housebuilding programme that increased rates and rents. For the poor, such state intervention as had occurred in the nineteenth century in the form of slum clearance had often produced a deterioration instead of an improvement. And the balance of power in most local authorities hardly commended them as agents disposed to radical and sensitive innovations on behalf of working-class people. In such circumstances, resort for many households to private strategies of housing improvement seemed more attractive. For many, housing problems were experienced as individual problems rather than as class grievances and both the ideology and the reality of private property rights were compelling.

COUNCIL HOUSING – A CONTINGENT SOLUTION

Continuing governmental success in avoiding the commitment of major public funds to housing provision; the limits placed on class conflict over housing by the perceived adequacy of market provision for many households; the frequently personal quality of landlord–tenant relations; and the suspicions of local authorities harboured by many workers and their preference for private housing strategies – our review of all these themes suggests that council housing may never have achieved its later importance without the emergence of particular historical circumstances. In this section we describe and then interpret some key events of the short period between the outbreak of the First World War and the end of 1919. These years saw the introduction of two related Acts of Parliament which brought a revolution in British housing history.

First, the Increase of Rent and Mortgage Interest (War Restrictions) Act of 1915 introduced controls on the rents of all dwellings up to a rateable value set sufficiently high to include the great majority of tenancies within the new controls. Rents were restricted to a 'standard rent' defined as that paid in August 1914. Although these unprecedented controls were introduced for the duration of the war and the following six months, the return to a fully free market in residential tenancies was still awaited in the 1990s.

Second, beyond these negative controls of the existing housing market the state finally assumed significant positive responsibility for the direct supply of dwellings through the Housing and Town Planning etc. (Addison) Act of 1919. This statute required local authorities to survey the housing needs of their area and to submit and enact plans for the provision of the necessary extra dwellings. For the first few years the rents of the new dwellings were to be based on the controlled rents of pre-war accommodation, with some allowance for the superior quality of public housing and for relatively high tenants' incomes. Crucially, beyond the product of a one penny rate all losses incurred would be met by subsidies paid to the local authority by the Exchequer. For the first time, therefore, central government both obliged localities to take substantial action to address the housing question and backed this directive by a major financial commitment of its own. Although government targets of 500,000 houses were not met in the years following 1919, 170,000 dwellings were completed using the Addison subsidies, sufficient to establish council housing in Britain as a significant tenure (Merrett 1979: 41).

Why, after decades of prevarication, did this major extension of state housing powers occur? Was it inevitable, the necessary final consequence of a long-term failure to secure the conditions of capitalist profitability through the satisfactory reproduction of labour and the related political upheaval? Is it to be construed simply as an important step in a natural 'social progress', a victory for rationality in policy development? Or were there more immediate, contingent, even accidental influences of war shaping events?

Certainly, the years preceding the First World War were ones of particular turmoil for private residential property, with increasing building costs (further raised by the requirements of the housing by-laws), higher interest rates, declining birth and migration rates, and stagnant wages combining to produce in many localities a collapse in property values and a dramatic decline in housing supply (Daunton 1984: 7). This has led many writers to identify this period as one when the chrysalis of council housing burst finally from its cocoon, responding, after so many false dawns, to the warmth of eventual acceptance by a sufficient weight of influential public opinion born of a finally unacceptable housing crisis. In such a view, the impact of war was to modify the speed but not the course of historical change. Indeed, Wilding argues that 'exchequer subsidies for housing would almost certainly have come sooner if war had not broken out in 1914' (Wilding 1972: 3).

Against these interpretations, however, we can set a view of the earliest state-funded dwellings not as the inevitable and permanent solution to a long-term crisis but as *emergency housing* (Dunleavy 1982: 13), a short-term expedient to meet more immediate exigencies. From this perspective both the fact and the form of direct state support for municipal house-building was a housing 'solution' unique among industrial capitalist nations, shaped by specifically British economic, social and political influences and by the crisis of war.

In support of this argument, it is possible to identify a disjunction between the pre-1914 housing debate and subsequent policy developments (Daunton 1984: 4; Swenarton 1981: 44ff.). Admittedly, the Parliamentary Labour Party had now joined other socialist groups in the campaign for municipal housing. Also, immediately before the war local Conservatives were pressing the case for the construction of low-rent houses financed by the Exchequer as a means of shifting the burden of taxation from the rates towards the general taxpayer. And by 1914 even the Liberal government contained members convinced of the need for state housing subsidies, and powers were sought to enable the Board of Agriculture to build houses in rural areas where the gap between wages and rents became especially marked (Wilding 1972: 15). However, in the late nineteenth and early twentieth centuries, Daunton argues, 'the housing debate ... was informed less by a new awareness of municipal socialism and central government subsidies, than by the land question' (Daunton 1984: 4).

For most Liberals, notably John Burns, President of the Local Government Board from 1906, state subsidies would merely serve as a grant to landowners, suppress private enterprise and exacerbate the housing shortage. The main Liberal strategy was not to subsidise rents but to reduce the high cost of urban land through the taxation of increased site values and the opening up of new land for garden city-style development.

Despite their recognition of the need for state building for the poor, the Conservatives remained committed to private enterprise as the dominant means of housing provision together with their policy of constructing a social 'rampart' linking substantial owners of real property and the rest of society through the promotion of a 'property-owning democracy' of owner-occupiers (Offer 1981, Chapter 9).

Surveying the debate of these years, therefore, Daunton concludes:

> There was, then, no single pre-ordained housing policy in the years just before 1914. There was a trenchant debate over the approach to be adopted which is missed if the end result of subsidised council housing is taken for granted. It is therefore necessary to explain why the particular solution of subsidised council housing was ultimately adopted.
>
> (Daunton 1984: 5)

Similarly, reviewing the policy of the Liberal government on the eve of war, Swenarton identifies a clear contrast with what followed:

> It was the First World War that was to create the conditions for a different kind of policy: a housing programme on a really large scale to be built not by state-aided public utility societies but by the state itself.
>
> (Swenarton 1981: 47)

For both writers, therefore, council housing was a response to the emergency of war rather than a reflection of what Wilding terms 'a product of the incrementalism which is the most obvious characteristic of the development of housing policy in this country' (Wilding 1972: 16). Nevertheless, in their detailed analyses, Daunton and Swenarton place differing emphasis upon particular aspects of the wartime 'emergency'. Swenarton stresses the political aspects of the crisis, identifying council housing as a device adopted by a hard-pressed state as an insurance against social revolution. Daunton pays fuller and more explicit attention to the economic roots of housing crisis, grounded in the especially severe and distorted market conditions produced by the conflict.

Regarding the first of these arguments, we have noted that Britain entered the First World War with the property market in a particularly depressed state. The move to a wartime economy, bringing a virtual cessation in new house construction, increased the shortage of accommodation and the crisis was compounded further in specific urban localities where rapid immigration was induced by the burgeoning of war-related industries. Stagnating supply and intense demand confronted even skilled workers with severely deteriorating living conditions and all workers with the prospect of large rent increases.

The result in many towns and cities was working-class direct action on an unprecedented scale, most notably in Glasgow where, in certain districts, landlords sought to exploit these market forces by raising rents by up to 23 per cent (Dickens 1981: 185). We should be cautious and avoid subscribing to what Englander terms 'the legend' that the Rent Act of 1915 was introduced simply as a response to the mobilisation of Glasgow tenants (Englander 1983: 205). This author cites research indicating that rent strikes, often involving over 1,000 tenants, were widespread in England and Wales and elsewhere in Scotland from a very early stage of the war. In many districts the war served to heighten the landlord–tenant tensions described earlier (see pp. 43–7). It is clear also that powerful additional interests, notably a growing proportion of industrialists, accepted the introduction of rent controls and, later, council housing subsidies.

Nevertheless, the exceptionally acute housing conflict which erupted in Glasgow in 1915 did become a focus of state attention. A committee of inquiry was established under Lord Hunter and 'it was the campaign on Clydeside that was decisive in shaping the measure that finally emerged' (Englander 1983: 210). Here, a particularly severe housing shortage was produced by the major immigration of new workers to the locality to meet the demands of war-related industries such as shipbuilding and munitions. Landlords responded to the intense demand for accommodation by raising rents.

The campaign against rent increases by Glaswegian tenants was made more intense and effective by a constellation of factors, some of which were specific to the locality. Thus, the particular nature of the Scottish legal rights of distraint, differences in typical tenancy conditions compared with those prevalent in England, the generally larger property holdings of Glaswegian landlords, and their consequent disposition both to mobilise as a landlord class and to employ agents to deal with tenants, and the historically high housing costs in the region, were all factors which produced particularly antagonistic landlord–tenant relations (see Englander 1983: *passim*).

The transformation wrought by the coming of the war was the power which it gave to tenants as *workers*. Articulated through the trades councils and the International Labour Party (which helped to establish the influential Glasgow Women's Housing Association) and other workers' organisations, a mass movement developed in Glasgow. This movement was composed of skilled, organised labour, with the city's slum dwellers playing little part (Englander 1983: 185). The action combined the actuality of district-based rent strikes, which by November 1915 had gained the support of 20,000 tenants (Damer 1980: 94), with the threat that the mounting industrial unrest would culminate in a general strike confronting the state with military defeat.

Substantial mobilisation over housing issues developed in other cities, and the solidity of the Glasgow action strengthened the resolve of workers in these other localities. Hence, aided by the conditions of war, working-class action played a central role in prompting the state to take a large step towards support for municipal housing with the introduction of rent controls on private housing in 1915.

Rent controls alone were sufficient to ameliorate but not quell the political tension produced by poor housing conditions. In 1917 Lloyd George established an inquiry to report on continuing unrest in key industries. Housing featured prominently in the causes of tension identified by the Industrial Unrest Commission which urged the government to indicate its commitment to increase housing supply. Subsequent months, which saw deepening industrial conflict and the Bolshevik revolution in Russia, strengthened the hand of those in the government who pressed for municipal housing. This political crisis pressed the state, Swenarton argues, towards council housing as 'an *ad hoc* response to an immediate political crisis' as 'an insurance against revolution' (Swenarton 1981: 81).

Interwoven with this account of the growing political pressure for housing reform in Swenarton's analysis is reference to the mounting economic obstacles to a return to minimal state intervention. It is this *economic* crisis provoked by the war, rather than the political turmoil, which is the focus of Daunton's attention in explaining the recourse to council housing. Daunton notes that Britain entered the war with the housing market so depressed that many subsequent commentators have argued that it was, at last, in terminal decline, so that the coming of state housing was ensured. However, Daunton suggests that the incapacity of the private market in normal times to revive should not be assumed. It was the war which compounded the housing shortage and increased the cost of new construction so sharply that the market mechanisms could not produce the rapid upsurge in supply required after the Armistice. Indeed, a central prerequisite for the market to make anything resembling an adequate response to the housing needs, the attraction of finance for housing investment through a substantial increase in rents, was of course prohibited by the rent controls of 1915. The dilemma for the state immediately after the war, therefore, was that rent controls were necessary because the shortage of houses permitted the imposition of scarcity rents; but the existence of rent controls hindered the provision of new houses to end this shortage (Daunton 1984: 9). The impetus for council housing, therefore, came more from the distorting effect of the war upon the housing market than from political pressure to use housing as an instrument of social control.

The purpose of our analysis, however, is not to adjudicate on the relative merits of these two perspectives. The important lesson for the present discussion is that neither writer interprets the rise of council housing simply as an inevitable, necessary reflection of system needs, or as the culmination of a long-term historical 'progress'. For both Swenarton and Daunton the municipal dwellings which began to appear in British towns and cities in the post-war years constituted 'emergency housing', forced upon the state by a constellation of political and economic contingencies.

A comprehensive history of the origins of council housing would examine many more specific influences in explaining why, alone among European nations, Britain adopted municipal housing as a major response to the housing question in the inter-war period. For example, the unusual political weakness of the landlord class in Britain (Englander 1983, Chapter 4; Daunton 1983: 127) and their separation from the more powerful demands of industrial capital was significant, as was the tradition of local autonomy in Britain against the centralism of France, for example, where state housing provision was later mediated not through municipalities but through new agencies answering directly to central government. We have had to be very selective. Yet the preceding discussion should serve to indicate that the emergence of major direct state provision of housing, although set against a backdrop of long-term market tensions and agitation for reform, occurred in particular historical circumstances. As we will show, the context of emergency in which the tenure developed was important in shaping the form and extent of subsequent council housing policy.

THE EMERGING POLICY – BIRTHMARKS AND BRUISES

This final part of the chapter traces the development of public housing from the introduction of central government subsidies in 1919 to the outbreak of the Second World War. It will be argued that, from the outset, council housing carried the marks of its birth and inherited a constitution which rendered it very susceptible to bruises inflicted by the harsh economic and political environment of the inter-war years.

Our previous discussion has shown that the infringement of private property rights through rent controls and the financing of local authority housebuilding was, in substantial measure, the state's response to working-class pressure. Although popular enthusiasm for municipal housing was not universal or unequivocal, the birth of council housing represented a major concession to working-class interests by a reluctant state. The new child carried the image of its working-class parentage, but it inherited far more from the continuing power of capital and the political objectives of the state. To repeat our earlier quotation from Gough, council housing seems a particularly clear case of where 'the threat of a powerful working-class movement . . . galvanises the ruling class to think more cohesively and strategically' (Gough 1979: 65). These birthmarks and bruises were some-times disguised, sometimes indeed exacerbated, but never removed by the policies of subsequent Labour governments and, as Chapter 7 will describe, resurfaced in the 1970s and 1980s to leave council housing unusually vulnerable to the general New Right assault on state welfare provision.

It has become normal in Britain to distinguish between 'public housing' and other tenures. This broad categorisation, however, gives little hint of the relatively narrow base on which it rests, the provision of state subsidies to bridge the gap between working-class wages and the rents necessary to secure acceptable living conditions. Of course, the significance of this development should not be minimised. Despite consistent failures to meet government housebuilding targets, council house completions up to 1939 still totalled over one million, 10 per cent of the stock, a development with far-reaching implications for the private rented market, for the relationship between many households and their local authority, and for wider socio-economic divisions and political alliances. Nevertheless, this dramatic change in British housing tenure patterns, together with the remarkable improvement in housing standards and other advances achieved through public housing investment, can detract from the very firm boundaries set around inter-war housing reform.

While the introduction of state housing subsidies indeed reflected the rising power of organised labour, it must not be forgotten that the legis-lation was framed by a Conservative-dominated coalition. Until the eleventh hour, opposition to this infringement of the principles of private property and the sanctity of the market remained strong within the govern-ment. In spite of Lloyd George's inspired rhetoric regarding 'homes fit for heroes', the commitment of central government funds for housing confronted Treasury hostility and Local Government Board irresolution (Swenarton 1981: 70ff.), until minds were concentrated finally by the Armistice of November 1918 and the findings of the Industrial Unrest Committee. By the time that revised, more radical proposals came before the Cabinet in March 1919, even Conservative members of the Coalition swung behind the need for a housing programme backed by both central funds and powers to act in default of resistant local authorities. However, this delayed conversion should not be allowed to obscure the underlying limitations in the proposed reform which reflect its origin in a capitalist political alliance and economic order.

First, the 1919 Act did not constitute a long-term strategic commitment to municipal housing as the dominant tenure for a wide cross-section of wage earners. Just as the rent controls of 1915 had been scheduled for removal six months after the war, so the Addison subsidies were envisaged as a temporary emergency device to relieve the intense housing shortage produced by the conflict so that the private sector could resume its historic role as the normal provider of new dwellings in an undistorted market (Daunton 1983: 298–9). Second, in the absence of other suitable agencies, and declining itself to assume full direct responsibility, central government resorted to the local authorities to expedite the required large and urgent housing programme. Policy was designed at the centre but implemented in the localities, where the political balance was often such that the requested housing drive achieved little momentum. For example, after an initial enthusiasm to use the 1919 subsidies to build council dwellings, the Conservatives of Leeds became much less energetic than other large urban authorities in using the subsidies established by the Labour Government's Housing Act of 1924 (Finnigan 1984: 109).

Third, the rents of the new council houses were such that the link between low incomes and poor accommodation was left largely intact. Until March 1927 rents were to be based on the controlled rents of pre-war housing, with an adjustment to reflect the higher quality of public dwellings and the incomes of their residents. Thereafter, to permit the progressive re-entry of private contractors into working-class housebuilding, rents were to rise to an 'economic' level to meet the construction, financial, management and maintenance costs, less central and local subsidy. Even before 1927, however, the rents for the Addison houses still excluded all but the most affluent manual workers and members of the lower middle class. This remained the case for all municipal dwellings built under the varying subsidy arrangements of the 1920s. The infringement of market processes implied by the Addison Act hardly amounted to a major redefinition of property rights. Early council housing addressed the discontent and the interests of more organised, secure sections of the working class, leaving the slums of the poor largely untouched. It can be argued that it was not until the launching of the slum clearance drive in 1933 that we encounter 'a landmark in the development of council housing, and one which pointed to its emergence as a social service' (Finnigan 1984: 116).

Finally, it is important to emphasise that the 1919 subsidies were offered within a market framework which, in most respects, remained intact. Hence, local authorities were obliged to finance the construction of the new dwellings using loans offered by the capital markets, usually at prevailing rates of interest. Local authorities had to compete with others in markets for land, building materials and skilled labour. And the vital Exchequer subsidies were vulnerable perpetually to national and international economic crises and fluctuations in the political balance of power. The state had put its money on the table after long delay and with great reluctance. Neither central government nor local authorities would necessarily continue to fund housing when the skies clouded or opportunities for disengagement arose.

All these circumstances surrounding the birth of council housing left it very susceptible to bruising by subsequent events and to progressive distortion from the ideals inspiring the Workmen's National Housing Council and the predominantly middle-class town planning movement. Immediate post-war boom conditions placed great pressure on municipal building programmes as, with building controls removed in December 1918, serious shortages of labour and materials arose with their attending increases in costs (Swenarton 1981: 115). However, as boom gave way to a dramatic slump and an abrupt decline in the demand for industrial building, so resources and labour were released for the housing programme heralding a decline in municipal house prices in 1920, which was to persist through the inter-war years (Merrett 1979: 38). Yet, before the end of 1918, market forces were constraining the housing programme in another, still more fundamental, way.

The recession strengthened the hand of those who had always opposed state subsidies for council house construction. The borrowing necessitated by the expense of war had forced a departure from the gold standard. This was seen as placing at risk the position of London as the pre-eminent international financial market and the viability of a British economy in which the imperial legacy had helped to elevate the power of financial capital and the role of foreign investment to a degree unique amongst industrial nations (Gamble 1985, Chapter 2). The prescribed route back to financial stability was via a reduction in public expenditure and an increase in interest rates. Hence, by June 1921 the 'homes fit for heroes' campaign had been halted by rising interest rates and progressive downward pressure on public spending, culminating in the termination of the Addison subsidies.

Reflecting and influencing these economic changes were the parallel political developments of the years between 1918 and 1921. With economic slump and rising unemployment, the power of labour waned considerably. Swenarton argues that this permitted Lloyd George to recant his commitment to housing welfare, as the threat of a general strike in the spring of 1921 passed (Swenarton 1981: 129ff.).

However, the end of a free market in housing signalled by the 1915 rent controls, together with other factors such as the downward pressure on wages caused by the planned return to the gold standard (finally achieved in 1925), discouraged a complete withdrawal by the state from housing subsidies. Even for the Conservative Government elected in 1922 there was a reluctant acceptance that municipal housing remained an 'unfortunate necessity' (Merrett 1979: 41). The Housing (Chamberlain) Act of 1923, therefore, retained Exchequer support, but at a level much lower than that advanced under the 1919 legislation with a flat-rate subsidy of £6 per dwelling payable for twenty years. A contribution from local rate funds was no longer required. The Conservatives' concern to reaffirm the private sector (now through owner-occupation) as the dominant source of supply was revealed in the fact that these subsidies were available to private enterprises as well as local authorities. Councils were encouraged to offer mortgage funds and council houses were to be built only if a local authority could show that they were necessary and could not be provided by other means. These measures, together with the introduction of extra subsidies for underwriting losses incurred in slum clearance schemes, mark an early contraction of council housing towards a residual tenure for households living in slum dwellings, a development delayed only by the election of a minority Labour Government in 1924.

In keeping with its foundations in a traditionally defensive trade union movement and its aspiration to manage the state to further workers' interests within a capitalist economic order, this Labour administration acted to bolster the existing machinery of state housing support rather than to forge its own. Hence

> the land was not nationalised; the construction industry and the financial institutions remained in the hands of the capitalist class; and the local authorities' building programme continued to be funded by loans from the capital market rather than by taxation.
>
> (Merrett 1979: 45)

The Housing (Financial Provisions) Act of 1924, introduced to Parliament by John Wheatley, a major figure in the Glasgow rent strike, proposed higher subsidies of £9 in urban areas and £12 10s. in rural areas and made receipt of these grants dependent upon a local authority rate-fund contribution to the value of half the central government subsidy. Unlike the Chamberlain Act, rents were to be limited in relation to controlled rents in pre-war dwellings. The Wheatley Act, therefore, embodied a view of council housing as a major tenure offering accommodation to a wide cross-section of the British population. Localities were no longer required to demonstrate that housing needs could not be met via alternative suppliers.

This increase in central funding, aided by falling building costs and the removal of restrictive labour practices, produced a major expansion of municipal housing, with over 500,000 houses being completed through the use of Wheatley subsidies until the repeal of the 1924 Act in 1933. The return of a Conservative Government after just nine months of Labour rule, and the subsequent reversal for the Left of the General Strike of 1926, did not bring the end of this support for municipal housing for general needs. The Chamberlain and Wheatley subsidies existed together until 1929, although the declining power of labour was reflected in the Conservatives' decision to prune both the 1923 and the 1924 subsidies for houses completed after September 1927. Many localities, particularly those under Conservative control, utilised the opportunities which both Acts offered to redirect central funds to finance private house construction (Finnigan 1984: 109; Dresser 1984: 164).

These years, therefore, witnessed relative consensus in housing policy, and the role of public housing was consolidated. Thousands of cottages for working-class households were constructed on land purchased, in the great majority of cases, at the periphery of existing towns and cities to designs and estate plans largely in conformity with the much enhanced standards recommended by the Tudor Walters Committee (see Chapter 4). Other households moved into popular inner-urban flats, again of radically improved amenity by historical standards.

Chamberlain and Wheatley did little, however, to rectify the key deficiency inherited from the 1919 Act – the failure of the public sector to meet the needs of those enduring the worst housing conditions. Although sharply declining building costs, cuts in standards pressed through by Chamberlain, and (under Wheatley) increased central and local subsidies all permitted some reduction from the very high rents charged on the earlier Addison dwellings, rents remained well above controlled private sector levels. The result was that the council housing of the 1920s served overwhelmingly to benefit those members of the lower middle and upper working class with relatively high, secure incomes and small families (Bowley 1945: 129; Merrett 1979: 48–9).

Against a deteriorating international economic context the second minority Labour Government, elected in 1929, did act quickly to prevent scheduled Conservative cuts in the Wheatley subsidies. The housing achievements of this administration, however, were limited by the Cabinet's inability and disinclination to alter the strong market parameters in which state housing had developed. As Labour turned its attention to the pressing need to rehouse much poorer households from slum dwellings through the Housing (Greenwood) Act of 1930, its scope for manoeuvre was further restricted. In the absence of massive subsidies to bridge the gap between the income of such households and prevailing rents, the major available strategies were a reduction in council housing standards, or an increase in the rents of more affluent tenants to permit a transfer of subsidy to the poor through a levying of differential rents and the introduction of a rent rebate scheme.

In fact, the 1930 Act employed a combination of these approaches to address the problems of the slums. Local authorities were required to produce a five-year slum clearance plan and obliged to rehouse those displaced by demolition. Support for this endeavour was offered through an entirely new form of subsidy based upon the number of people rehoused. This incentive to reduce council housing standards was reinforced by additional subsidies to build flats where authorities incurred high clearance costs on central sites. The Act also empowered localities to levy 'reasonable rents' and to initiate rent rebate schemes. This encouraged the development of differential rents, with more affluent tenants required to cross-subsidise their poorer neighbours.

It was a Labour Government, therefore, which sanctioned a major departure from the 1919 practice of subsidising the construction of low-density, high-quality, predominantly cottage estates, with support which emphasised quantity rather than quality. Moreover, Labour antagonised many of its own supporters through attempted sponsorship of rent rebates and differential rents, although this option was not taken up by most local authorities (Malpass and Murie 1987: 64; see also Chapter 5, this book).

The assistance which Labour had given to a process of 'residualisation' of council housing, away from its definition by Wheatley and other socialists as a tenure of high quality homes for a wide section of the British population, was mitigated temporarily by the co-existence of the 1930 Housing Act with the Wheatley subsidies. However, the MacDonald administration was short-lived. Amidst economic crisis, a further weakening in the power of labour, and acute pressure to reduce public expenditure, the Conservative-dominated National Government, which held office from 1931 until the end of the Second World War, abolished the Wheatley subsidies in 1933 and placed pressure on local authorities to build smaller houses and flats. Moreover, the trend to differential rents was given impetus by the Housing Act of 1935 which required local authorities to establish a single Housing Revenue Account to replace the multitude of separate accounts for houses built under different Acts. This arrangement permitted 'rent pooling' which allowed localities to relate rents to the use-value of different dwellings and the consolidation of all the various Exchequer subsidies and local contributions into a single fund for the disbursement of rent rebates, although these schemes remained unused by most councils (Merrett 1979: 58; Malpass 1990: 44ff.).

The Conservatives' escape from 'general needs' public housing was eased greatly by the massive upsurge in private housebuilding for owner-occupation from the mid-1920s. Writers differ in the relative weight which they accord to the factors sustaining this trend. Apart from the growing availability of building society mortgages, regarded by Richardson and

Aldcroft (1968: 50) as 'the vital permissive factor', and the negative
consequences of rent control for investment in private rented dwellings, the
slump in the wider economy actually fuelled a boom in housebuilding.
Alternative investments became less attractive than housing. Also, as
prices, including those of building materials and mortgages, fell, so
demand for home ownership increased as the wages of many of those
remaining in work fell more slowly (Richardson 1967: 105–11). Private
housebuilding output rose from an annual average of 131,000 between
1925 and 1933 to nearly 260,000 per annum in the years leading to the
Second World War. By 1939, 60 per cent of middle-class households had
become owner-occupiers and many clerical and manual workers had
entered into house purchase (Merrett 1979: 50–3), notably in areas where
unionisation, rearmament and a predominance of skilled labour protected
wages (Furbey 1974: 207). In this way, owner-occupation became established as the dominant tenure, with council housing relegated to the residual, sanitary role of public housing prior to 1914. It was the Coalition
which presided over this erosion of the status of council housing. Yet, in
addition to initiating the change nationally, many Labour-controlled local
authorities also accepted lower standards and a residual status for council
housing (see, for example, Dresser 1984: 167).

CONCLUSION

A necessary precondition for state housing in Britain was the continuing
gap between wages and the rents required to secure acceptable accommodation. This contradiction evoked a working-class response in the form
of sporadic protests, often individual but sometimes organised and widespread, against private landlords. By the beginning of the twentieth century
the rising strength of working-class political influence was being reflected
in a broader analysis of the housing question and a demand for state
intervention.

Support for public housing amongst the working class, however, was
never complete. The failure of the housing market was not absolute, and the
ability of more secure households to make private provision tolerable
limited housing conflict: so too did the prevailing ideology of private
property, the distinct form of property represented by housing, and the role
of the home for working-class people as a shelter from wider social
processes. The fact that state housing provision was through the
traditionally distrusted local authorities served merely to encourage a
reliance upon private landlordism or, increasingly, owner-occupation.

It appears, therefore, that tensions between capitalist production and
social reproduction provided a necessary context for state housing pro-

vision in Britain, but the rise of council housing was not an inevitable response to system needs. It was the contingencies of the First World War which offered the historical circumstances in which long-standing cyclical housing market deficiencies and their related miseries and conflicts sharpened sufficiently to confront the state with an economic and political crisis of housing provision.

The origins and early history of council housing reflect successful working-class pressure for reform. However, if inter-war council housing reflected working-class influence it also, in the end, underlined capitalist control. Certainly, Labour Governments increased output and, until the 1930s, maintained housing standards. But council housing was born in a wider capitalist context which remained broadly intact, where the power of organised labour waned and where economic conditions served to constrain public spending while stimulating the private housing sector. In such circumstances the resources to establish a universal high-standard housing service, always a more expensive proposition than a universal education or health service, were never forthcoming. By the 1930s, even Labour had accommodated itself to a much more limited vision for state housing, a retreat witnessed by the supersession of 'homes fit for heroes' by a greatly inferior product. And, as we shall see in Chapter 3, this limited view of council housing soon emerged again in the period following the Second World War.

3 The post-war experience
State housing and the welfare consensus

In this chapter, we follow our analysis tracing the progressive disengagement of public housing from other services which formed the basis of the post-war welfare state in Britain. The thirty years following the Second World War are now regarded as an era of bipartisan support for the social democratic principles underlying the welfare state. Both Labour and Conservative Governments gave ideological and financial support to universal state provision in health and education, with 'safety net' provision through social security and the personal social services. The accommodation of principles for collective social care with Keynesian economic management techniques prompted a flurry of new initiatives and legislation, including the extension of mass secondary education following the 1944 Act, the creation of the National Health Service, the introduction of National Insurance and Family Allowances, the establishment of the National Assistance Board, the adoption of new town planning controls and the development of welfare services for children and the elderly.

We will argue that government policies towards public housing differed in their emphasis and orientation in the thirty years after the war. There are several points of difference. First, council housing – unlike other services – had already developed into a major tenure before 1939, as outlined in Chapter 2, and post-war policies were derived out of a basic framework established nearly thirty years earlier. Second, state housing never attained the status of a comprehensive, universalist service like health and education. Third, government policies residualised and marginalised public housing well before the adoption of similar strategies for other welfare services in the 1980s.

The direct provision of services is not a necessary condition for a welfare state. Government support can be provided through an alternative approach of guaranteeing a basic income through benefits or tax concessions. Post-war housing policy contained both approaches, but increasingly support for direct state provision was withdrawn in favour of a more selective approach of directing subsidies towards housing consumers to help meet the gap between disposable household income and high housing costs. This process was virtually unique to housing in the period 1945 to 1979, although it paved the way for the policies towards health and education pursued by the Thatcher Governments during the 1980s.

We do not intend to provide a simple chronology of housing policies in the post-war era. Instead, we wish to focus on underlying themes which illuminate the process whereby council housing became uncertainly integrated, and then progressively detached, from the post-war infrastructure of state welfare. We will show how council housing was relegated to a second-class service, meeting residual rather than universal needs, marginalised by economic pressures and political priorities and largely discredited as an efficient or equitable housing tenure. This is demonstrated by reference to the limited vision for council housing in the immediate post-war era, the impact of subsequent policies favouring mass home ownership, the switch in emphasis for local authority housebuilding programmes and the redirection of subsidies towards a residual model of public housing. As a result of these changes, council housing was an easy target for the forthright attack launched by the Conservative Governments during the 1980s.

THE IMPACT OF THE SECOND WORLD WAR

It is impossible to discuss the genesis of the modern British welfare state without acknowledging the effects of the wartime experience on generating a collectivist spirit, support for government intervention and a determination to avoid a return to the means-tested ravages of the inter-war depression (Marwick 1990). The development of the welfare state was a key factor in the wider political and economic programme of post-war reconstruction. The groundwork had been laid during the war by the Coalition Government. The key text was the 1942 Beveridge Report, which provided the foundations for National Insurance, Family Allowances and the National Health Service. The Coalition Government introduced Family Allowances, the 1944 Butler Education Act and, in the same year, the Conservative Minister of Health, Willink, published a White Paper outlining a scheme for a comprehensive health service. The Ministry of National Insurance was set up in November 1944. These measures demonstrate the extent to which post-war provision had bipartisan origins founded in the rigours of wartime.

Strands of dissent to these policies were evident from the Right and the Left, but these were sidelined. As George Orwell noted at the time of the Beveridge Report,

Thirty years ago any Conservative would have denounced this as state charity, while most socialists would have rejected it as a capitalist bribe. In 1944 the only discussion is about whether it will be adopted in whole or in part.

(Orwell 1970: 29)

The battery of legislative measures introduced by the 1945–50 Labour Government was, therefore, the realisation of a popular mood for state planning, control and intervention on an unprecedented scale in peacetime. The purpose of these measures was, in Atlee's words, 'to give security to all members of the family' (quoted in Pelling 1984: 117). The Labour Government was swimming with the tide, as Addison points out

The demand for jobs, homes and social security was the very reverse of revolutionary, but it was nonetheless radical – for these modest needs had never been satisfactorily met by the system of political capitalism. The Labour Party reaped the benefit.

(Addison 1977: 248)

A degree of state intervention was necessary to regulate the market, equalise opportunities and ensure a measure of social justice, while stopping well short of a fully collectivist system.

There was one omission from the services undergoing sweeping post-war legislative reform: housing. The future role of public housing was never subject to the radical reappraisal accorded to National Insurance, education, services to children, National Assistance, town and country planning and health. There was little evidence of any fundamental thinking about the role of government in housing, and the relationship between housing and other activities such as income maintenance, town planning and population dispersal policies. As a result, and in terms of capitalising on a widespread public optimism and support for state provision as a means of achieving a fairer society, council housing missed the boat.

There were several reasons behind the absence of bold new strategies for public housing. Most obviously, the war had left a visible legacy on the condition of the housing stock. Adolf Hitler proved a more decisive influence than William Beveridge in shaping the housing requirements of post-war Britain. Subsequent policies were dominated by a single objec-tive: meeting the housing shortage. Council housing programmes de-veloped as a peacetime equivalent of the type of government intervention, control and economic direction which had characterised the war effort. The drive to meet production targets completely overshadowed any attempt to reconsider the state's responsibilities for meeting· a basic social need or achieving a more equitable housing system.

HOUSING AFTER THE WAR: A PRAGMATIC STRATEGY

During the war 218,000 properties were destroyed, a further 250,000 were made uninhabitable and nearly three million houses damaged to some extent (Holmans 1987; Merrett 1979). Only 190,000 properties were built during the war and little repair work was carried out. Meanwhile, the number of households had increased from 11.75 million to 12.25 million. By 1945 the Ministry of Reconstruction estimated that three-quarters of a million new dwellings were required for every family needing one, and a further half million properties were needed for slum clearance and over-crowded households (Merrett 1979: 237). Alan Holmans has calculated, however, a real shortfall of two million dwellings in 1945, by making an allowance for married 'concealed' households. This was the largest housing shortage ever recorded – 500,000 greater than in the period after the First World War (Holmans 1987: 92). In this context, it is hardly surprising that the resolution of the 'housing problem' was defined in terms of building new units of accommodation through any available means.

In the 1945 election campaign, housing figured prominently. Ernest Bevin had claimed that a Labour Government would build the incredible number of four to five million houses to meet the shortage, although the Labour Party's manifesto did not mention whether this would be achieved through the public or private sector. The Conservative manifesto merely referred to the need for subsidies to local authorities and private enterprise alike (Craig 1970).

As in 1919, so it was in 1945. The expansion of council housing was driven by the need to meet numerical targets for new building, rather than to erect one of the pillars of socialism (Donnison and Ungerson 1982: 145). The fulfilment of the Labour Government's promise to provide a separate dwelling for every family was susceptible to the economic vagaries of post-war reconstruction. Building costs, for example, had risen sharply during the war, with the average tender price for a three-bedroomed house rising from £376 in 1939 to £1,045 in 1945. The difficulties of meeting an ambitious housing target were compounded by the shortage of materials (especially timber and brick) in 1946, the shortage of skilled labour, poor weather conditions (1946/7) and the imposition of Treasury spending controls from 1947 onwards, in response to a balance of payments crisis and dependence on American loans.

The Coalition Cabinet had set a target of 220,000 units in the two years after the war, but this was not achieved. Nevertheless, local authority housing starts in England and Wales were 163,518 by 1946 and continued roughly at this level, reaching 170,857 by 1951. In addition, 124,455 prefabricated dwellings had been constructed in England and Wales by 1948 (Holmans 1987).

The selection of local authorities as the vehicle for the housebuilding drive was pragmatic, rather than an explicit statement of faith in the virtues of state housing. Private developers operating in market conditions could not be relied on to meet the nation's need for new houses – hence Aneurin Bevan's famous observation that the speculative builder was not 'by his very nature, a plannable instrument' (quoted in Foot 1975: 71). As a result, private housebuilding only accounted for about one-fifth of total output in the five years following the War. But the criticisms of the private sector were less forthright in housing than in other areas of social policy. In health, for example, the virtues of a free and comprehensive system of public provision were continually contrasted with the iniquities, costs and selectivity of private health care. Private housing – whether rented or owned – was subjected to greater controls than before under the Labour Government but the principles of a market-based system were never seriously challenged.

As in the inter-war period, central government used various financial levers to regulate the scale of local authority housebuilding. Subsidy levels were increased under the 1946 Housing (Financial and Miscellaneous Provision) Act to £16 10s. per dwelling, with a compulsory Rate Fund Contribution of £5 10s. The government also eased the cost of borrowing by only allowing local authorities to borrow from the Public Works Loan Board, at the relatively low interest rate of 2.5–3 per cent from 1946 to 1951.

However, the pressure on the costs of the housebuilding drive was not met entirely by central government subsidy. Council tenants themselves had to pay more. The 1939 Rent and Mortgage Interest (Restriction) Act had frozen rents so they were over one-third lower in real terms by 1946. Average rents increased from 7s. a week in 1938/9 to only 7s. 6d. by 1946/6 – a policy which, according to Holmans, 'had long-lasting effects on tenants' attitudes and expectations about what rent levels were reasonable' (Holmans 1987: 95). The level of building productivity after the war was lower than expected, and as a result central government support was insufficient. In 1946 subsidies were intended to cover a capital cost of £1,175 per house – in practice, the average cost was about £1,500. The balance had to be met from the local authorities' own housing revenue or repairs account, putting pressure on council rents. By 1950, rents had risen to 10s. per week for pre-war, and 14s. per week for post-war, properties.

In the event, the housebuilding drive from 1946 to 1951 did not attain its target. Larger-scale building programmes were postponed in 1947 and the following year, 'like a rerun of the Coalition movie of 1920–1, the Cabinet decided to cut back and contain the municipal housing effort' (Merrett 1979: 243). The Labour Government fell short of its targets by 240,000 properties a year – one of the reasons for its defeat in the 1951 election. In a 1949 Gallup poll, for example, 61 per cent of those interviewed had said that they were not satisfied with the government's housing record (quoted in Short 1982: 47).

In retrospect, this electoral judgement seems rather harsh. The post-war housing programme achieved more than its First World War equivalent. In the six years after the First World War 475,000 properties were completed, compared with 1,017,000 after the Second World War (including prefabricated dwellings). The programme kept pace with the rapid growth in households, although there was no net improvement overall.

1945–51: THE HIGH WATER MARK OF STATE HOUSING?

In his analysis of council housing, Peter Malpass has claimed that state policies in the late 1940s were consistent with more general principles laid down for the modern welfare state. 'The emphasis was on breaking down the barriers and distinctions between groups in society, opening up public services to all on the basis of need, without investigation of ability to pay' (Malpass 1990: 74).

Malpass claims that there was no need for reforming legislation for public housing in this period, as the principles and framework had already been established after the First World War. Aneurin Bevan's view that 'council housing was for everyone' (Community Development Project 1976: 16) is taken as further testimony to this commitment for a comprehensive state service.

Writing from a different standpoint, Peter Saunders has also argued that the 1945–51 Labour Governments were committed to the eventual abolition of private landlordism so that 'council housing was seen in the same universalistic terms as the new National Health Service and state education system' (Saunders 1990: 27).

We disagree sharply with this analysis of the 1945–51 Labour Governments' housing policy. We would emphasise by contrast the limited horizons set for state intervention in the housing market, the acquiescence in the dominant role of the private sector and the inability to meet acute housing needs through public provision. The reasons are partly historical. The basic function of council housing had been established in the inter-war period and this was not seriously questioned by the 1945–51 Labour Governments. The role of public housing focused on issues of national production, rather than equity between tenures, the extent of housing need, or local variations in housing markets. Any grandiose claims about achieving a greater degree of social justice were soon consumed by the interaction of interest rates, building costs, political hostility, pressures on public expenditure and the implications for the private market. The extent of historical continuity is very strongly imprinted on the housing programme from 1945 onwards. The Labour Government's approach to council housing appears as simply a more effective version of the post-1919 strategy rather than as an embodiment of the radical universalistic thinking behind health or education reforms.

We do not wish to minimise the significant advances made by the 1945–51 Labour Government in its housing programme – and not just in achieving relatively high housing output. There are occasional glimpses of a more universalistic approach to council housing. This is partly due to the influence – or at least the rhetoric – of the Minister responsible for housing from 1945 to the start of 1951 – Aneurin Bevan. He fostered a view of council estates consisting of mixed communities which cut across class and income barriers and offered a superior quality of life to private estates. The removal of the term 'working classes' from the 1949 Housing Act also carried symbolic force in affirming that the purpose of council housing was to meet general needs, rather than those of a particular social class.

Bevan's commitment to council housing also moved beyond the need simply to meet building targets at all costs. Higher standards were introduced for new council dwellings, even though this inevitably increased unit costs. The average size of council houses increased from less than 800 sq. ft. in the 1930s to the minimum of 900 sq. ft. recommended by the Dudley Report in 1944, with an average floor area for three-bedroomed council houses of over 1,000 sq. ft. between 1946 and 1951. The impact of changing standards is discussed in more detail in Chapter 4.

However, these glimpses of a more comprehensive view of council housing are overshadowed by the clear differences between the ethos of housing policy and the Labour Government's overall social welfare strategy. The two main political parties differed in their approach to the costs of the new welfare state, the proportion of funding from National Insurance and general taxation, and the extent to which the public sector should aspire to a redistributive role, reducing social inequalities. But there was bipartisan support for the guiding principles of universalism – in education and health care – and securing a minimum level of subsistence – through social security. State provision was necessary to protect the casualties falling prey to Beveridge's five 'Giants' of Want, Idleness, Disease, Ignorance and Squalor. Yet public housing fell well short of meeting either of these objectives. It was neither universal in coverage nor did it assist those in greatest need. In many respects, the strategy was contradictory. Bevan's commitment to higher standards of construction, for example, forced up rent levels, inhibiting the capacity of low income households to gain access to council housing. Poorer households were excluded from state provision in the immediate post-war period. They remained in the private sector of rented housing.

We noted in the Introduction that housing differs from other welfare services because of its commodity form and its high capital and revenue cost. These features drove a further wedge between state housing and other public services such as health and education which were 'free' at the point of use. Housing costs can be reduced by government intervention, through subsidies directed to properties or to consumers. But the ability of the 1945–51 Labour Governments to lower costs were continually thwarted by economic pressures. Central government subsidies to local authorities were not increased after 1946 and by 1949–50 'the pressure on rents arising from standards and costs was resulting in both high rents and widespread extra subsidies from the rates' (Malpass 1990: 80).

If property subsidies came under increasing pressure, subsidies to consumers fared even worse. The number of rent rebate schemes – discretionary systems to help poorer council tenants meet housing costs – actually declined. Malpass claims that this was justified by reference to the rising real value of wages, the provision of family allowances and the creation of National Assistance. As the new social security system had been introduced to abolish poverty, extra help with housing costs was quite simply unnecessary; and the poor at least had access to relatively cheap privately rented housing.

The 1945–51 Labour Governments' approach to private provision offers a further point of difference between their housing policies and the broader social welfare strategy. We have argued that council housing was promoted out of economic necessity, and not as the first step towards universal state provision. In fact, the private sector remained relatively unscathed. Measures were introduced to control rents and improve security of tenure in the private rented sector, for example, but there was little discussion about changing the pattern of ownership through the wholesale municipalisation of a tenure which at that stage housed the majority of the population. Similarly, the growth of middle-class owner-occupation, which had taken place during the inter-war period, remained unchallenged. The slower pace in the expansion of home ownership in the late 1940s was due to the direction of the building programme, the response of private developers and pressures on consumer spending, rather than on the Labour Government's ideological abhorrence of private provision *per se*.

A distinctive feature of policies towards state housing in any period is the umbilical link with overall national economic performance. Of course, all welfare services – especially health – came under pressure to contain expenditure in the late 1940s, due to balance of payments problems and competing claims, especially from the defence budget. However, housing was especially vulnerable. In evoking the vocabulary of reconstruction and in gaining the support of the Prime Minister, Aneurin Bevan achieved some success in insulating state housing from economic pressures. At least the building programme was maintained, favourable loan rates for local authorities secured and subsidy levels held firm – in absolute, if not in real, terms. Yet the pressures to curtail spending were inexorable, and the development of high quality public housing at a reasonable cost to the consumer eventually gave way.

When Bevan resigned from the Atlee Government early in 1951, his housing responsibilities were taken over by Hugh Dalton (as Minister of Local Government and Planning). Three months later, Dalton issued a circular (38/51) reducing costs and standards in council housing. This established a precedent which Conservative Governments were not slow to follow during the rest of that decade.

We have concentrated here on the housing policies of the post-war Labour Government because this was such a crucial period in the formation of the British welfare state. The objectives of this network of state services and benefits have been summarised as 'universality of population cover- age, comprehensiveness of risks covered, adequacy of benefits and the citizenship notion of the social services provided as of right to all and not as a form of charity to the few' (Mishra 1984: 7). In housing, however, the government's policies towards state provision, dwelling subsidies and help to meet consumers' housing costs clearly had more modest objectives. At a time of acute shortage, the expansion of local authority housing was merely the preferred 'bricks and mortar' response to the country's key housing problem. As Short suggests, 'public housing was the solution adopted because it seemed the best one in the circumstances, not because it was perceived as an inherently socialist model for building a better society' (Short 1982: 47). It is illuminating to reflect on the weakness of support for state housing in this period compared to other services by reflecting on the contribution of the ideology which underpinned the development of the British post-war welfare system – Fabianism. The weakening political resolve to develop council housing in the post-war period was not, we suggest, merely the result of changing economic conditions and govern- ment priorities. It reflected a wider theoretical disquiet and ideological uncertainty about the purpose and function of the British welfare state.

In the post-war period, a prescriptive, ethically informed approach was the hallmark of Fabian ideology. The approach laid particular emphasis on the values of citizenship and social equality. Welfare policy would promote citizenship through the provision of social rights and the development of universal services. The market failed to provide services of an adequate standard, and the losers in the capitalist lottery were effectively denied the right to participate in the community, as they were dependent on residual second-class and stigmatised benefits and services. Universal provision, on the other hand, ensured a higher level of public support, especially from middle-class consumers, and therefore promoted higher standards. The Fabian welfare state also enhanced economic efficiency through ensuring a more productive, healthy, better educated and housed workforce. There was no inherent conflict between the socialised welfare sector and the market economy: the former aided and nourished the latter, and then reaped the reward by taking its share of the surplus generated by economic growth. Commitment to equality in Fabian ideology derived from its concern with the unequal distribution of resources under market mechanisms. For Fabians, a more equal society, guided by public intervention, would achieve social cohesion, enhance integration, develop the quality of altruism and promote social mobility through extending opportunity. The framework of the capitalist economy was accepted but the 'diswelfares' of economic change needed to be reduced. Public provision was designed to meet those social needs ignored, neglected or distorted by the market economy.

What did the Fabian perspective contribute to understanding the development of welfare state policies, and the changing role of council housing? It was assumed that governments achieved their objectives by relying on expert knowledge, professional judgement and applied research. The welfare state contributed to social progress by implementing ever more enlightened policies which responded to general public needs, rather than serving specific economic or class interests. Fabian theorists were aware of the unequal distribution of political and economic power, and became increasingly concerned about the barriers to introducing incremental reform. But at the heart they took a pluralist view of the state – in which power was not concentrated in the hands of an élite, but dispersed among different groups with cross-cutting interests and influences (Mishra 1984).

The Fabian model of the welfare state also entailed a distinctive view about the mode of organisation of social service provision, which was combined with a faith in the virtues of professional expertise and efficient administration. Resources were most effectively allocated through centralised bureaucratic systems, so that benefits and services could then be 'delivered' to recipients at a more local level. The process of professionalisation was central to the development of the Fabian welfare state. As long as defined codes of practice and procedures for self-regulation were devised, professionals could be given ample discretion in carrying out their roles. Their expertise could be dispensed to those in need. There is little hint in most Fabian writing about the disadvantages which might arise from this approach to service provision – such as the abuse of professional power, the rigidities of welfare bureaucracies or the lack of consumer influence or involvement.

The attention of Fabian academics and politicians was not devoted equally to each aspect of the welfare state. Their influence was most penetrating in the fields of income maintenance, personal social services and health. The approach was less confident in an analysis of housing provision, as this diverged most clearly from the Fabian ideal of social welfare. As we have seen, the state's contribution was more limited, and public provision fell well short of universal coverage. The market was dominant throughout the post-war era. The expense of housing as a commodity, and its consequently high direct cost to the consumer, brought it within the purview of *laissez-faire* economists – the Fabians' main antagonists. The delivery of the public housing service was also problematic. As we shall argue in Chapter 5, housing management proved more resistant to the process of professionalisation than other state welfare services.

The fragility of Fabian analysis of housing provision in a welfare state system reflected underlying weaknesses in the overall perspective, which became more evident once the period of sustained economic growth came to an end during the 1970s. Fabians assumed that the structural relationship between the welfare state and the market was basically neutral – conflict was confined to different aims and values. This position became more tenuous when the welfare state, buoyed up on the tide of economic growth, foundered on the rocks of recession and 'stagflation'. Critics from both Right and Left uncovered the blindspots and weaknesses of the Fabian vision – its reliance on an expanding tax base to finance welfare reform, its failure to recognise the tenacity of market mechanisms, its assumption that the boom–slump economic cycle was over for good, its neglect of class forces and interests. Above all, the Fabian view was challenged on the basis that the welfare state had failed to achieve its objectives of social justice and greater equality.

Many of these difficulties could be seen in the rather muted Fabian analysis of housing policy and provision in the post-war period. From the start, public housing was permeated by market prerogatives, which stunted its expansion and distorted its subsequent development. These features did not fit easily within a Fabian analysis wedded to an expanded state working in harness with the market to provide universal social services. Furthermore, Fabianism concentrated on the mechanics of provision rather than the qualitative experience of the service consumers – and, as we show in Part II, this latter aspect tells us a great deal about the perceived shortcomings of council housing for many of its tenants.

The limitations of Fabian solutions to problems in the post-war housing market were reflected politically in the Labour Party's growing ambivalence towards council housing. The Labour Party shifted its ground on state housing well before any other element of the welfare state, accepting the dominance of owner-occupation and consigning the public sector to a residual role; as Clapham *et al.* claim:

> The affirmation by Labour of owner-occupation as the normal tenure signalled acceptance of only a limited role for in-kind provision, and acknowledged the legitimacy of subsidised market provision . . . . This flew in the face of the social democratic ideals behind council housing . . . . Instead of integrating council tenants into society, the party has helped to exclude them by identifying them as poor and unable to provide for themselves in the market place.
>
> (Clapham *et al.* 1990: 44–5)

The consequences of the Labour Government's restricted and pragmatic approach to council housing were to unfold during the 1950s and 1960s. State housing was not a permanent monument to the virtues of public provision: it was an expedient service, intermittently making good the shortcomings of the private market. Council housing was, therefore, more amenable to attack and transformation than state education, health or social security. This brittleness was increasingly exposed by new government priorities, changing public attitudes and spending patterns and the impact of low growth and sporadic crises in the British economy. The period from 1950 to 1980 affirmed the dominance of the private sector – while witnessing a major shift from renting to owner-occupation – and the growing residualisation of public housing provision.

EMBRACING HOME OWNERSHIP: 1950–79

From 1951 onwards both Conservative and Labour Governments' housing policies reinforced the role of state provision as subservient to the private market. The delicate shield constructed by Aneurin Bevan around levels of investment and standards in council housing was quickly shattered, and patterns of housing tenure changed sharply. Between 1953 and 1981, owner-occupation became the majority housing tenure (rising from 32 per cent to 58 per cent of households). Public sector housing increased from 18 per cent to 29 per cent of households although, as we will see, the sector moved towards a more residual form of provision. The private rented sector collapsed. We will argue that this process of tenurial transformation can best be understood by reference to the failure to establish universal public provision as the basis of post-war housing policy, as had been the case in health and education. This failure was manifested in different ways – in changing patterns of new housebuilding, in the modification of housing subsidies and in wider changes across all housing tenures. Each of these will be examined in turn.

We have already seen how the post-war period was dominated by the urgent requirement to achieve a building programme to meet the housing shortage. The commitment was carried forward in the early years of the 1951–5 Conservative Government, which aimed for a target of 300,000 properties a year. This determination was graphically expressed by the then Housing Minister, Harold Macmillan: 'the fierce and almost frantic pursuit of the housing target filled my mind . . . to the exclusion of everything not directly related to the achievement of our purpose' (Macmillan 1969: 377). In order to achieve this objective, large-scale public housebuilding had to continue, albeit at reduced standards and unit costs. Housing subsidies were sharply increased in 1952 (from £16 10s. p. a. to £24 15s. p. a. per dwelling) to protect housebuilding from rising interest rates. The policy led to the construction of 939,000 council properties between 1952 and 1956 – an unprecedented scale of activity. However, the balance had already started to shift in favour of 'releasing' the private speculative housebuilder to take on the dominant role for new construction.

During the 1945–51 Government, a stringent licensing system had held private housebuilding in check – although, in the early stages, economic conditions were hardly favourable to private development in any case. As part of the strategy of encouraging private enterprise, the Conservative Government liberalised the licensing system, and finally abolished it in 1954 in a more promising economic climate for private housebuilding. The taxation of development values had been abolished the year before, building costs were falling in real terms, credit was easing, interest rates were fairly steady and demand was increasing. As a result, the proportion of new housebuilding in the private sector increased from merely 15 per cent in 1952 to 63 per cent in 1961. As Stephen Merrett claims, 'Private construction was encouraged to surge ahead whilst public housing was once again confined to making up the shortfall of speculative output below the aggregate target' (Merrett with Gray 1982: 28). This basic philosophy remained unchanged during the 1960s and 1970s, under both Labour and Conservative Governments, although the capacity of the public sector to make up the shortfall was continually thwarted by economic circumstances.

Various attempts were made during the 1950s and 1960s to squeeze more completions out of limited housing investment – by raising productivity, cutting costs or reducing standards. Harold Macmillan's 'Peoples' House' of 1952 was an early example, reducing the size of the average three-bedroomed house by 50 square feet. Industrialised building methods were increasingly adopted to cut down costs: contributing, at their peak in 1967, to 43 per cent of public sector output. The pressure on land prices and favourable subsidy arrangements advanced the trend towards flat construction in the public sector. High blocks (above five storeys) rose from

9 per cent of council housebuilding in the late 1950s to a peak of 26 per cent by 1966 (Burnett 1986: 186; Dunleavy 1981a). There were significant local variations, concealed by these national trends. In London, for example, 91 per cent of the homes built by the GLC in 1967 were in flats – and two-thirds of these were in high-rise blocks (Power 1987: 45).

The objective of promoting local authority housebuilding to achieve specific targets was a recurring motif in housing programmes. It was most evident in the policies of the Labour Governments during the mid-1960s and mid-1970s. However, there was no Aneurin Bevan to show the necessary political determination to maintain public housing investment in the teeth of economic crisis. True, the sheer shortage of housing was less compelling than in the immediate post-war period. But the reduction of council housebuilding programmes also reflected the loss of support for state housing in a Labour Party now wedded to the notion of mass home ownership.

The National Housing Plan of the 1964–70 Labour Governments, for example, sought to achieve the completion of 500,000 units a year overall. In the event, 1.8 million properties were built between 1965 and 1969 (half of them in the public sector) – 28 per cent short of the target. The reasons were both economic and political. The 1967 balance of payments crisis, culminating in the devaluation of sterling, resulted in public spending cutbacks. Economic strategy turned towards greater private sector invest-ment to expand exports and reduce imports. However, the downturn in the programme also reflected the waning faith of the Labour Government in the capacity of local authorities to operate as the vehicle behind this great housing drive. As Minister for Housing and Local Government in the 1964–6 administration, Richard Crossman's attitude to local councils was rather different from Aneurin Bevan's: 'Most local authorities don't want to build houses and, if they do, are grossly incompetent and drive any contractor crazy by the arbitrary methods of their committees and their sullenness and incompetence' (Crossman 1975: 625). In fact, Crossman's frustration anticipated future political obstacles for the Labour Government – many local authorities came under Conservative control following the 1967 and 1968 local elections, resulting in land sales to private developers, reductions in council building programmes and the promotion of council house sales.

The general costs of housing production spiralled in the early 1970s as a result of inflation, rapid rises in interest rates and an explosion of land prices. Public investment was especially vulnerable to these pressures and, under the 1970–4 Heath Government, council housebuilding fell until it was at its lowest level since 1947. The attempt of the 1974–9 Labour Government to expand local authority housebuilding appears in retrospect as a paler version of its Housing Plan in the 1960s. The targets were less ambitious, the upswing was shorter, the crisis more immediate and the decline in investment more dramatic and permanent.

The overall strategy of the Labour Government was guided by the need to regenerate British industry and contain 'unproductive' public expenditure. In 1975 the Chancellor of the Exchequer, Dennis Healey, cut £1 billion off the public sector borrowing requirement for 1975–6, and a further £3 billion for 1976–7. In exchange for the infamous $5 billion loan from the International Monetary Fund in 1976, a further £1 billion reduction in public spending was required for 1977–8. Much of this fell on capital investment, as a less painful means in the short term of cutting back spending for a Labour Government then clinging on to power with the help of Liberal Party support. The housing programme suffered because of its large capital component, and because cuts would not have an easily identifiable impact on particular groups (Cooper 1985). There would be a time lag before the consequences of reducing the building programme were felt, and there would be savings on future debt charges and subsidies.

Local authority housing investment therefore fell from £2,580 million in 1975–6 to £1,934 million in 1977–8. The number of council housebuilding starts in England and Wales fell from 156,000 in 1976 to merely 72,000 in 1979 (Holmans 1987: 157). While overall housing expenditure fell by 19 per cent between 1974–5 and 1978–9, capital expenditure declined by fully 35 per cent. The 1976 economic crisis proved to be the death knell of large-scale council housebuilding in Britain.

As we have seen, the expansion of council housing after the Second World War was propelled by pragmatic economic reasoning and not as a convincing attempt to promote universalist state provision. When economic and political circumstances changed, the private sector could take on the dominant role, sustained by benign government financial policies. The intermittent function of council housing – as a means of achieving imposed government building targets – diminished, as political support grew fainter and the most pressing issues moved from housing production to issues of finance, rehabilitation, allocation and distribution. In the event, housing investment in the public sector was no greater in real terms in 1979 than in 1949. It is instructive to compare this trend with expenditure on other elements of the post-war welfare state. Obviously one cannot simply assume that rates of expenditure growth simply mirror government priorities, so that the most favoured services receive the most money. Other factors influence the trends – such as demographic changes, the differential extent of central government control, technological requirements, political expediency, perceived public resistance and changes in demand. Nevertheless, the contrasts are stark. Compared to the static level of expenditure on public housing investment, spending on social security increased on average by 4.9 per cent *per year* between 1951 and 1978; education spending increased by 4.4 per cent, health by 2.6 per cent and personal social services by 5.7 per cent (Gould and Roweth 1980: 347).

Overall public expenditure on housing did increase between 1951 and 1979, but the composition of this expenditure changed considerably. Instead of spending on new investment, public expenditure was taken up by subsidies on current spending directed in various ways to local authorities, tenants, owners and landlords. Here, the cumulative effect of increasing rates of inflation, rising costs and nominally high interest rates placed ever greater pressure on the maintenance of high quality public sector housing provision. It soon started to crumble.

The second key factor in government housing policy until 1979 concerned the distribution of housing subsidies. In the early 1950s, council tenants were protected from bearing the market costs of public housing by various means – lower interest rates for local authorities, government subsidies for new building, rent rebates (in some councils), contributions from local authority rates and rent fixing on the basis of historic costs. Over the next thirty years, the complex mesh of subsidies, benefits and costing procedures came increasingly to reflect market-based principles. The overall approach individualised the costs of public housing, both in investment for new building and in ongoing revenue costs. Greater reliance was placed on the consumer and less on public subsidy. This policy prefigured strategies pursued by the Conservative Governments during the 1980s towards expenditure on all state welfare services. However, in the thirty years after the Second World War, the health and education services remained largely financed from general government taxation. In council housing, however, tenants – or at least more affluent tenants – had to bear a much higher proportion of the costs of the service.

From 1919 the structure of flat-rate subsidies for new council dwellings had underwritten the function of state housing as a means of achieving building targets. Changes in subsidy level reflected the priority accorded to the building programme by the government of the day. However, the Conservative Governments of the 1950s used their control of subsidies to influence not just the rate of new building but also the character of council housing. Subsidies were reduced in 1954 following the attainment of the magic figure of 300,000 annual completions. The 1956 Housing Subsidies Act introduced differential subsidy levels. A £10 'general needs' subsidy was introduced (only to be abolished later in the year apart from one-bedroomed dwellings for the elderly) and a £22 slum clearance subsidy was established to promote local authority redevelopment programmes.

Financial protection for council tenants was further reduced in 1956 by the removal of the requirement on local authorities to make a rate fund contribution to housing revenue accounts. Further changes in the 1961 Housing Act produced a dual subsidy system to encourage low-cost local authorities to raise rents (Malpass 1990).

The system of council housing finance was further exposed to the open market by changing interest rate policy. The rate charged by the Public Works Loan Board was raised from 3 per cent in 1951 to 5.75 per cent by 1956. In addition, local authorities were given the freedom to borrow directly on the open market. This was made a requirement from 1955 onwards, unless local authorities could not raise the necessary funds in this manner. Local councils were therefore forced to pay considerably more for loans raised on the capital market to fund new building. By the late 1950s, over 60 per cent of local authority housing expenditure was devoted to interest payments (Short 1982: 51).

Malpass (1990) claims that the most significant shift towards a self-financed local authority housing service was produced by the introduction of rent pooling in 1955. Local authorities were to pool rents across the entire stock, thereby protecting tenants in newer properties from higher costs resulting from inflation and interest charges. This policy persuaded local authorities to charge higher rents for older houses, increasing total rental income and reducing dependence on Exchequer subsidies. The only alternative was to increase rate contributions, or cut costs, maintenance and development programmes.

The essence of these changes was that council tenants now had to 'pay their way'. An increasing proportion of local authorities' housing revenue expenditure was met from rents, although there were widespread local variations according to past rent policies, the extent of rate support, the age of the stock and management and maintenance costs. Overall, council rents increased on average by 7.7 per cent between 1955–6 and 1965–6 – a process which 'attempted to drive the affluent worker out of their house and into the market' (Merrett 1979: 252).

These policy changes reinforced the crucial differences between the funding of the state housing service and other welfare services. The principles behind health and education finance were to minimise costs at the point of use by the individual consumer and to socialise expenditure commitments through local and central government taxes and national insurance. The balance between public subsidy and costs charged to the consumer in housing, however, was continually disturbed by the initiatives described above. While other elements of the 1945–51 welfare state remained intact, the uniquely high costs of the public housing service were too much for the Conservative Governments of the 1950s to countenance. Tenants had to pay more.

Rents continued to rise faster than pre-tax earnings or retail prices during the 1964–70 Labour Governments, due to increasing costs in repairs, maintenance, management and new construction (DoE 1977a: 186–7). However, Exchequer subsidies also rose sharply – from £68 million in 1963–4 to £124.6 million in 1969–70 (Malpass 1990: 103). The government had raised subsidy levels in the 1967 Housing Subsidies Act in order to expand housing output. The subsidy was not a fixed subsidy per dwelling, but was based on differences in loan charges (between a nominal 4 per cent and the actual rate of interest). Building costs were to be regulated by the housing cost yardstick, but interest rate increases were not limited. While this provided roughly the same benefits to council tenants as owner-occupiers gained through mortgage tax relief, the resulting cost of the subsidy was later represented as 'a staggering addition to the nation's tax burden' (HMSO 1971).

Despite its short life on the statute book, the 1972 Housing Finance Act represents a turning point in the post-war policies towards rents and subsidies. More than any other measure, it foreshadowed the philosophy, if not the practice, of the Thatcher Government's strategy towards state housing. The Act, introduced by the 1970–4 Heath Government, was an explicit attempt to impose market principles on the creaking system of council housing finance. While detailed analysis of the Act's provisions is available elsewhere (Lansley 1979; Cooper 1985), the underlying premises merit some consideration, as they broke with the shaky post-war orthodoxy towards rents and subsidies.

'Fair rents' had originally been introduced by the Labour Government for the private rented sector under the 1968 Rent Act. They were rather confusingly defined as market rents disregarding the effects of scarcity. The 1972 Act introduced fair rents for the public sector as well. This measure ensured that council rent levels would change according to current values and conditions in the private sector, rather than as the product of historic costs, loan charges, management and maintenance expenditure and cross-subsidy from the rates. The cost of a state service to the consumer was therefore to be dictated by reference to market pricing – a unique financial policy for the public sector during the 1970s. This policy also constrained local authorities' freedom to set rents, and was a major step towards greater central government direction and control.

The objectives of the 1972 Act were to raise council rents, soften the blow for lower income tenants with a compulsory rent rebate scheme, boost the private rented market and reduce Exchequer subsidies (Parker 1971). The adoption of a system designed for profit-making landlords and the phased increases in council rents provoked widespread resistance from tenants and local authorities. In the event, only two local authorities refused implementation until 1974 – Bedwas and Machen in South Wales and Clay Cross in Derbyshire. The disqualification of Clay Cross councillors created a *cause célèbre* in the struggle of local authorities against undue central government control (Skinner and Langdon 1974; Sklair 1975).

The impact of the 1972 Housing Act was not as intended by the government. In a period of sharply rising land prices, construction costs and interest rates, local authorities were actually assisted by the workings of the new subsidy system. Tenants were also protected by the transition to 'fair rents' in a period of high price inflation. The purpose of the Act was to lay a higher proportion of the cost of council housing at the doors of tenants. Yet subsidies almost doubled in real terms over the two years following its passage into law (DoE 1977b: 41). Unique economic conditions had simply forced a reluctant government deeper into the mire of subsidisation.

The 1972 Housing Act was quickly repealed by the 1974–9 Labour Government. However, subsequent measures merely underlined the lack of a systematic strategy to fund council housing in accordance with principles of universalism or social equity rather than a market-based paradigm. The growth of mass home ownership, the waning confidence of the Labour Party in the principles and operation of state housing, the narrow parliamentary majority of the second Labour administration and the consequences of the 1976 sterling crisis – these factors all conspired to reproduce a chaotic system of subsidies and controls which, in the words of the future Secretary of State for the Environment, Anthony Crosland, 'distribute aid to housing in a whimsical manner' (Crosland 1971).

The 1977 Housing Policy Review was intended to cut a swathe through the system of housing support to all tenures. The Review contained thorough research and analysis but it was 'almost entirely a non-event in terms of its policy recommendations' (Lansley 1979: 218). The reasons are not hard to find. Council housing had progressed too far down the road of a minority, residualised tenure for the poor for any sweeping changes to be palatable. The *realpolitik* of maintaining current tenure relationships was imprinted on every page. The Review supported the continued growth of owner-occupation and noted that 'the overall level of public sector housing investment should decline in response to changing circumstances' (DoE 1977a: 44). Some firm proposals were advanced. Central control over local authority capital expenditure was extended through the introduction of housing investment programmes. Subsidies were to be linked to deficits arising from councils' income and expenditure records rather than loan charges – an echo of the 1972 Act's formula.

Council rents fell in real terms by an average of 4.3 per cent a year between 1974 and 1979, declining from 7.4 per cent to 6.7 per cent of average earnings. Again, changing rent levels were not the result of any fundamental reappraisal of the role of council housing – they were the accidental consequence of high inflation, falling building costs and restrictions on capital expenditure commitments. In retrospect, it now seems that the Housing Policy Review was the last opportunity to stake a political claim for a distinctive public housing sector in Britain operating on different principles to the private market. The attempt to equalise financial support to each housing tenure and to direct subsidies and tax expenditure to those in households in most acute need had failed. The resultant confused system of public housing finance therefore tottered along, clearing the way for the decisive policies of the Thatcher Government from 1979 onwards. Council housing could by then be effectively presented as an anachronism – financed on a basis for which it was not designed, divested of its traditional function in supporting new building programmes and under severe criticism for its record in management, maintenance and design. By this time, Bevan's dream of a relatively low-cost, high-quality service serving a wide range of households was well and truly dead.

The third feature of post-war housing policies was the influence of consumer 'preferences' on the development of housing tenures. The twenty-five years following the 1945–51 Labour Governments were a period of reasonably consistent (if sluggish) economic growth and rising real incomes. In the thirteen years of Conservative Government from 1951, for example, real disposable incomes rose by 54 per cent and average *household* income increased even more, due to the higher proportion of women going out to work (Holmans 1987: 103). In theory, this could have provided fertile ground for the expansion of public housing along the lines envisaged by Aneurin Bevan. Poorer households would have more disposable income so that they could afford higher council rents to secure better standards and amenities than in the private rented sector. Existing council tenants could have paid their rent and spent their remaining income on consumer durables, or leisure activities. As the income level of council tenants increased, local authorities could have maintained a high level of service, active maintenance and repair programmes, and built to high standards. Modest rent increases could have been levied without causing too much distress, supported by a constant level of Exchequer subsidy.

In short, the sustained post-war consumer boom could have prompted the expansion of a council housing service which genuinely cut across class and income barriers. Of course, this did not happen. The newly affluent workers bought their way into home ownership rather than council renting. Why did the growth in consumer expenditure lead to the expansion of owner-occupation during the 1950s and 1960s, thereby consigning state housing to a narrower function in the housing market?

The explanation for this transformation is open to dispute. Certainly, changing financial conditions played a part. As we have seen, from 1951 onwards subsidy levels to local authorities were subject to constant modification, as successive governments juggled between the need to expand housebuilding and to reduce public expenditure on council housing. Finance of owner-occupation, on the other hand, was more readily available to a wide group of households during this period.

In comparison to other elements of the welfare state, the actual service offered by local housing authorities was also inadequate. The prevailing values in housing management were often patronising, oppressive and inflexible. In part, this reflected the tardy professionalisation of housing management compared to, say, planning or social work. Yet the different emphasis also stemmed from the overriding need to collect the rent – to recoup the costs of the service directly from consumers. This 'policing' role added a different quality to the work of housing practitioners compared to colleagues in other local government departments. Above all, council housing had not been established as a comprehensive form of provision: the private sector remained dominant throughout.

The preference for owner-occupation was not, therefore, the result of free choices made by consumers assessing available options in the housing market, gaily swapping their rent books for long-standing mortgage commitments. As always, the distinctive features of housing as a commodity – its immobility, durability and high cost – meant that consumer expectations were crucially shaped by the determinants of available *supply*. In the post-war period, the supply of new council housing was intermittent and – in England and Wales, at least – never approached universalist status. The quality and cost of the service varied widely at the local level, and access was restricted to households in particular categories (such as those already resident in the local authority area).

State health and education services were based on principles of universalism, ready access and equality of opportunity. During the 1950s and 1960s, few consumers showed signs of using their new found affluence to buy their way into private provision in these services. Housing was the only public service where state provision denied access to many in need, placed a significant proportion of costs directly on to consumers, and was dominated by provision through the private market. These unique features constrained the expansion of the public sector and led ultimately to the erosion of the early post-war hopes for council housing. We therefore need to consider this process of tenure change in some detail.

Access to owner-occupation was eased through various financial measures. Schedule A tax (on imputed rental income on properties) was abolished in 1963 and two years later domestic property was exempted from Capital Gains Tax liability. In 1969, the Labour Government made loan repayments subject to taxation – but mortgages were excluded due to the anticipated electoral repercussions. The government also introduced the option mortgage scheme to benefit households whose income fell below the tax threshold. Many households were therefore induced to buy rather than rent by the straightforward financial calculus that it was cheaper and more beneficial in the long term.

Authors such as Short (1982) and Cockburn (1977) have claimed that the financial advantages of home ownership were sought by governments eager to divide working-class interests, promote market principles, encourage privatised and consumerist life-styles and stifle the potential for industrial conflict by landing workers with long-term debt. Certainly, it is not hard to identify a consistent ideological message from post-war governments in homage to owner-occupation. Prior to the 1950 General Election, for example, the Conservatives had extolled the virtues of owner-occupation in the following terms

> Private property is an equipoise to political power. The more men and women there are whose property gives them a security, a status and an influence independent of officialdom, the greater is the guarantee for the freedom of fellow subjects.
>
> (Conservative Political Centre 1950)

Fifteen years later, the Labour Government had accepted the expansion of owner-occupation as 'normal' and a 'long-term social advance' (Ministry of Housing and Local Government 1965b). By the time of the Housing Policy Review undertaken by the Callaghan Government in 1977, reference was made to a 'basic and natural desire to own one's own home'. The preceding Conservative Government had meanwhile expressed its support for home ownership more lyrically as 'the most rewarding form of housing tenure'. 'It satisfies a deep and natural desire on the part of the householder to have independent control of the house that shelters him and his family' (HMSO 1971).

It is evident that the expansion of owner-occupation from the early 1950s onwards received bipartisan blessing. It is more debatable to suppose that this tenure change was carefully cultivated through the complex financial manipulation of subsidies, grants and tax relief measures by successive governments. Owner-occupation expanded in the 1950s and 1960s, due largely to overall economic strategies towards consumption and borrowing and changing market conditions in both the private and public rented sectors. The rise in home ownership was not a social revolution engineered by government policies solely designed to divide the interests of working-class households or to promote allegiance to market values.

Many chose to become home owners simply because alternative housing choices were either unavailable or unedifying.

Our emphasis on the characteristics of housing supply as a crucial influence on tenure change follows the approach taken by Hamnett and Randolph in accounting for the decline of private renting during this period:

> The causes of the decline of private landlordism and the rise of owner-occupation this century owe more to the structure of taxation, interest rates and financial opportunities for investors than they do to rent control *per se* or the idea of natural preference on the part of home owners . . . . The structure of tenure opportunities in the private sector is essentially a product of the profitability of different forms of supply, not consumer choice and preference.
>
> (Hamnett and Randolph 1988: 10–12)

This shifts our focus in explaining the triumph of owner-occupation away from any notional 'basic desires' and towards the limitations on other sources of housing supply – and, in particular, the restricted function of state housing. Throughout this period, access to council housing was limited by various factors – notably household income and composition, previous housing history and patterns of mobility. We would argue that much of the success behind the growth of home-ownership can in fact be traced back to an earlier failure – the failure to establish a genuinely universalist public housing service as an integral feature of the post-war welfare state. As a result, private home owner-ship became a much more attractive and viable option for those households seeking to move out of the private rented sector. Skilled working-class and middle-class households did not rush to spend their new found affluence on private services in health and education in the post-war boom (Papadakis and Taylor-Gooby 1987). In these areas, the state offered ready access to a decent standard of provision. Council housing, on the other hand, usually meant long waiting lists, variable standards, relatively high rents and indifferent service delivery. Saunders (1990) has argued that the growth of post-war home ownership represented the ability of households to fulfil their need for emotional expression, security, autonomy and control. We would suggest that these new home owners had not, in fact, seized on a new opportunity to meet natural desires which had been thwarted in the pre-war housing market. More prosaically, owner-occupation was attractive because the private rented sector was collapsing, and council housing was not worth a long wait.

Would patterns of tenure change in post-war Britain have taken a different configuration if state housing provision had been more comprehensive? We have seen that the post-war function of council housing was to achieve ambitious targets in the construction of new dwellings. Yet new additions obviously represent only a small percentage change in terms of the housing stock overall. A genuinely universal public housing service would have had to transform the *existing* tenure balance, not just provide a 'top-up' for the housing service. In particular, it would have had to provide for the majority of households after the war who were living in the private rented sector.

Indeed, the expansion of owner-occupation in the post-war era was the consequence of tenure switch from the private rented sector as much as the product of building programmes. The proportion of newly owner-occupied dwellings resulting from purchase from private landlords rather than new construction was 60 per cent from 1953–61, 35 per cent from 1961–71 and 36 per cent from 1971–81. A different post-war housing strategy might have channelled this exodus of private tenants into the public rather than owner-occupied sector.

In fact, the wholesale municipalisation of the private rented sector never got on to the agenda of the 1945–51 Labour Governments, even though it might have helped to achieve the balanced social communities in council housing sought by Aneurin Bevan. The government's policies towards private renting were confined to rent control and enhancing security of tenure. It is, of course, not difficult to see why municipalisation was given scant consideration. The costs of the large housing programme were difficult enough to sustain, without the added legal complications of transforming property ownership rights, the financial and political complexities of compensation arrangements and the administrative strain placed on local authorities. But it remains the case that, if council housing was ever to become a universalist service, *existing* tenure patterns had to be changed through radical and far-reaching controls. It was simply not possible to build one's way to a comprehensive form of public housing provision. The distinctive nature of housing as a durable commodity ensures that the legacy of previous policies and circumstances constrains the room for manoeuvre for even the most ambitious government.

If a strategy of widespread municipalisation had been adopted after 1945 – resulting in a National Housing Service which rivalled the other NHS as a key ingredient in the post-war welfare state – it remains a matter of conjecture how far this would have checked the growth of mass home ownership. But it is conceivable that many households in the poorly maintained private rented sector would have moved into a system of municipal ownership if security of tenure, good management, reasonable rent levels and high standards had been guaranteed. A more comprehensive and securely funded public housing service would at least have provided a firmer edifice to withstand subsequent financial and ideological attacks by post-war governments.

As it was, the buoyancy of house prices, declining rates of return and the ill-conceived attempt to revive the private rented sector under the 1957 Act all conspired to induce landlords to sell up, whether on the open market or to sitting tenants. Even then, many of those who bought in the 1950s and 1960s had to be convinced of the value of taking on the financial burden of home ownership rather than continuing to rent (Hamnett and Randolph 1988: 88–90). Alan Holmans, for example, refers to 1960 survey evidence which shows that 21 per cent of owner-occupiers with a mortgage said they would have preferred to rent rather than buy – and 27 per cent of those where the head of household had a net income of £10 or less. As Holmans states, the evidence is important 'in showing how recent is the near-universal preference for owner-occupation that by the late 1970s had come to be regarded as axiomatic' (Holmans 1987: 188). The triumph of owner-occupation, therefore, owed much to the changes in the private rented sector, the priorities of both major parties and continuing public expenditure pressures which consigned state housing to a minority role – out of reach to many in the greatest housing need and overlooked by more affluent middle- and working-class households. This was a very different outcome to access to the public health services – where middle-class consumers actually used the service more, and where the expansion of private sector alternatives remained modest.

As a result of the transformations in housing tenure from the early 1950s, the character of council housing itself changed. We will now consider how this process further weakened the principles on which the service had been based in the immediate post-war period.

THE RESIDUALISATION OF COUNCIL HOUSING

In the 1960s, Richard Titmuss drew a distinction between 'institutional' and 'residual' models of social welfare (Titmuss 1974). In the institutional model, values of universalism, mutuality and collective purpose are promoted through the development of public social services. In the residual model, the state only provides for those who cannot rely on support from their family, or further their own interests through the market place. At the time Titmuss was contributing to an academic debate in social policy. He could attack right-wing economists such as Hayek, Friedman and members of the Institute of Economic Affairs in the secure knowledge that their influence on government welfare policy was marginal. Titmuss himself was a bearer of the broad Fabian, social democratic tradition which had underpinned the foundation of the post-war welfare state. Labour and Conservative Governments alike were pursuing social welfare strategies broadly consonant with the principles of collective public provision designed to meet specified social needs.

Council housing was different, however. Increasingly during the 1950s and 1960s the character of public housing came to reflect the axioms of the residual model of welfare, as Stephen Merrett has made clear:

> Since 1953 the role of state housing has been perceived by the leadership of both major political parties, when in power, as the residual activity of carrying through what speculative building for owner-occupation and private rehabilitation were unable to achieve.
>
> (Merrett 1979: 281)

This transformation did not result from governments vigorously pursuing housing policies as part of an ideological crusade on behalf of a residualist, anti-collectivist model of state welfare. Rather, as we have seen, the changing function of council housing emanated from wider economic processes, such as high interest rates, price inflation and high land prices, social and demographic factors and an underlying antagonism to direct state control over property relations and the housing market. The combined effect of these influences unpicked the shaky commitment to an institutional view of council housing as a comprehensive service along the lines of state education or health.

The concept of residualisation has been prominent in housing policy literature (Clapham and Maclennan 1983; Forrest and Murie 1983; Malpass 1990), and one needs to be precise about the nature of this process. It does not mean the retreat of state involvement in the housing market in favour of the private market. Indeed, the influence of the state remained pervasive throughout the period 1945–79. The public housing sector increased steadily in size, public subsidies to housing consumers increased sharply and regulation of the private sector (for example, in rent control) was maintained. Rather, the process refers to the changing social composition of consumers in the public sector, and the redirection of financial support away from collective provision in favour of 'subsidised individualism' – whether in rent rebates to tenants, or tax concessions to owner-occupiers. Until 1979, this shift in emphasis was distinctive to housing provision: by comparison, the character of other public services remained largely unchanged.

The changing nature of tenants in the public sector in the post-war period has been well documented. In 1938, 47 per cent of heads of households, for example, were skilled manual workers; 46 per cent were semi or unskilled manual workers; and only 7 per cent were pensioners or widows (Holmans 1987: 171). This tenure profile began to alter significantly from the early 1960s onwards, due to the influx of greater numbers of elderly people, large family households and Supplementary Benefit (SB) claimants. From 1960 to 1976, for example, four-fifths of the increase in households on Supplementary Benefit below pensionable age was accounted for by council tenants. From 1962 to 1978, 1.25 million of the additional 1.9 million households in public sector housing had no employment earnings. The proportion of council tenants who were economically inactive increased from a mere 4.8 per cent in 1961 to 28 per cent by 1981 (Hamnett 1984; see also Forrest and Murie 1988).

While the rise of mass home ownership produced a more heterogeneous sector in the housing market than before, council housing increasingly became the tenure for the poor. Bentham (1986) demonstrated that the median income of council tenants declined from slightly below the overall median in 1963 to a mere 58 per cent of the median (and only 45 per cent of home owners' median income) by 1983. During the 1970s, the proportion of Supplementary Benefit recipients in owner-occupation barely changed (from 17 per cent in 1970 to 19 per cent by 1980), despite the expansion of this tenure. The proportion of SB recipients in council housing, by contrast, increased from 51 per cent to 61 per cent in the same period (quoted in Murie 1983). There are several factors which prompted this change. The move away from 'general needs' housing in the mid-1950s set in motion a longer-term trend. In 1955, the Ministry of Housing and Local Government had noted that local authorities 'should be encouraged in future to concentrate their main housing efforts on slum clearance and overspill building, which only they can tackle effectively' (MHLG 1954: 3). The introduction of specific subsidies for those displaced by slum clearance and for one-bedroomed dwellings for the elderly led to a sharp increase in the proportion of non-earning households in the sector. The introduction of a compulsory rent rebate scheme, to sweeten the pill of fair rents under the 1972 Housing Finance Act, brought a further turn of the lever in the direction of welfare housing. The number of council tenants on rebate increased from 270,000 in 1972 to 945,000 only four years later (DoE 1977b: 10).

Such financial changes were aided by a changing ethos in administrative procedures governing access to council housing. The 1969 Cullingworth Report advocated a 'needs-based' approach to the allocation of council housing, derived from points-based systems rather than those based on waiting time alone. While the intention of such proposals was to promote a more welfare-orientated approach in housing management, the consequence was that council housing began increasingly to resemble what Michael Harloe termed 'an ambulance service concentrating its efforts on the remaining areas of housing stress and dealing with a variety of "special needs" such as the poor, the homeless, one-parent families, battered wives and blacks' (Harloe 1978).

The social profile of council tenants changed not just as a result of the type of households moving into the tenure, but also due to the characteristics of those moving out. We noted earlier the drive towards more 'economic' rents in the public sector. As early as 1952 the government was only constrained in its enthusiasm to raise rents by the overriding need to build more houses, as Harold Macmillan later confessed: 'The time had not yet come to deal with the problem of rents. The houses must go up before the rents' (Macmillan 1969: 407). Once the boom in public sector house-building began to subside, council rents *did* go up. The introduction of rent pooling and the need to limit public subsidy to council housing soon took their toll. Council rents had been 25–30 per cent lower in real terms in 1955 than in 1939. By 1970–71, they were 85–90 per cent higher. The newly styled 'affluent worker' was being effectively pushed out of state provision and into owner-occupation.

A further element in the process of residualisation from the early 1950s to 1979 concerned the sale of council houses to sitting tenants. This policy did not hold centre stage in government housing policy as it did during the 1980s, but the cumulative effect was nevertheless significant. General consent to the sale of local authority housing to sitting tenants was granted in 1952, subject to conditions on price and the right for local authorities to pre-empt resale within five years. By 1967, local authorities could sell at prices up to 20 per cent below market value and this prompted a flurry of activity from larger Conservative-controlled councils, such as the Greater London Council and Birmingham. Although restrictions were imposed in certain urban areas the following year, by 1970 local authorities had the discretion (under circular 54/70) to sell at up to 30 per cent discount, subject to conditions of pre-emption after eight years.

Altogether, 210,185 dwellings were sold to sitting council tenants in England and Wales between 1969 and 1979 (Forrest 1982). This only represented one-fifth of the total number of new council dwellings built during the same period and it remained a discretionary policy for local authorities. But council house sales acted as a further catalyst in attracting the traditional tenants of council housing – skilled manual workers – away from the sector and into home ownership.

CONCLUSION

In this chapter, we have traced the process whereby council housing was deflected from its embryonic status as a universal public service in the post-war welfare state. It came increasingly to serve a more selective and residualised function by providing for those households excluded from the 'private' market. This trend was fostered by the redirection of public financial support away from supply subsidies to stimulate local authority housebuilding in favour of subsidies aiding housing consumption across all tenures, but especially in the owner-occupied sector.

By 1979, the weaknesses of state housing were manifold. Its consumers were increasingly drawn from the ranks of the economically inactive, dependent on social security benefits – a group wielding far less political or economic power than the skilled and semi-skilled working-class households which constituted the original council tenants. The professional status of housing managers remained uniquely weak and uncertain, so that they could not operate as an influential lobby in defence of the service. The extent of local government control over the management and financing of its housing stock was severely diminished; and both Conservative and Labour Governments pursued strategies which fed the expansion of home ownership. Alone among the basic services of the welfare state, the supporters of council housing were outnumbered by the critics.

It seemed that state housing had not merely failed to meet the aspirations of the architects of the post-war welfare state, it had failed its own consumers. The potent symbol of the 1960s council tower block seemed to speak volumes – impersonal, poorly and badly designed, often expensive to maintain, and completely out of step with consumer preferences. Universal state housing was a half-formed idea which had gone hopelessly wrong.

In 1945, the expansion of state housing offered hope to the millions of households trapped in the private rented sector or without a home at all. The only disadvantage was actually gaining access to the service, despite vigorous housebuilding programmes to ease shortages. Thirty-five years later, the wheel had turned full circle. Local authorities were faced with the new problem of 'difficult to let' estates (DoE 1981b). In many urban areas, it seemed, the ingenuity of housing managers was no longer being taxed by coping with ever lengthening waiting lists: the real challenge now was to persuade households to take up council tenancies at all. What clearer signal could there be of the sector's failure and unpopularity?

This process was crucial in shaping the entire social policy strategy of the Thatcher Governments from 1979 onwards, as we shall see in Part III. Propelled by its populist instincts, Thatcherism could begin its long haul to 'roll back the frontiers of the state' by concentrating on its most vulnerable and discredited service. The post-war experience had laid the ground for a strategy which made state housing seem a temporary aberration in the overall transition from private renting to private ownership in the British housing market.

We should, however, be cautious before accepting a priori the unpopularity of council housing. The changing status of the tenure in post-war Britain has thus far been assessed according to a familiar discourse in housing policy analysis – identifying financial measures, economic trends, changes in tenure, social forces and allocation and management practices. This seems to provide fertile evidence to support the view that council housing had failed as a service, not least in the eyes of its consumers. Only wistful academics or romantic socialists (often the same thing) would mourn its demise as a major housing tenure. By 1979 this was the received view of council housing – but it remained a partial view, limited by its emphasis on macro-economic forces, state policies and observable social and demographic trends.

This perspective tends to emphasise quantitative concerns and assess the problems and advantages of council housing from the vantage point of the academic observer. Such an approach pays only passing attention to the more qualitative and immediate concerns which preoccupy tenants. While there is growing pressure for tenant participation in housing policy, there seems to be ample scope also for more tenant participation in housing research and analysis.

The distinctiveness of a tenants' perspective can be indicated by reference to the six major attributes or 'predicates' operating to influence a household's choice of dwelling and tenure suggested by Merrett (Merrett with Gray 1982: 57–9). These are: the physical character of the house; the control exercised over its use by the occupier; the quality of the surrounding environment; the access to other locations afforded by the dwelling's location; the future mobility prospects offered by the dwelling; and the financial advantages of the dwelling. While conventional analyses of housing policy can shed important light on all these issues, notably in the case of the comparative financial advantages of different tenures, several of these 'predicates' are often approached only incidentally and rarely fall under the academic spotlight.

Merrett's taxonomy is unusual in highlighting the importance of the *'use-value'* of the dwelling. He employs this term in a specific sense, departing from Marxist convention, to express 'a holistic conception of the attributes of the dwelling possessed by a household and which can be measured or described in terms of the first four of my predicates' (Merrett with Gray 1982: 65). Hence, while issues of mobility and finance relate more to the 'exchange-value' of a dwelling, its physical character, the degree of control it offers, its environmental amenity, and its spatial location relative to other facilities constitute the home as 'the major environmental influence in the life activities of every household' (Merrett with Gray 1982: 65). It is this latter, broader conception of the dwelling which is absent in so much housing policy literature, yet it encompasses dimensions which must be examined if we are adequately to assess the past record of council housing and its potential for future reform and revival. The widely assumed poor use-value offered by public housing has been a major justification for the support of other means of provision and the decline in the tenure. If council housing lacks popularity, and there has been limited resistance to privatisation and residualisation, perhaps this is because tenants have been in receipt of a bad all-round package.

What is therefore required alongside our historical overview of government policy is the 'inside story' of council housing during this period – not as an object of policy but as a lived experience for millions of households in Britain. The policy-driven account provides a framework for understanding the reasons for the decline in state housing – but it conveys little about what consumers themselves felt about their homes, the amenities and standards of their houses and the service they received from local authorities. Before we make any conclusive judgements about the popularity of council housing among its consumers, we need to assess empirical evidence on precisely these factors – on the standards achieved in design, the impact of professional and managerial control and, above all, what the tenants themselves felt about this apparently discredited service. We take up these themes in turn in Part II and, as we shall see, the evidence falls some way short of a complete indictment of the idea and the reality of state housing as an enduring feature of the British housing market.

Part II
Council housing in use

4 Council housing design and standards

Strengths + weaknesses

In summarising a review of competing theories of the rise and decline of council housing, Dunleavy distinguishes his own view by stressing 'the importance of the *physical products* of public housing for their success or failure', placing this almost on a par with the social mix of tenants or the level of subsidy given to people in council housing: 'my explicit claim is that if the policy-making process had produced more successful housing with the features people wanted, then the policy would not be in its current parlous state in Britain' (Dunleavy 1982: 47, emphasis in original).

Dunleavy's assessment of the physical amenity offered by British public housing is shared by commentators across the political spectrum. From the New Right, Robinson suggests that 'the council house, for good or ill, has become a byword for drabness, inelegance and uniformity' (Robinson 1983: 82), while on the Left, George Orwell offers this bleak description of the inter-war estates of northern England:

> The Corporation building estates, with their row upon row of little red houses, all much liker than two peas, are a regular feature of the outskirts of the industrial towns . . . at their very worst the Corporation houses are better than the slums they replace [but] in very many cases, perhaps half the cases, I found that the people in Corporation houses don't really like them. They are glad to get out of the stink of the slum, they know that it is better for their children to have space to play about in, but they don't really feel at home . . . in a Corporation estate there is an uncomfortable, almost prison-like atmosphere, and the people who live there are perfectly well aware of it.
>
> (Orwell 1937: 59–62)

More recently, Seabrook has recorded his impressions of council schemes completed in Blackburn during the 1950s and 1960s:

> The estates have been constructed with the greatest parsimony of compassion and amenity. They are sketchy, spare and denuded, a child's drawing of a dwelling place . . . . They invite violence and negation: and the best to be hoped for from the people who are compelled to live here is a sullen and passive indifference.
>
> (Seabrook 1971: 14)

And more importantly, often with equal eloquence, some council tenants too have expressed their anger and dismay at their physical surroundings. Interviewed by Tony Parker, Audrey Gold describes her life in a London tower block in these apocalyptic terms:

> To me living here on the sixteenth floor on my own, apart from the kids who're at school all day, is as near I could imagine as to what it must be like living in hell. When I was a kid I used to read in books hell was down under the earth somewhere; but it's not, it's up here in the sky.
>
> (Parker 1983: 54)

The apparent 'failure' of the design and physical quality of council housing was certainly a theme exploited by the Thatcher Governments in the 1980s to justify the virtual cessation of financial support for new council housebuilding and the intensifying drive for privatisation. During this decade, vandalised, lawless and decaying high-rise developments became strongly consolidated as the dominant image of public housing, an example of, in Ruth Glass' memorable phrase, a 'cliché of urban doom' (Glass 1989).

Indeed, the failings of council housing architecture have been promoted as the source of a whole range of social problems in post-war Britain, notably through the influential research of Coleman. Prompted by a paternalistic 'utopianism', Coleman argues, this architectural 'creation of officialdom' departed from the principle of individual natural selection to create quite avoidable problems for people 'most of whom could cope perfectly well with life in more traditional houses' (Coleman 1985: 3) supplied through a free market (1985: 184).

To judge by these observations from varying quarters, we might conclude that council housing has always offered at best mediocre, and at worst appalling, use-values to its residents. Yet we suggest that many commentators are too selective in their perceptions of the design, standards and general amenities of British public housing and fail to give adequate recognition to its frequently high quality in comparison with the products of the private sector and to its popularity with consumers. This chapter, therefore, will balance the image of a tenure in crisis with evidence which points to the very real success of much council housing in offering greatly enhanced living standards to millions of British households.

It is important to accept that there have indeed been major failures in the physical design and production of many council estates. But, as Malpass suggests in his rejoinder to Coleman, these shortcomings derive to a significant extent from the status of public housing in Britain as 'a residual-ised, neglected and chronically under-funded tenure' (Malpass 1988: 143).

Part I of this book traced the manner in which a generally hostile context first constrained the development of council housing and eventually in-duced its decline. These same constraints clearly also impaired the physical quality of the dwellings produced. However, to blame the capitalist environment surrounding council housing as accounting for all its weak-nesses is to conceal other important influences which confront the Left with disturbing questions concerning the ideologies and practices which have guided municipal building programmes. Only a broader analysis of the causes of failure can enable us to absorb the appropriate lessons in moving towards a reformed public housing tenure in the final part of the book.

A VARIED PRODUCT

The blanket disparagement of council housing design and standards ad-vanced by so many critics serves to obscure an essential characteristic of British state housing: the considerable *unevenness* of its physical quality and design. This section examines this variability, sketching the ebb and flow of government resolve to improve housing standards in the face of external pressure, opportunity, and crisis. The emphasis here will be upon the basic physical standards achieved, upon such aspects of use-value as floorspaces, dwelling densities, and levels of household equipment. Only passing reference will be made to wider, and crucial, issues of design and architectural symbolism, as these will be explored later in the chapter.

The post-Armistice promise of a programme of 'homes fit for heroes' involved a commitment not only to a quantitatively large programme of public housebuilding, but also to a qualitatively superior dwelling form to win the confidence of working-class households. The year 1918 saw state involvement in the control of building standards develop in quite a new direction.

In accordance with the sanitary principle of the nineteenth century, the state's previous intervention had been through local authority by-laws and regulations designed to prevent the erection of homes which threatened safety and health through such defects as inadequate drainage, poor site preparation, insufficient ventilation, poor materials construction, and low ceiling heights. From 1918, however, faced with a shortage not only of housing for the poor but for many other sections of the population, the state extended its concern beyond the policing of minimum standards to the elaboration of recommended standards designed to promote the construction of homes of a higher quality to meet people's aspirations for a life which offered more than mere survival (Cullingworth 1966: 132–6). This new intervention in the control of housing production was signalled by the publication in 1918 of the Tudor Walters Report (Local Government Board 1918). This provided the specification for 'the greatest advance achieved during the twentieth century in the standards of new housing' (Donnison and Ungerson 1982: 90).

In July 1917, Sir John Tudor Walters, MP, was invited to chair a committee established by the Local Government Board to examine the issue of housebuilding and design for the working class. The ensuing report, published in November 1918, announced its objective as being to 'profoundly influence the general standard of housing in this country' (quoted in Burnett 1986: 223), including the private sector, although its most obvious impact was to be upon the new public housing programme. Whilst the Local Government Board remained wedded to a pre-war view of appropriate housing standards and to the confinement of local authority housing as a safety-net for the poor, the Committee shared common ground with the Workmen's National Housing Council and the wartime Ministry of Reconstruction that the opportunity should be taken to seek a radical improvement in *general* housing conditions (Swenarton 1981: 89–91). The Committee's key figure was the architect Raymond Unwin, a prominent member of Ebenezer Howard's Garden City Association and influenced by the socialist utopianism of William Morris. Unwin was to have a powerful influence over the public housing programme as chief architect for housing and town planning at the Ministry of Health until 1928 (Ravetz 1980: 29).

The Tudor Walters Report endures as a highly progressive document, especially when judged by the standards of its time. The Committee argued that Britain already possessed sufficient obsolete dwellings and sought to advance standards which would stand at least as minima for the next sixty years. It advocated two-storey vernacular cottage-style houses built at the low density of twelve dwellings per acre or less, with at least 70 ft between facing homes. These houses would be of a novel design, quite unlike the old by-law terraces, with wider frontages to permit more light, air and garden space. According to local needs and the means of the inhabitants, the Report presented specimen internal plans for different types of dwelling. All had three bedrooms upstairs but alternative arrangements were advanced for the ground floor and the location of the bath. The space standards for the dwellings – 855 sq. ft. for the non-parlour houses and 1,055 sq. ft. for the parlour types – were generous by historical standards and the Committee argued that a high proportion of completions should meet public demands for a parlour, even if this had to be achieved by reducing the size of the other downstairs rooms (Cullingworth 1966: 137).

Larger homes, lower densities, gardens instead of small rear yards, luxuries such as a bath, a WC, hot water, and the other features advocated by the Tudor Walters Report offered a revolution in working-class living standards. Moreover, the Committee had anticipated the obvious criticism that such dwellings would require massive state subsidies to bridge the gap between construction costs and working-class incomes. Unwin argued that the long-term costs of building socially obsolete dwellings would be greater; that expertise and simplicity in design, economies of scale, and standardisation of components and fittings would reduce tender prices; and that the use of culs-de-sac instead of traditional streets would permit adherence to low densities by reducing roadbuilding costs.

How far was the Tudor Walters ideal translated into reality in the years following 1918? Certainly, much of the shine was removed from the utopian vision, first by the way central and local government implemented the policy, and second, by the financial and political context confronting the inter-war public housebuilding programme examined in Chapter 2.

Concerning implementation, the Committee's emphasis upon the role of sensitive, locally attuned architecture in the development programme did not accord well with the emergency nature of the housing drive which began with the Housing and Town Planning Act of 1919 or with the resources available to most local authorities. Only the largest authorities could justify and afford the appointment of their own salaried architects and, after the scale of fees for private architects working on municipal schemes was reduced in 1921, councils could not attract the most talented practitioners (Swenarton 1981: 141). Many authorities adopted the pre-war practice of using borough engineers to design their estates (Ravetz 1974: 136).

The Tudor Walters recommendation that new public housing developments should be varied in dwelling type and social class was often ignored, resulting in many huge, undifferentiated schemes (Ravetz 1980: 19). Further, Unwin's awareness of the importance of cheap, efficient public transport to link this new suburban world with workplaces, urban centres and relatives, together with the need for a range of local community facilities, was too often not shared in localities where estates were constructed simply as dormitories.

Beyond the locality, the progressive ebbing of commitment to 'general needs' council housebuilding, engendered by the search for public economy and permitted by the weakening of working-class power described in Chapter 2, also produced a partial retreat from Tudor Walters principles. The first Addison schemes of 1919–20 were of very high quality. Indeed, the *Housing Manual* issued by the Local Government Board in 1919 for use by the housing committees being established by most authorities actually recommended space standards which were higher than those advanced in the Report and many councils began building to still higher specifications. But subsequent changes almost invariably marked a decline from this zenith. As early as February 1921, local authorities were informed that tenders would be approved only where 'a very substantial reduction on past prices is secured', leading to simplified designs, the use of cheaper materials, and standardised dimensions. Later in the same year, councils were requested to make further economies (Swenarton 1981: 151 and 154–5).

Estates completed under the Chamberlain and Wheatley Acts have the marks of continuing economies whereby the minimum standards advocated by Tudor Walters became the maximum, so that the three-bedroomed dwellings built after 1923 were of between 750–850 sq. ft. instead of the average 900 sq. ft. suggested in the 1919 *Housing Manual* (Burnett 1986: 232).

Nevertheless, although we will return to the significance of both these retreats and the gap between original Tudor Walters design principles and working-class aspirations, Burnett concludes that

> What these changes meant in practice was not a major departure from Tudor Walters layouts and plans, but generally smaller, cheaper houses which cut down on what were regarded as inessentials . . . . There is little doubt that the great majority of council tenants approved of what was offered to them and took a new pride in their homes, gardens and possessions.
>
> (Burnett 1986: 232 and 236)

Moreover, it seems clear that the Tudor Walters Report did realise in significant measure its aim of influencing *general* housing standards in Britain. The rise of the speculative private housebuilding industry and the production of over 250,000 owner-occupied houses per year by the mid-1930s secured, for all the accusations of jerry-building, greatly enhanced housing standards for middle-class and, increasingly, working-class households. While this urban transformation was achieved through a uniquely favourable constellation of circumstances, including low land prices, falling building costs, cheap credit from the growing building societies and intensive demand for family housing, these much improved private sector housing conditions were also influenced by the standards for working-class homes proposed by the Tudor Walters Committee. Indeed, it was Raymond Unwin who was appointed as the first chairman of the National House-builders Registration Council, established by the industry in 1937 to set private housebuilding standards.

Any shortcomings in the council housing programme of the 1920s, therefore, were not primarily in terms of their functional physical amenity. Ravetz's description of the estates as 'unlovely and unloved' may have validity in relation to broader considerations of estate layout and architectural symbolism. But it is a judgement which accords more with the perceptions of these schemes in the present day than those of the first occupants of the houses. Even today, many of the estates, with suitable maintenance and modernisation, compare favourably with recent, densely packed private sector schemes. In fact, the main failing of this time lay in the failure of the Addison, Chamberlain and Wheatley subsidies to secure a more focused assault on housing poverty.

As noted in Chapter 2, the response came in the Labour Government's Housing Act of 1930. This Act introduced subsidy arrangements encouraging a reduction in housing standards and the construction of city-centre flats in an attempt to provide housing for poorer families. In fact, vernacular cottages continued to be the main form of provision, with Tudor Walters layouts and densities retained. However, the necessary savings were achieved through further reductions in the standards of the dwellings themselves, with more emphasis on two and three-bedroomed non-parlour houses (Burnett 1986: 245–7). The local authority flats of the 1930s, although targeted initially at the poor, came to house a wider cross-section of the working class. For reasons discussed by Ravetz (1974), they disappointed policy-makers by proving unexpectedly expensive and rents net of rates amounted to over 20 per cent of unskilled workers' wages (Ravetz 1974: 127). Certainly, the good level of space, amenity and comfort experienced by the occupants of these flats, compared with similar households remaining in the private rented sector, is often overlooked. However, by sanctioning housing in the suburbs which was still of poorer quality for poorer occupants, and by encouraging the use of flats, a dwelling form associated with the disreputable tenements of the nineteenth century, to tackle the slums, the government had reduced the status of council housing as a tenure offering model housing standards, especially with the withdrawal of 'general needs' subsidies in 1933. Council housing form came to reflect the internal differentiation of the working class and, by 1939, the sector was identified increasingly as offering minimum sanitary standards as the National Government looked to owner-occupation to provide mainstream housing. In this manner, many of the 'problem estates' identified by the 1970s were built by government design.

FROM THE VERNACULAR TO THE SPECTACULAR

If inter-war council housing was marked by a growing diversity of quality and design, the post-war years were to produce a still more extended hierarchy of desirability in the public sector. Just as the first municipal housebuilding programme had been in response to the shock of war, so this further differentiation of the council stock was initiated by the emergency produced by the conflict of 1939–45 and the reinstatement of state housing as a 'general needs' tenure.

In a context of acute housing shortage, the wartime Coalition Government established a new committee to review the standards of new housing appropriate to the post-war era. The Dudley Report of 1944 (Central Housing Advisory Committee 1944) advanced less revolutionary specifications than those proposed by Tudor Walters in the context of 1918, but it was still an important document.

First, it called a halt to the gradual pre-war retreat from the Tudor Walters ideal for space standards, recommending a minimum of 900 sq. ft. for three-bedroomed houses compared with the 750–850 sq. ft. for dwellings built after 1923 (Holmans 1987: 118). Second, it anticipated the peacetime rise in popular expectations in its proposals for the internal design and equipment in new homes. These centred on the enlargement of the traditional scullery into a kitchen, permitting not only the cooking but also the eating of meals, and the provision of a small utility room for laundry and other tasks. The bathroom would now be upstairs and the Dudley Committee argued that all new homes should have better heating provisions, hot running water, better kitchen fittings and facilities for cooking, improved plumbing and sanitary fittings, and more sunlight, storage space, and light and power points (Cullingworth 1966: 142).

Aneurin Bevan committed himself to the construction of high-quality council housing which met and exceeded the Dudley minima. The three-bedroomed 'Bevan houses' completed during the period 1946–51 averaged 1,044 sq. ft., boasted most or all of the detailed improvements recommended in the Report, and incorporated two lavatories – a controversial feature which provoked charges of extravagance. Reflecting Bevan's concern to avoid the creation of drab, predictable, low-income public sector colonies and to demonstrate the superiority of planning and public provision, therefore, local authorities were encouraged to build to a diversity of designs and for higher income households (Forrest and Murie 1988: 23). Appropriately maintained and upgraded, the products of these years endure as some of the best of the public housing stock. They proved particularly desirable purchases in the early Right to Buy sales of the 1980s. But, as we showed in Chapter 3, the increased production cost of such dwellings, adding over a quarter to the capital outlay for a standard house in 1947, proved unsustainable in Britain's straitened post-war economic circumstances and in the changing political environment of the early 1950s. By putting quality first, Bevan was sacrificing output, with completion rates further reduced by a shortage of building labour and materials and the severe winter of 1947. The balance of payments crisis of the same year brought compromises in housing standards even before the Conservatives, promising a major increase in housing production, were returned to office in 1951.

Although the Conservative Government of the 1950s expanded public sector housing production to over 200,000 homes per annum in the peak years and raised the Exchequer and rate fund subsidies paid per dwelling, the quality of completed houses declined significantly. Dimensions were reduced, with three-bedroomed, five bed-space dwellings 150 sq. ft. smaller than the Bevan equivalents being recommended in the Ministry of Housing and Local Government's specimen designs. Local authorities were encouraged to build more two-bedroomed and three-bedroomed, four bed-space houses (Holmans 1987: 119). Further savings were made in the equipment of homes and in reduced standards of design. In this way, the quality of the new council dwellings reflected the Conservatives' concern to displace public housing as the dominant mode of provision. Principally, the Conservatives looked to an expansion of owner-occupation, with council housing beginning to revert by the late 1950s to a residual tenure associated with the rehousing of slum dwellers.

However, as annual completion figures declined in the late 1950s, the pressure for state action grew, and the government was obliged to review the limited role assigned to council housing, especially in view of mounting public criticism about the quality of new public sector homes. The initial response was to establish another committee, chaired by Sir Parker Morris. The ensuing report (Ministry of Housing and Local Government 1961) provided the framework for yet another differentiation in public sector housing standards, by basing its recommendations for today's housing upon the needs of tomorrow's more affluent households.

Concerning floorspace, the Parker Morris recommendation of a minimum of 910 sq. ft. plus 50 sq. ft. storage space for a five-person terraced home, calculated through an estimation of the space required for basic household activities, marked no advance on the Tudor Walters or Dudley reports. Nevertheless, this standard was significantly more generous than that specified in the Ministry of Housing and Local Government's design manual of 1952 and 1953 which advocated 900 sq. ft. as the maximum rather than the minimum. To render the extra space in the home usable in all seasons the Report argued that public sector houses should now be constructed with at least partial central heating and have other improvements reflecting changing life-styles and expectations: better kitchen fittings, more electric sockets, more bedroom cupboards, and (in a five-person or larger dwelling) a second toilet with a handbasin. These improvements were costed by the Committee and were calculated to raise the capital outlay on a five-person house by 11 per cent, with the additional floorspace accounting for about half the increase (for a fuller discussion of the cost implications of Parker Morris standards see Goodchild and Furbey 1986).

Although a limited number of local authorities did adopt the Report's proposals, it was not until 1969 that Parker Morris floorspace and heating standards (but not the Committee's other recommendations) were made mandatory. However, the same Circular 36/67 which issued this instruction also introduced the 'cost yardstick' whereby subsidies would be paid to local authorities only when the costs per bed-space of a scheme fell within annually reviewed limits, with loan sanctions being withheld altogether where tenders exceeded 110 per cent of the cost yardstick (Merrett 1979: 105). Merrett notes that this double constraint of higher standards and low costs produced some poor designs and the search for short-term economies in the use of materials which produced higher long-term running costs (Merrett 1979: 105), an issue to which we return on p. 103.

The Parker Morris recommendations on housing standards applied to the private as well as the public sector, but the Committee did not suggest the enforcement of any standards for private housebuilders. In 1967 the speculative housebuilding industry established its own minimum standards through the National Housebuilders' Registration Council (since renamed the National House Building Council) as a response to government pressure, press criticism and the risk of competitive downward bidding of standards. However, these private sector controls made no reference to overall floorspace, household activities or furniture requirements, and private developers have resisted the enforcement of floorspace norms on the grounds that they would entail higher costs and also because housing standards (beyond a basic standard of fitness for health and safety) are not a proper subject for state control. In Circular 22/80 (DoE 1980) issued during the first Thatcher administration, developers were supported in this view as the document identified the consumer as the best judge of appropriate standards. Indeed, this market-led approach was established as the guiding principle for the limited public sector development of the 1980s after Circular 9/81 (DoE 1981a) replaced Parker Morris standards by granting councils the freedom to build to their own chosen standards, provided that the development was not inordinately expensive. In practice, the comparables, in calculating the 'value for money' of a scheme, were likely to be drawn from the private sector.

The lack of information on housing standards by private housebuilders makes comparison difficult, but a study by the Building Research Station of the plans of eighty new private sector dwellings by four large building firms in 1966 found that nearly a quarter fell below Parker Morris standards

(Burnett 1986: 319–20). More recently, faced with soaring land and materials costs, private builders have reduced space standards still further, prompting one critic to remark that in modern private sector developments

> The physical footprint has shrunk to the barest minimum consonant with the claim that the 'features' on which it sells are actually present. Bedrooms in some new homes are so small that they fail to meet not only the Parker Morris space standards of the 1960s, but the space standards recommended by the Tudor Walters report of 1918.
>
> (Pawley 1986: 15)

This 'minimalisation' of the private sector dwelling was given pronounced expression in the 'starter homes' constructed in the early 1980s after the encouragement of successive governments (Goodchild and Furbey 1986: 90–4), with a floor area approximately 53 per cent of a typical Parker Morris three-bedroomed house. Such developments have enjoyed only limited success with consumers and have elicited a strong re-endorsement of Parker Morris standards in professional circles (Institute of Housing/ RIBA 1984). In 1989, with public sector starts reduced to a derisory level in favour of an expanded role for private and voluntary agencies, the Royal Institute of British Architects produced a highly critical report which, looking ahead, warned that

> the quality of much new housing will be poor . . . . None of the new housing procurement agencies are being given central advice on design matters; nor are they in turn setting minimum criteria for the housing which they create. Value for money is the sole consideration yet this apparently totally disregards achieving the required standard, cost in use, or long term maintenance. The Institute urges most strongly the re-introduction of design and space standards, to prevent housing built today from becoming the sub-standard houses of tomorrow.
>
> (RIBA 1989: 5)

This underlines the contribution by the public sector both as a direct provider of dwellings and as an indirect influence upon the private sector. Economic crises and political changes have indeed caused retreats from the principles of Tudor Walters, Dudley and Parker Morris, and some dwellings have proved cramped and otherwise defective. Yet the preceding discussion has shown that the prevailing image of council housing as universally mean, drab and inappropriate is a crude caricature. Council housing is a varied product and when the focus is upon issues of floorspace and other aspects of internal functional amenity, its record is generally good.

If council housing specifications have been frequently high, therefore, why have so many critics, from both Left and Right, attacked the tenure

precisely in terms of its physical aspect? It seems that, while the establishment of recommended standards of housing amenity may be a necessary, if
contested, element of housing policy, adherence to principles of amenity
and design is not sufficient in guaranteeing the production of dwellings
which meet the long-term needs and aspirations of their users. A narrow
focus upon space standards and equipment levels ignores other vital physical aspects, such as technical and architectural innovation, the external
environment, and the symbolic meaning of design.

The importance of these factors became undeniable in the years after the
Conservative Government's Housing Subsidies Act of 1956 when large
urban local authorities in England used the enhanced subsidies for flatted
developments of four storeys and above to construct over 330,000 high-rise
units between 1956 and 1970. A similar growth in output of high-rise flats
occurred in Scotland where, in the peak year of 1967, such dwellings
constituted 29 per cent of 40,000 public sector approvals (Dunleavy 1981a:
40–2). It is this episode, which added still further to the variety of the public
housing stock, which Dunleavy identifies as 'a central element or theme in
the current delegitimisation of public housing' (Dunleavy 1981a: 354). The
high-rise era highlighted endemic shortcomings in council housing design
and construction processes, which remained largely concealed (at least to
public officials) as long as output consisted overwhelmingly of traditional
two-storey family dwellings and as long as policy debates centred mainly
on internal amenity standards. Underlying all these shortcomings, it may be
argued, was the strong concentration of power in the hands of the producers
of council housing and the political marginalisation of its consumers.

PRODUCER POWER

Part I of this book, while underlining the importance of the political
pressure applied by sections of the working class in provoking the inception and growth of a public housing tenure in Britain, emphasised the
enduring control exerted by other aspects of the wider social, economic and
political context upon housing policy. Responding to the vicissitudes of the
British economy and to changing conditions, and operating in an environment in which land, labour, finance and the construction industry were
normally shaped by private interests, the state was able (or obliged) to place
firm limits on the costs, subsidies and output of public housing.

But beyond these contextual constraints, and despite the original soundness of most council houses, the 1980s brought a mounting crisis in the
physical stock which underlined as never before a further crucial factor: the
past predominance of producer interests in this housing sector. In the
thirty-five years from 1945 local authorities failed to invest in repair and

modernisation of the existing stock and favoured new construction in response to central government priorities. This produced growing disrepair and obsolescence in the traditional brick-built dwellings which form the majority of the public housing stock. Many of the inter-war dwellings, built to reduced space and amenity standards with the retreat from Tudor Walters guidelines, came to require costly modernisation to provide amenities and fittings appropriate to the late twentieth century. An Association of Metropolitan Authorities (AMA) study estimated that 450,000 out of 1,200,000 inter-war council houses in England and Wales remained unmodernised by the mid-1980s (AMA 1985). Moreover, original parsimony in design has added considerably to the expense of modernisation and this has also limited the proportion of homes improved (Cantle 1986: 60).

To obsolescence may be added the issue of repair. Common defects in dwellings now up to 70 years old include rain penetration through solid walls, poor thermal insulation, cavity wall-tie failure, defective roofing, and the need for rewiring in many houses. The need for investment is not confined to pre-war homes. By the mid-1980s approximately 200,000 traditionally built post-war council houses required repairs and improvements (AMA 1985: 29) and the total cost of tackling the problems of the entire traditional stock had reached £15,000 million.

The physical deterioration of the traditional stock is serious enough, but the deficiency of the non-traditional and industrialised system-built stock – and the ability of the state as producer to impose such housing 'solutions' – has attracted the greater publicity and caused still more intense hardship for tenants. The history and current problems of this form of public housing have been reviewed succinctly by Cantle (1986: 65–78). Experimentation began with the construction of 52,000 non-traditional dwellings in the inter-war period, but it was in the years after 1945 that first Labour and then Conservative Governments placed heavy pressure upon local authorities to build 500,000 dwellings using untried and under-researched techniques involving varying use of prefabrication and new materials, notably concrete. The new methods were seen as a means of achieving a rapid increase to meet urgent need by circumventing shortages in skills and materials and the high costs of production.

In fact, although the proportion of flats in public sector housing output rose to over 50 per cent in the 1960s, it should be recalled that blocks of five storeys or more constituted at most only around a quarter of annual total production (Malpass and Murie 1987: 81) so that, in fact if not in popular perception, houses and low-rise flats continued to be the dominant forms within the municipal stock. However, as a short-cut to cheap and accelerated output, the decade following the Housing Subsidies Act of 1956 brought a bipartisan central government sponsorship of approximately one million industrialised and system-built dwellings, incorporating both low-rise and high-rise flats. Many of these later 'units' were built to Dudley or Parker Morris standards, but their subsequent history offers depressing confirmation of the earlier observation that space and amenity standards alone are not enough. Varying combinations of poor basic design and inadequate on-site procedures have frequently produced a legacy of decay, premature obsolescence and, in some cases, early demolition, reflecting such deficiencies as materials failure, poor insulation, inappropriate and ineffective heating systems, inadequate fire stopping, and water penetration. These crimes of omission and commission, of failure to repair and modern- ise and of imposing flawed designs on tenants, constitute a substantial counterbalance to the original high quality and soundness of council housing stressed in the previous section. The blight on people's lives caused by the physical condition of many estates by the 1990s is difficult to overstate.

These physical shortcomings of public housing can be explained in terms of the unpropitious environment in which the sector developed, and by reference to the long-standing obstacles limiting tenants' ability to play an active part in formulating and enacting the housing development and maintenance processes (see Chapter 6). Also, the public housing pro- gramme has been influenced significantly by producer interests outside the state itself. For example, Dunleavy indicates the importance of the market interests of large national contractors in impelling the state towards its fateful support for industrialised building techniques and high-rise development (Dunleavy 1981a: 59ff.). However, British council housing reflects not only the material framework of national and international capitalism and the continuing attempts of Conservative politicians in central and local government to contain its quantity and quality. The bricks and mortar, glass and concrete of council estates also embody theories and ideals central to dominant definitions of socialism in Britain and to archi- tectural principles absorbed with seemingly little difficulty into Fabian and Labourist strategies.

If support for a reformed public housing is ever to be revived, the implications of these ideas for the rise and later decline of the tenure require critical appraisal. In the remainder of this section, therefore, the related influences of Fabianism and architectural functionalism on council housing design will be highlighted. The final part of the chapter will then explore the tension between these ideological forces and the perceptions and aspir- ations of many tenants moving into their new homes.

Our brief review of Fabianism in Chapter 3 noted its commitment to the rationality and efficiency of socialism compared to market capitalism, in addition to its moral superiority. Fabian thought reflected a utilitarian concern for progress towards human 'happiness' through the rational evaluation of alternative courses of action, illustrating the strong connection between Fabianism and the empirical tradition in social science. More importantly for our purposes, it explains the crucial role assigned by Fabians to the professional technical expert within the state who directs welfare services as the logical response to the practical problems posed by urban-industrial society. If power was to be achieved through the institutions of parliamentary and municipal representative democracy, the emphasis thereafter was on professionally and bureaucratically administered services, with only a subsidiary place for participatory democracy in Fabian and Labourist debate. Despite their influence at all levels of the Labour Party, therefore, there is a clear detachment between the Fabians and the working class. Their relations with organised labour have often been marked by mutual distrust, with Fabians evincing an élitist unwillingness to cede rights of self-determination to the masses, preferring to accord to themselves the roles of educators and leaders in the march towards socialism.

In other respects there has been a greater congruence between the ideologies of Fabianism and rank-and-file Labourism. Fabians have often conceived of society as an organic whole and, in the nineteenth century, shared with the social imperialists a concern for 'national efficiency' and the superiority of the British race. Furthermore, the biological model of society brought the Fabians into association with the racist theories of the Eugenics Society (Jacobs 1985: 7). This imperialist stance was often paralleled by nationalism and racism in the working class, the trade unions and the Labour leadership.

Black people are merely one group which both the intellectual and the proletarian wings of British Labourism have consigned to marginal status. For both, the model household has been the 'deserving', 'respectable' white family headed by a male breadwinner and it is to such households that the expansion of the welfare state after 1945 was principally directed. The need to pay due regard to the particular relationship of women to welfare services remained neglected, and many Fabians shared the popular view that the state should impose strict discipline on less 'deserving' groups suffering social deprivation.

Fabianism must take its place as an important contributory ideology to producer power in council housing. In Chapter 5, we explore its relationship with council housing management. Its connection to council housing design, however, must be seen in conjunction with the architectural and planning ideologies which have joined with Fabianism and more material factors to shape the tenure's physical form.

The design principles influencing British council housing can be traced to two main traditions, the Garden City model and the ideas of the Modern Movement. Although marked by obvious differences,

> One surprise was the level of agreement between the Garden City movement and the Modern Movement of architecture . . . . On the face of it no compromise was possible between the Garden City vision of low-density new towns or suburban cottages and the Modern Movement's slab blocks or Corbusian glass towers . . . . [Yet] both sides believed deterministically that social problems were soluble through properly designed environments; both agreed on the need for total redevelopment, for hierarchy and segregation. Neither questioned the assumption that it was right for professional planners and designers to make all the decisions about an environment.
>
> (Ravetz 1980: 55–6)

These shared sentiments found further accord with many of the main tenets of Fabianism, particularly after 1945. The Fabian commitment to massive state-directed reconstruction, based on rational planning conducted by technical experts, was matched by design professions possessed of utopian visions of a new society attainable through the application of their scientific expertise and artistic flair.

The digestion of these design traditions in state policy was not straightforward or immediate. In the case of the Garden City ideal, both Ebenezer Howard's original vision (Howard 1902) and Raymond Unwin's architectural style were influenced by William Morris, not only in their rejection of the ugliness of the industrial *laissez-faire* city and recourse to the vernacular romantic picturesque cottage as the predominant housing form, but also in their interest in the principle of guild socialism as a means of empowering and dignifying each household.

However, even in its original conception, the Garden City blueprint embraced principles which indicated an affinity with Fabianism. Mellor observes that Howard succeeded in 'articulating the fabric of thought of radical, conservative and liberal elements of the middle classes of Victorian England' (Mellor 1977: 131). Indeed, the town planning movement to which Howard's plan gave rise was an essentially middle-class pressure group and the Town Planning Institute, founded in 1913, was aligned closely with the Fabians in terms of ideals, strategy and membership (Mellor 1977: 127), with Unwin contributing a Fabian pamphlet in 1902 on *Cottage Plans and Commonsense* (Cherry 1988: 63). The Fabian emphasis on central state collectivism was muted in Howard's scheme; but the commitment to peaceful social progress and efficiency through planning, and the focus on the private, respectable, orderly household as the object of his proposals struck chords with Fabians and other, more conservative, political constituencies.

It is from this broad class and ideological rapport that Ravetz traces the gradual and pragmatic accommodation of the original crusading town planning movement, with at least a toe in the water of radical co-operative socialism, to the 'public corporation idea' (Ravetz 1980: 30). A vision invoking decentralised power yielded to one to be 'delivered' by the state and its experts. Thus, by the mid-1930s, Unwin's position had shifted:

> In 1909 he had argued that successful planning could only come from the expression of a truly common life, but by 1936 planning itself was to assist in the 'co-operation between men' on which a successful society depended . . . . His socialism did not prevent [him] putting over his ideas in a way that was acceptable to government, and the middle classes generally.
>
> (Mellor 1977: 140)

The radical elements in the Garden City tradition became accommodated progressively to Fabian ideals and to producer power.

The housing design and estate layout of the suburban single-dwelling, two-storey public housing schemes can be traced to the Garden City movement. The ideological origins of the high-rise and system-built schemes of the post-war years, on the other hand, owe much to the Modern Movement, although the spheres of influence of the two traditions have not been confined rigidly to one housing and estate form. The Modern Movement in architecture, which paralleled upheavals in other visual arts and in music, emerged in continental Europe in the early decades of the twentieth century as a reaction against what it considered to be the obsolete and oppressive classical style of the old pre-industrial world. In its place, Modernist architects in many countries, most notably Le Corbusier in France and the Bauhaus school headed by Walter Gropius in Germany, sought to develop a new design principle whereby architecture could improve humanity's condition by utilising rationality, science and technology to produce an urban environment appropriate to the social advance signalled by the arrival of the industrial era. Essential to the Modern Movement was its commitment to the view that 'form should follow function' in architecture, and that design should eschew 'bourgeois clutter' to reflect closely the *use* to which a building would be put. The search was for the universal house which could satisfy, at minimum cost, the basic living requirements of space, light, and air. Once identified, techniques and materials of mass production could be employed to permit the complete redevelopment of existing towns and cities and the production of entirely new settlements, all arranged in accordance with a rational plan. In a machine age, in Le Corbusier's famous dictum, 'the house is a machine for living in'.

In the inter-war years Britain bore few marks of the Modernist revolution and 'remained wedded to its Unwin-esque traditions in housing
design and layout' (Cherry 1988: 107). Even in the heady atmosphere of
post-war reconstruction in 1945 the ideas of the Modern Movement had
limited influence among senior architects and planners. From the 1950s,
however, sustained by the growing seniority of its professional adherents,
Modernism became established in the mainstream of British architecture.
Its impact upon housing style was largely confined to the public sector and
is most obvious in the high-rise and system-building boom from the late
1950s to the early 1970s. However, the functionalism of the Modern
Movement both coincided with, and underwrote, the more long-standing
attempt to define officially recommended design and amenity standards in
housebuilding. Hence, the Parker Morris Report defined user needs in
explicitly functionalist terms, stating that 'the problem of design starts with
a clear recognition of . . . activities and their relative importance in social,
family and individual lives' (Ministry of Housing and Local Government
1961), and then moved on to assess the conditions necessary for their
pursuit. The *method* of the Modern Movement (or at least methods shared
with the Garden City traditions), therefore, were embodied in the design of
many public sector schemes which, at first sight, appear antithetical to the
Modern *style*.

As with the Garden City tradition, it would be wrong to read the huge
'Brutalist' council estates as an entirely literal translation of Modernism.
Le Corbusier's ideal was compromised severely as less gifted local
architects, working within tight economic, political and bureaucratic constraints, designed schemes which reflected an accommodation with central
government, local politicians, construction companies and other
professions (Malpass 1975: 24–6). Yet in relation to *central* government's
broad housing strategy the architectural profession achieved significant
influence in the crucial years of the 1960s (Dunleavy 1981a: Chapter 1),
which owed much to the common ground between the ideals of the Modern
Movement and the Fabianism of Labour and, at this stage, the 'reluctant
collectivism' of the Conservatives. The points of contact were many,
including rationalism and the belief in science and technology as the route
to economic growth and human happiness; commitment to comprehensive,
centralised planning; reliance upon the crucial role of the professional
expert to identify and satisfy needs; and an élitism and authoritarianism
which, for all the social idealism and concern on both sides for the masses,
kept the users of the built environment at arm's length, in the role of those
who require 'education' in the appropriate direction of policy. Christopher
Booker expressed a common view when he described Le Corbusier as 'a
totalitarian on an heroic scale' (Booker 1979). Within the gender division

of labour of the western European civilisation from which it emerged, the architecture of the Modern Movement can thus be seen as reflecting a broadly 'masculine' perspective – an issue to which we return below.

The Fabian ideology which shaped so much of Labour's post-war policy agenda (and met with substantial bipartisan support) therefore found professional sustenance for its producer-led approach to housing provision from the apparently antagonistic architectural and planning approaches of the Garden City tradition and the Modern Movement. Earlier chapters have indicated many other forces shaping British public housing, many of them stemming from the unsympathetic market context in which the tenure developed. But the distinctively British approach to the housing question was also the product of contingent and distinctive political doctrines which achieved dominance within Labourism. Some of the consequences of producer power and architectural functionalist philosophy for users' experiences of council housing must now be assessed.

FUNCTIONALITY, MEANING AND HOUSING USERS

Although standards have varied according to economic and political events, British council housing has offered a considerable improvement in physical living standards for millions of households. This public house-building programme, however, has reflected the influence of strong producer ideologies and practices which have established functionality as the dominant criterion of design. In the evaluation of council housing as a physical product this last aspect of the tenure poses two important questions. First, does a preoccupation with functional design by producers involve the neglect of other dimensions of crucial significance for housing users? And second, despite the improved space standards and internal amenities, how successful has the public stock proved in specifically functional terms for all its diverse inhabitants?

Focusing on the first of these questions, in stressing the functional character of the relationships between people and architectural space, it has been suggested that the dominant approach in the British design professions has been to 'posit causal links between space and behaviour; they treat the former as active and the latter as passive facets of a determinate relationship' (Lipman and Harris 1980a: 415). Mirroring the epistemological pre-eminence of positivism in the natural sciences, therefore, many architects and planners have proceeded upon the assumption that design can be based upon the elucidation of laws concerning human reaction to the environment. This approach has become known as 'architectural determinism' (Broady 1968) and, at its simplest, rests upon a straightforward view of urban residents as passive objects responding in predictable ways to their physical surroundings. Such a model assigns central importance to the task of architects and planners who can engage in powerful social engineering as they alter the architectural form and spatial structure of urban areas.

It is worth noting, however, that mediating this simple determinism in Britain have been 'the ideas that architects and government decision makers have had about "proper" working-class family life and the role of women' (Boys 1989: 39). Hence, design has been directed at the realisation of a succession of social objectives from classlessness and 'social mix' in the early new towns to the 'honesty', 'solidarity' and 'egalitarianism' of working-class 'community' in the brutalist deck-access flats of Manchester's Hulme and Sheffield's Park Hill and Hyde Park, to the emphasis in the 1970s and 1980s upon neo-vernacular housing for an individualistic and 'respectable' working class aspiring to 'territory', privacy and domesticity (Boys 1989: *passim*). Believing that they understood the nature of social conflict and popular aspirations, design professionals have sought to combine these shifting images of the working class with physical determinism to resolve social problems (Boys 1989: 51).

Prompted by the frequent failure of the public to respond in the predicted way to new residential environments, the last two decades have brought a developing critique of this positivist, deterministic and functionalist approach to urban design, a response which has been associated with an emerging, if disparate, 'post-modernist' reaction against the Modern Movement (Goodchild 1991). Rapoport summarises such an alternative view:

> It appears that people react to environments in terms of the meanings the environments have for them . . . . One might say that 'environmental evaluation is more a matter of overall affective response than of a detailed analysis of specific aspects, it is more a matter of latent than of manifest function, and it is largely affected by images and ideals'.
>
> (Rapoport 1977: 60; and 1982: 13)

Far from being passive recipients of external environmental stimuli, people are active subjects, making their own particular sense of their surroundings and endowing them with meaning. According to this view, householders' perception of their home is likely to be more in terms of its generalised image, meaning and symbolism than of its more functional attributes. Architecture and spatial boundaries are used as

> a means of communication, as a way of exchanging meanings which tell others about oneself and/or about one's social group. The ability symbolically to represent elements of one's situation – physical as well as social – facilitates the exercise of control over one's daily life.
>
> (Lipman and Harris 1980a: 417)

The meaning of the urban environment and the home, the way in which buildings and space are interpreted as a form of non-verbal communication, is culturally relative both between and within societies. In modern capitalist societies the importance of housing as a badge of social identity is probably greater than in many pre-industrial civilisations (Duncan 1981). Even within a single society, people develop their perception and evaluation of their surroundings through the filter of their particular cultural experience, constraints and priorities. Hence, the meaning which people assign to a particular residential environment will depend crucially upon their active response to its message in the light of experiences, past and present, deriving from class, gender, race, nationality, the media, and many other individual and collective encounters and aspirations.

This understanding of environmental perception as the active, socially mediated interpretation of the meaning of the urban landscape is of great importance in assessing a producer-led public housing programme. Design has often rested, therefore, on a straightforward architectural determinism, emphasising function rather than meaning. Alternatively, it has involved the predominantly white, male, middle-class professionals presiding over a process which has attempted to incorporate social objectives and communicate meanings through schemes embodying an equally deterministic 'super-functionalism' (Pawley 1971: 86), encompassing both physical and social 'variables'. Either way, non-comprehension and conflict between producers and users seem inevitable.

This gulf between producers and users can be illustrated by reference to the recurring tension over the external appearance and ornamentation of council dwellings. During the inter-war years central government, with continuing regard to cost minimisation, urged local authorities to avoid merely decorative architectural features in favour of simplicity in design, relying on sensitive layout to achieve aesthetically pleasing housing schemes. To Unwin, whose ideas the Local Government Board followed closely in its 1919 *Housing Manual* for local authorities,

> There could be no doubt that external features should not be superimposed for effect but should derive from the internal arrangement of the building . . . . But local authorities and tenants did not belong to this architectural tradition. They could see no reason for omitting decorative features which, in their view, effected improvements in appearance very much greater than the increase in cost.
>
> (Swenarton 1981: 146–7)

Residents' preoccupation with decorative, movable elements of housing as opposed to intrinsic architectural form stood in still sharper contrast to the principles of the Modern Movement, with its emphasis on the development of an 'honest', functional, unornamented housing form and its willingness to impose this style in 'an attack on users' meaning' (Rapoport 1982: 22).

The combination of public sector housing design and restrictive tenancy conditions prohibiting alterations to dwellings by their occupants has often removed from tenants the power to impose their own meaning, symbolism and control upon their homes and project their own sense of social identity to the world. The spatial segregation and architectural distinctiveness of many estates, most notably the post-war flatted developments, involved the powerful imposition of producers' meanings and symbolism on working-class households. Such architecture announces to society the 'differentness' of the scheme's residents, underlining the marginal status of many inner-city households and prompting the question, in the context of concern about 'problem housing estates', as to why people should be expected to care for the symbols of their own social inferiority (Reade 1982). Many dwellings, it seems, have been overdesigned as 'housing' rather than 'homes', denying to users opportunities for 'personalisation', i.e. the control of their residences through possessing, completing and changing them.

British council housing, therefore, has tended to emphasise functionality and producers' meanings at the expense of users' meanings, a factor helping to explain the preference of many households for private sector dwellings with fewer amenities and poorer space standards. In purely functional terms, the standards of most council houses outlined earlier in the chapter brought significant improvements in living conditions and the general approval of tenants. Yet *even at the level of function*, council housing has exhibited important shortcomings which have also highlighted the gulf between producers and users.

In addition to the obvious physical design and construction failures of many homes built by innovatory techniques discussed earlier, the social and economic consequences of slum clearance and relocation of households away from physically heterogeneous inner urban areas to segregated suburban estates have long been debated (for example, Willmott and Young 1960; Dennis 1970 and 1971; Ravetz 1980: Chapters 5 and 9). We should allow for the strong element of romantic nostalgia in the concern for working-class 'community' and note subsequent evidence that many found the long-term experience of relocation congenial (for example, Coates and Silburn 1980). Nevertheless, the new estates were often conceived with little understanding of the practical considerations of tenants' incomes, kinship ties and responsibilities, social networks or employment opportunities. The focus of policy was on either the rapid production of sufficient 'units' or, in the better times, on the standards of the dwelling itself. This was counterbalanced by a neglect of the functionality of housing areas in the context of a wider locality and employment market, an oversight which has particularly affected women. With reference to British new towns, for example, Lewis and Foord show that while a major stimulus to the development of several such centres was the existence of a plentiful supply of female labour,

> access to services and employment in these towns assumes traditional gender roles. This is especially evident in the lack of nursery and public transport provision and in the physical layout of the towns. Low or inadequate service provision and gender-blind design has hindered women's social as well as physical access to a wider selection of educational, employment, health and recreational opportunities.
>
> (Lewis and Foord 1984: 45)

Moreover, these effects are reinforced by gender inequalities in access to private car usage in the face of diminishing and more costly public transport (Pickup 1984 and 1988).

In fact, in what Ravetz describes as 'by far the most significant input of women into house design' (Ravetz 1989: 194), the Women's Sub-committee to the Ministry of Reconstruction, advising on housing design and amenity for the years following the First World War, placed a singular and often unheeded emphasis on the need to look beyond the individual dwelling and to relate housing policy to planning policy through the provision of play space, social centres and other facilities to meet the needs of housewives and mothers (Ravetz 1989: 195–6).

Much more attention was paid to the functionality of the dwelling designs themselves than to broader planning concerns, but here too deficiencies emerge which can be traced in part to the gap in perception and political interest between producers and users. For ethnic minorities, not only the location of council housing (Robinson 1980) but also its size-mix and internal design often paid little regard to household structure or cultural distinctiveness (Ross 1985).

An assessment of the utility of the design of state housing raises further questions about gender inequalities in the development process. It seems that, when actually consulted, working-class women have generally colluded with the official assumption that they have a distinctive 'expert' view in their role as housewives in a conventional gender division of labour (Matrix 1984: 31; Ravetz 1989: 200). From within this role-affirming perspective, government plans which offered much increased space and equipment to ease the burden of domestic labour, together with greater privacy, elicited high degrees of support and satisfaction (Ravetz 1989: 202). Nevertheless, women have also made distinctive demands, given notable expression in the conflict between Unwin, who opposed the division of homes into smaller specialised rooms in favour of a more 'flexible' layout, and the Women's Subcommittee to the Ministry of Reconstruction which demanded a separate front parlour to permit women to escape from unfinished work elsewhere in the house, and placed especial emphasis upon the need for a separate bathroom and for labour-saving facilities such as hot and cold running water and improved cooking equipment (Matrix 1984: 28–32). After 1945, although the parlour or 'best room' was deemed obsolete in the Dudley Report (Matrix 1984: 76), many of these demands eventually received greater recognition through the Parker Morris Report which confirmed 'the public demise of the "parlour"' (Burnett 1986: 306), but which acceded to popular post-war enthusiasm for kitchens with adequate space in which to eat meals (indeed providing for separate dining rooms in the designs of larger houses) and which recommended that houses for families should include a downstairs room for activities requiring privacy and quiet.

However, as our earlier discussion indicated, removed though the members of the Tudor Walters, Dudley and Parker Morris committees may have been from the experience of working-class women, these reports mark points of relative (and significant) enlightenment in housing standards and design. It is women who have borne the worst effects of the repeated retreats from these benchmarks and the impact of the largely unresearched shift to industrialised and flatted schemes which pose major problems for child-rearing and household management.

Although council housing has not always met the functional requirements of women in the dominant prescribed domestic role in a nuclear family, public sector designs have certainly embodied assumptions concerning the 'normality' of this household form. Hence, the plans advocated by the Dudley Report 'strongly reflect the post-war idealisation of family life, seeing the house as a cheerful and comfortable place where wives would find homemaking a pleasure and not a burden' (Matrix 1984: 74) and more recent official design guides project 'value-laden assumptions about women's social role and family life' (Matrix 1984: 83). As such, council housing has brought important, if incomplete, functional benefits for women in a domestic role, but by giving architectural expression to broader gender inequalities it has often been dysfunctional for women seeking, or already committed to, an alternative life-style or pattern. In many homes the absence of privacy for women makes little concession to personal needs and interests beyond those of wife and mother, and the overwhelming emphasis on the construction of housing for small nuclear families in the public housebuilding programme (Watson with Austerberry 1986: 71ff.) has failed to address the needs of the large and increasing proportion of women in non-family households.

CONCLUSION – BETWEEN UTOPIA AND DYSTOPIA

During the Thatcher years the departure from the various ideals of the Garden City Association and the Modern Movement – with the decline in new public housebuilding in favour of the rehabilitation of the older housing stock and the extension of owner-occupation – became a headlong flight. These 'utopias' having been rejected, however, the housing debate in Britain showed signs of succumbing to yet another panacea. Now on offer was a 'dystopia', a 'post-modern metaphysic' (Lipman and Harris 1988) given popular and exaggerated written expression in the work of Coleman (1985) and material enactment in the state housing strategy of the 1980s. This later orthodoxy proclaimed a *general* failure of public housing, the particular failure of modernism and its associated architectural functionalism, and the imperative of establishing a housing system based not upon ideals of collective social change and progress but upon individual concern for a place within the existing scheme of things; a defensible, neo-vernacular house with a garden in which to raise a family, an objective to be sought through the 'natural selection' of the market.

This chapter has sought to avoid both the naïve utopianism of the past and the fashionable dystopianism of the present. Certainly the deficiencies of council housing as a physical product, long ignored by the Left, have to be faced. The failure to maintain standards, the failure to interpret design guides imaginatively, the vulnerability of users facing strong producer interests and ideologies, the neglect of issues of meaning and identity in favour of a preoccupation with function, the failure adequately to maintain and modernise the stock, the insensitivity of clearance and the broader planning of new areas and the limitations of many designs at the level of function itself, particularly for non-nuclear households, women and minority groups – all these shortcomings require frank recognition. But, even in accepting all this, it is important to keep in view the very real merits of British council housing.

The dominant image of public housing has become the forbidding, vandalised high-rise block, flats of all kinds (including low-rise schemes) constituted less than 30 per cent of the total municipal stock prior to the large-scale privatisation of the 1980s. Many critics have condemned tower block living *tout court*, but there is evidence that, given the ongoing investment in management and maintenance necessary for this building form (Bulos and Walker 1988) and the opportunity for appropriate allocations procedures, even this housing can prove successful for many households (Anderson *et al.* 1985). The remaining majority of public dwellings, mainly two-storey houses with gardens, when suitably maintained and upgraded, offer space and amenity which generally compare well with the physically shrinking, cost-inflating offerings of the private sector.

Even the contrast between functionality and meaning can be drawn too sharply for, if the external appearance of many council dwellings fails to convey the desired social image for its occupants, the comparatively generous internal space provision offers much more scope for 'personalisation' than many 'first-time' private sector homes in which room sizes rigidly dictate the dimensions and arrangement of furniture and fittings. Indeed, the Parker Morris recommendations were themselves advanced with an explicit acknowledgement that an increasing number of people expected not simply a dwelling to meet basic functional requirements but to offer opportunities for self-expression. While Parker Morris standards had a basis in functionalism, they incorporated also a recognition of social change (Ministry of Housing and Local Government 1961: 2) and, for all their assumptions concerning gender roles, they offered wider scope for variation in home life. In interpreting the enthusiastic response to the Right to Buy provisions of the 1980 Housing Act, the large discounts on market price were not the only crucial factor. The very quality of much that was on offer also exerted its effect in prompting tenants to invest in the purchase of their homes.

All this suggests that, in rejecting the crasser expressions of architectural determinism, we should still recognise the contribution that design standards can make to people's lives and to their opportunities for establishing their personal identity through the personalisation of their homes. Future policy should *combine* a framework of official housebuilding standards with varying forms of resident involvement and empowerment to produce homes which both reflect and permit personalisation, external as well as internal, by their occupants. In fact, after the rejection of modernist designs and industrial building methods in the early 1970s, the subsequent restricted public housebuilding programme reflected a growing willingness to recognise and address successfully the lessons of the past.

A central lesson to be drawn from this chapter is that many of council housing's physical problems derive from the gulf between powerful producer interests and the relatively powerless users of the service. The main response of the Conservative Government to this imbalance in the 1980s was to use privatisation as a means to diminish the power of municipal landlords and as a device to empower the consumer. It may be, however, that such empowerment can be more profound and less capricious in its impact if steps are taken to reform public housing rather than to abolish it – an issue to which we return in Chapter 8. First, however, we look beyond the production of public housing to its management in Chapter 5, and then in Chapter 6 to tenants' overall perceptions of the deal which they have received. It is in this fuller light that the future role for the state in housing can be properly assessed.

5 Council housing management

There were many reasons for the unusually rapid and far-reaching withdrawal of the state from direct provision of housing during the 1980s. We
have examined the physical housing standards on offer. A further cause
which invites consideration is the erosion of support for state housing
produced by tenants' experiences at the hands of housing management.
That so many households exercised the 'Right to Buy' their council homes,
and that the Conservatives were able to advance their housing policy as one
of their major achievements during the 1980s, may indicate not only the
popularity of massive discounts on purchase prices and the promise for
some of substantial capital gains, but also the *un*popularity of council
landlords. Had council housing conferred on its occupants extensive
citizenship rights, had it offered autonomy to each household, a genuine
choice of dwelling, opportunities for mobility, and a trained, efficient,
responsive and accountable management, then it is possible to imagine
opposition to state withdrawal from direct housing provision in Britain
bearing some resemblance to that confronting the growing financial short-
falls in the National Health Service in the 1980s and 1990s.

Certainly both Conservative cabinet ministers and right-wing commentators have stressed the subordinate status of council tenants in arguing
for the pre-eminence of market forces in housing provision. In the words of
one critical observer,

> The policy of encouraging local authorities to build and manage a large
> housing stock has created a separate, second class and stigmatised status
> for council tenants . . . . It is a status which involves 'degradation
> ceremonies' in which potential tenants are sifted and sorted by means of
> intimate, demeaning and socially devaluing allocation procedures. It is
> a status in which control of almost all aspects is vested in others . . .
>
> (Robinson 1983: 88)

This attack from the Right in the 1980s has been mirrored by criticisms of council housing by writers on the Left. Echoing George Orwell's remarks in *The Road to Wigan Pier* on the prison-like atmosphere and drab uniformity of some early council estates quoted in Chapter 4, more recent neo-Marxist commentators have identified council housing as a means of labour reproduction and social control, 'a form of public landlordism rather than a more benevolent welfare service' (Ginsburg 1979: 139).

The same approach is followed here as in the previous chapter. As with council housing design and standards, so with council housing management, a conventional wisdom exists which emphasises its inefficiency and remoteness. Such a stereotype has constituted an important context to policy debate yet, as noted in a key research project undertaken for the Department of the Environment by researchers at Glasgow University, 'there has never been a well-established knowledge base regarding how social landlords manage housing, let alone the effectiveness of management' (Centre for Housing Research 1989: 1). In exploring the available evidence on the nature of British council housing management, the following discussion will seek to avoid an easy acceptance of both the complacency of the more distant past and the apocalyptic gloom concerning the 'unreformability' of public housing which has characterised recent debates.

However, the balance of our argument will be more critical of council housing management than our relatively supportive analysis of public sector design and standards in Chapter 4. We shall first make a preliminary indication of the gulf between the vision for council housing as a tenure based upon principles of social needs, high quality and social rights and the reality of much local authority housing management in the past. We shall then explore those factors which combined to limit the equity, efficiency and responsiveness of council housing administration, and sketch some of the main consequences of the interaction of these factors in housing practice. Finally, we shall consider whether it confirms the widely held view that future housing policy should focus not on the reform of the tenure, but on its supersession.

COUNCIL HOUSING AS 'PUBLIC LANDLORDISM'

The nature of council housing management can be interpreted by reference to those structures, institutions and interests which, together and in interaction with each other, shape the local government policy process. In analysing local government services it is common to identify the varying influences of the political and class relations implied by the continuing existence of market capitalism as the context for state policy; the statutory and financial framework for local services established by central government, bolstered in specific spheres by more detailed controls; the structures and processes of local government and the relative influence on policy of councillors and local government officers; and the role of public opinion exercised through the ballot box and through pressure groups, including users' associations.

The relative importance of these influences fluctuates over time. For example, the contextual changes, recently intensified, which have produced social polarisation and the long-term residualisation of council housing have had a significant effect in changing the emphasis of housing management. Further, the reorganisation of local government and reforms in the internal management structures of many local authorities during the 1970s promised to enhance the role of local senior housing management professionals in the policy process, before the legislation of the Thatcher administrations brought a challenge to local professional power. Despite such changes, it is still possible to make some important generalisations about council housing management, particularly if we focus our discussion upon the decades of the tenure's growth, and leave until Chapter 8 a more developed consideration of the emerging managerial reforms which attended the severe challenge to public housing in the 1980s. In particular, there has been an enduring disparity between the hopes for council housing as a radical and liberating break with earlier models of landlord–tenant relations and the reality of much traditional local authority housing management practice.

Although our discussion in Chapter 2 indicated the need for caution in characterising all tenancy agreements in the private sector as unequal, oppressive and lacking in personal warmth and sentiment, it remains the case that the nineteenth century saw the progressive 'displacement of a moral by a political economy in rental housing' (Kemp and Williams 1987: 4). While scope remained for individual altruism, private landlords were increasingly inclined to regard their relationship with their tenants and their property in purely economic terms, with the realisation of an adequate profit on their investment as the overriding goal. Questions of household need were subordinated to the priorities of maximising rents, minimising costs, discrimination in lettings, and retaining strong control over tenancy conditions.

In the face of the exploitation, insecurities, indignities and physical privations which so often attended private landlordism, the aspiration of many who campaigned for municipal housing was that the tenure would bring not merely a revolution in material living conditions but also a substantial enhancement of households' legal rights and the quality of their relationship with their landlord. The birth of council housing as a significant tenure in 1919 was to herald landlord–tenant relationships founded upon quite new assumptions and conditions. Even representatives of the state shared the expectation that council housing would be based upon new criteria. Hence, in its annual report for 1929–30 the Ministry of Health registered its acceptance that local authorities could not 'be governed by the same considerations as other property owners' (quoted in Ryder 1984: 73). In more recent years council housing has been included with housing association, co-operative and charitable trust accommodation in the category of 'social rented housing'. This term implies that

> the purposes underlying provision are social rather than commercial, that allocation will take place according to need rather than profit, and that the interest of the tenants will be uppermost amongst a landlord's considerations.
>
> (Inquiry into British Housing 1990: 36)

How far has council housing management embodied these hopes and expectations? Have the interests of tenants really been uppermost in the administration of public housing?

The following two sections explore the particular patterning of the policy process in local authority housing management which resulted in the failure of council housing to offer the radical break with private land-lordism. The terms and services so often offered to consumers seem to be well encapsulated in the phrase 'public landlordism', which evokes images of old antagonisms rather than of a new partnership.

LOCAL DISCRETION AND POLITICAL INFLUENCE

Formally at least, the development of council housing management has been a matter for discretion on the part of each local authority. It is only in the last fifteen years that the centralisation of policy affecting all local services has begun to extend substantially to the detailed administration of the municipal housing stock. Of course, we have seen that local freedom in housing policy has been exercised within a series of non-local constraints deriving from the economic, political and ideological structures and pro-cesses of Britain as an essentially market capitalist society and the manner in which these have been mediated by the framework for municipal housing provision established through the statutes and financial arrange-ments set by central government. This non-local context of council housing management was a central theme of Part I. In such an environment, the definition of good housing as a social right to be underwritten by the state even at the expense of private property interests never secured more than a precarious foothold. These continuities in the economic, political and ideological context of council housing have formed a powerful set of parameters for local housing management practice.

Although central government can exert significant influence, the rules in which local housing authorities work were for many years much less prescriptive than in other service areas. In contrast with, for example, the mandatory responsibility of local education authorities to provide an education, free at the point of delivery and subject to independent inspection, to all children and young people to the age of 16, local housing departments have not had a parallel responsibility for the housing conditions of the whole population, even since the Housing (Homeless Persons) Act of 1977 required councils to provide accommodation for certain categories of homeless people. While central government has set the parameters, the *implementation* of local housing policy in Britain has been vested to a unique extent with local authorities.

Councils have had considerable discretion, therefore, over how many dwellings should be built and, once completed, how the stock should be managed. Certainly, there has been a long history of central government advice in the form of circulars and reports. Gallagher (1982) quotes some early advice to local authorities in a Ministry of Health periodical published in 1920:

> Whatever system is adopted arrangements will have to be made for carrying out the following objects:
>
> 1 The careful selection of tenants;
> 2 The elimination of unsatisfactory tenants;
> 3 Constant supervision of the property and its occupants by officials directly employed and paid by the owners;
> 4 Systematic and punctual collection of rents.
>
> (Gallagher 1982: 135)

Such guidelines, which sit uneasily alongside the Ministry's identification of the social dimension of public housing provision quoted above, steered councils unambiguously in the direction of 'public landlordism'. During the 1960s and the 1970s an attempt was made to influence local management policy through the reports of the centrally constituted Central Housing Advisory Committee (replaced in 1976 by the Housing Services Advisory Group) and, in Scotland, the Scottish Housing Advisory Committee (Gallagher 1982: 135; Malpass and Murie 1987: 89; Laffin 1986: Chapter 8). However, the response to this advice remained a matter for judgement on the part of each council. Given this scope for discretion, we can now turn to examine local decision-making in housing.

From the very earliest years of council housing, local authorities were obliged to employ salaried staff to manage their housing operations. The values and practices of these professional employees are of considerable significance in assessing the nature of council housing management and the relationship between local authorities and their tenants. This issue will be considered shortly. However, formal statutory decision-making authority has rested with the full council so that, with the recent exception of Northern Ireland, it has been local *politicians*, in theory at least, who have determined the housing policies which their officers then enact. Reality undoubtedly departs from this constitutional model but, before examining the role of professional power in council housing, it is important to devote some attention to the actions and perceptions of those who, in law, are the tenants' actual landlords – local government councillors.

The willingness of local politicians to intervene in service delivery has been greater in housing than in other areas. The reasons for this will be appreciated more fully after our discussion of the relative weakness of the housing management profession below. Initially, it can be observed that the relatively strong influence of local politicians in shaping local housing services stemmed from three sources. First, we can point to the early establishment of housing as a local authority service function before the general consolidation of professional power in welfare service delivery after 1945. An early tradition of councillor involvement in the detail of local housing policy was established, which persisted into the post-war era of expansion. Second, the relative absence of mandatory requirements in housing legislation has left ample opportunity for local political interpretation. Finally, compared with apparently less tangible and straightforward services such as education, civil engineering, public health, social work and town planning, councillors have often regarded housing as devoid of mystique, a matter of common sense, and of particular immediacy to the individual households and communities comprising their own electoral power base. In housing affairs, therefore, local politicians have been both more confident and disposed to intervene.

Local political preferences have found expression in the decision as to whether or not to take advantage of central subsidies to build council houses. In Chapter 2, for example, we saw how the power of organised labour in Sheffield was crucial to the development of council housing in that locality even before central subsidies became available in 1919. Subsequently, the greater power and radicalism of working-class politics in Sheffield compared, for example, with Leeds, is reflected in the varying use of the Wheatley and Chamberlain subsidies in the 1920s so that public sector housing output was nearly twice as high in Sheffield (Dickens *et al.* 1985: 166). Activity in Leeds was relatively biased towards the use of the Chamberlain subsidies with their greater encouragement of owner-occupation (Finnigan 1984: 109).

More recently, with regard to council house sales, Birmingham

Corporation under Conservative control in the late 1960s and early 1970s was particularly enthusiastic in selling its stock well before the Right to Buy provisions of the 1980 Housing Act (Malpass and Murie 1987: 278). Conversely, Norwich City Council under Labour control in the 1980s attempted to minimise its sales in the wake of the introduction of mandatory sales, so provoking the Secretary of State to use central government's powers of intervention to appoint a representative to administer council house sales in the city (Malpass and Murie 1987: 233–40; Duncan and Goodwin 1988: 158–9).

But it is in the important management matter of the *allocation* of council houses that the influence of councillors has been recognised most frequently. Local politicians have sometimes exercised their authority as landlords in a purely capricious way, for example, to favour political supporters, friends, acquaintances or others judged to be 'deserving' in the allocation of tenancies. This was particularly common in the years before 1974–5 when housing authorities were often small and councillors could adopt a very personal role in managing the stock. Writing of the numerous councils in County Durham during the inter-war years, Ryder records that

> in most cases . . . the decision to award a tenancy rested with councillors, who consequently found their goodwill to be much in demand. The proffering of bribes, though rarely mentioned in council records, was probably quite common.
>
> (Ryder 1984: 73)

Although the growing scale of the housing operations of many localities brought a delegation of management functions, including allocations, to professional officers, the more recent study of housing management by Glasgow University indicated the enduring significance of councillors' discretion in determining housing allocation policy in some smaller authorities (Centre for Housing Research 1989: 51). Almost three-quarters of council housing staff interviewed by the Glasgow researchers in a survey of a cross-section of local authorities said that it was councillors who took policy decisions (Centre for Housing Research 1989: 29). Similarly, a recurring complaint in the Audit Commission's major inquiry into council housing management was the relative power of councillors in relation to housing professionals in many of the least efficient authorities and the consequent inability of managers to manage (Audit Commission 1986: 14 and 29–31). In identifying a continuing involvement of councillors in detailed policy implementation, contributors to the Widdecombe Inquiry on the practice of local government selected housing as the policy sphere in which to exemplify detailed member intervention:

To combine their most questionable qualities into a representative but manufactured example, small rural district councils still exist in which councillors appoint all staff, with personal linkages and nepotism amongst the considerations used in staff appointment; allocate all council houses, and frequently ignore waiting list criteria in so doing, with similar considerations operating to those involved in staff appointments; [and] allocate improvement grants on a similar basis.

(Gyford *et al.* 1989: 159)

This tendency was given a new momentum with the polarisation of political debate during the 1980s, the rise of 'manifestoism' and a more ideological form of local politics, and the growing prominence of 'professional' councillors, particularly in metropolitan districts. Hence, Conservative councillors have become increasingly disposed to establish detailed investigations into the internal management of services in pursuit of 'value for money' (Gyford *et al.* 1989: 151), while Labour politicians have been similarly interventionist in launching decentralisation strategies to build support for council services (see Chapter 8).

The relatively high involvement of local politicians in council housing management might be expected to result in wide differences between localities according to variations in the political balance of power. Certainly, there has been evidence of the impact of local political discretion, especially in the setting of rent levels, the use of rate fund contributions before 1989 to subsidise rents, and the resistance by some Labour councils to attempts by central government to secure increases (Hartley 1973; Sklair 1975; Skinner and Langdon 1974). There is also evidence that a minority of councils have been willing to raise their rents to pay for a higher level of management services to tenants (Centre for Housing Research 1989: 108). In the end, however, whilst recognising these and other signs of the traditional local autonomy in housing affairs, the important *similarities* in housing management policies and styles between localities through many decades must not be overlooked. In general, it seems that local politicians would not, or could not, use their apparent powers of intervention to produce models of housing administration to challenge the epithet of council housing as 'public landlordism'. Some of the main results of this prevailing stance will be considered later in the chapter. Here the focus is upon why the great majority of councillors accepted such a limited definition of 'social housing'.

Apart from the inhibitions of the non-local context of council housing and the very tangible personal consequences of moving beyond the boundaries set by statute, housing committees have confronted additional, although related, pressures operating at the local level itself. In particular, any liberality by councillors in allocation policies, rent levels, or in attitudes towards tenants' rent arrears have required justification to the ratepayers. Policies favouring one group of tenants or applicants for housing at the expense of another have also carried the risk of political and electoral penalty.

In the case of councils under continuing Conservative control, or at least that of a majority of conservative-inclined independent members, there has often been a direct link between the interests and values of those with local political power and ratepayer concern to confine council housing to a residual role, involving strictly limited public resources. Dresser's research on inter-war council housing in Bristol, for example, reveals a Housing Committee dominated by business and professional men, many of whom were drawn from occupations central to the private housebuilding industry, including contractors, a wallpaper and paint manufacturer, a quarry owner, a major landowner, and at least three members of building society boards (Dresser 1984: 165–6). Although some such interests may have been served by a major public housing programme during times of recession in the speculative housebuilding trade, in general such a group regarded council housing as a regrettable necessity to plug the gaps in market provision. Their own perceived interests and those of their political sup-porters did not lie in the development of a local authority housing stock which in size, amenity and management standards necessitated inflated transfers from the general rate fund to the housing account.

However, it is the practices and the ideologies of local Labour poli-ticians which are of greater interest. It was Labour, at least in some periods and in some localities, which moved beyond the 'reluctant collectivism' of other parties to support the principle of council housing as a progressive 'general needs' tenure. It is to Labour councils, therefore, that we might reasonably look for approaches to public housing management which transcend the parameters of 'public landlordism'. In practice, however, the energy and visionary quality of the building programmes undertaken by many Labour councils were accompanied by a prevailing conservatism and lack of imagination in the management of this stock.

For an explanation of this general failure of Labour to secure a radical departure from traditional landlord–tenant relations in council housing it is important to stress again the essentially conservative aspects of both Fabian political philosophy and British labourism. Both these influences on Labour Party policy and practice were identified in relation to council housing design and physical standards in Chapter 4. The predominantly reformist character of Britain's labour movement also forms a theme in our discussion of tenants' responses to council housing in the next chapter. The purpose here, therefore, is to indicate briefly the influence of these traditions in placing firm limitations on the distinctiveness of housing management in Labour-controlled localities.

We have identified earlier a central strand in Fabianism as its emphasis on the delivery of efficient public services through rational bureaucratic organisation. This theme became still more pronounced as the early enthusiasm for municipal initiative waned and was replaced in later decades by Labour's commitment to national economic planning, larger units of local government and the adoption of corporate management systems in local authorities. In other service areas this development strengthened the position for professional managers within local government. This trend was apparent also in housing, as the next section of the chapter will show. However, for the reasons identified above, councillors were more able, more disposed and more confident to assume a prominent role in the management of housing than in the delivery of other local services. Housing, therefore, remained a 'top-down' service distinguished from other welfare sectors by the heightened importance of political discretion. To the extent that Fabian ideas exercised an influence among local Labour politicians they served to confirm a paternalistic stance and an approach to people similar to that attributed by G.D.H. Cole to Sidney Webb. Cole wrote of Webb,

> He still conceives the mass of men as persons who ought to be decently treated, not as persons who ought freely to organise their own conditions of life; in short, his conception of a new social order is still that of an order that is ordained from without and not realised from within.
>
> (quoted in Lee and Raban 1988: 79)

Other elements of Fabian thinking are evident in the history of council housing management. Particularly important is the preoccupation with the conventional nuclear family and the need to use the state to support and, if necessary, discipline and control it. Parallel with the drive for economic and organisational efficiency, the concern with 'appropriate' housekeeping standards, with rewarding 'respectable' households with the better dwellings, and with offering basic, 'sanitary' provision to others, all echo the quest of the early Fabians for 'national efficiency'. Finally, viewed from a later vantage point, the interest of the early Fabians in biological theories of racial differentiation, central to 'scientific' debate at the beginning of the twentieth century, surface in the later reluctance of Labour politicians, both national and local, to open public housing to colonial immigrants and their British-born children (Jacobs 1985: 7–10).

As Gamble has observed, Labour has never become a party dominated totally by managers and has continued to rely upon the support of trade union leaders and the rank and file activists of the constituencies (Gamble

1985: 95). While Fabian ideas exercised a direct and powerful influence upon the perspectives and actions of the Party at Westminster, therefore, at local level the discretion of Labour politicians during the decades of council housing growth was informed also by the essentially defensive working-class values of the labour movement. Just as the British trade union movement, rooted in the skilled manual (predominantly 'male') crafts, used corporate action to pursue limited interests relating to wages and employment conditions – leaving aside wider questions of economic control – so the 'gas and water socialists' of the local councils used a political power resting in the same constituency to humanise the life of working-class households through the vigorous development of public services such as housing. The rise of the New Left in the early 1980s brought an attempt to build support upon a diverse constituency of the shop stewards' movement in industry, the women's movement, black groups, environmental organisations, the peace movement, gay rights groups, and other organisations to mount a more explicitly ideological challenge to capitalist interests using community campaigns (Stoker 1988: 193–4). By contrast, traditional municipal socialism owed its power to organised, relatively affluent, male, white workers and sought pragmatically to use available levers to extend service provision from the town hall to 'our people'.

This priority of action over vision ensured that far more attention was given to the production rates of new housing units and to questions of allocation and rent levels crucial to continuing political support than to exploring radical new definitions of landlord–tenant relations. In some circumstances, the lack of an explicit countervailing ideology left local Labour groups unable even to challenge the Conservatives on the most basic housing decisions. For example, Dresser analyses the diminishing radicalism of the minority Labour group in Bristol in the inter-war years, noting that by 1930 party differences in housing policy had become limited largely to those of 'political style', with most Labour members of Bristol Council 'forced into increasing accommodation with a residualist housing policy' (Dresser 1984: 167). Dresser confirms that Labour's housing policy in Bristol in this period reflected the wider conservatism of the trade union movement and the Party at national level. This included a disregard for women's housing needs and an acceptance of the bureaucratic and un-democratic management of the city's housing estates (1984: 168).

In general, local Labour parties have used power not to develop in-novatory approaches to housing management but to ensure that rent levels and allocations systems have been arranged to the benefit of their natural supporters. When this priority has been forgotten or subordinated to other goals – as in the introduction of a deeply unpopular differential rents scheme in Leeds in 1933 to permit the rehousing of the poor (Finnigan 1984: 114–22) or with the introduction of a 'lodger tax' in Sheffield in the late 1960s (Lowe 1986: 94ff.) – the price has often been paid at the ballot box.

Through most of council housing history, therefore, local authorities have been allowed considerable discretion in matters of housing management. Furthermore, local politicians have shown a greater willingness to involve themselves in the routines of housing administration than in most other service areas. However, this discretion has not amounted to the development of new, democratic and participatory approaches to landlord–tenant relations. National and local economic and ideological pressures, together with, in the case of Labour councils, the specific nature of the ideological strands which combined to inform British municipal socialism, ensured that local authority housing management has rarely moved beyond the parameters of 'public landlordism'.

In other service areas, notably education, it has been through the influence and organisation of a relatively strong profession that changes in practice have been obtained and services defended. Having examined the influence of politicians, we now turn to the impact of professional housing officers on council housing management.

HOUSING PROFESSIONALS – THE TRANSLATORS OF POLICY

In this section we develop a discussion of the general influence of the professions in public policy and then seek to apply this analysis to the specific case of local government housing managers.

Although in the early years some councils did hire the services of private firms to collect rents, all local authorities have appointed full-time officials to administer their housing stock. By the 1990s the number of local government housing officers totalled more than 55,000 – a figure which far exceeds those employed, for example, in town planning. If size alone were a determinant of influence, this would be a formidable force shaping state intervention in housing. We shall argue, however, that housing professionals have been more the translators of public sector housing policy than its creative authors.

The extent of professional power in the formulation and implementation of public policy is a matter of long-standing controversy. In attempting to explain the social and spatial inequalities of post-war British cities, Pahl (1970) identified local government officers as prominent among the 'urban managers' which he termed the 'independent variables' determining the flow of land, housing, education and other resources to local populations.

By the late 1970s, however, the emerging consensus, influenced strongly by Marxist structuralism, was that the 'urban managerial thesis' in its original formulation overstated the autonomy and power of local government professionals. Pahl himself accepted this in subsequent writings (Pahl 1975).

Yet the Marxist critique of his work contained its own deficiencies and fostered a premature dismissal of some important insights gained from the managerialist perspective (Williams 1982). As argued in Chapter 1, while a strength of Marxist analysis is to encourage close examination of the capitalist parameters of state policy, such an emphasis on its own can yield only a partial account of the policy process. In particular, while accepting the crucial importance of patterns of ownership and control of capital, the *independent* impact of professional groups needs to be reassessed.

Indeed, the issue of independence is at the core of most recent analyses of professionalism, with many writers following Freidson in defining a profession as 'an occupation which has assumed a dominant position in the division of labour, so that it gains control over the substance of its own work' (Freidson 1970: xvii). In securing this privileged position the imprimatur of the state is essential. From the state, an aspiring profession seeks enforcement of a monopolistic right to practise its particular occupation. It seeks the right to control the number and calibre of recruits joining its ranks and the length and content of their training. And it strives to gain acceptance of its right to determine the content and conditions of its members' everyday work. In the case of welfare professions, essential to this last demand is the right to define clients' problems and needs and the way in which these are to be addressed. Success in this endeavour would involve strong professional influence well above 'shop-floor' level, through bodies with power to formulate policy and to guide its implementation. Typically, a profession's case is sustained by claims to specific technical competence of benefit to society, guaranteed standards of service, and commitment to a strong ethic of professional service.

Why should the state accede to such demands? It is clear that some professions operate very effectively within a context of 'interest corporatism' (Dunleavy 1981b) whereby the state enters into alliances in which it underwrites the power and privileges of a profession in return for the delivery of a service broadly consistent with the state's overall objectives. In making such corporate representation, the chances of success for a profession are enhanced if it is backed by the tradition of a long history and also congruence in the social background of its members and those holding the reins of economic and political power in business, Parliament and other state institutions. But in seeking professional influence, success as a well-organised lobby in a process of interest corporatism remains dependent upon the profession in question being able to offer a contribution to public policy which is attractive to the institutions of state. Wilding has suggested that the state is drawn into an alliance with various professions because it 'needs professions to fulfil the responsibilities which modern governments assume, to legitimate state power, to make available expertise, to deal with the common situations of industrial society' (Wilding 1982: 65). Or as Cousins suggests,

> the relationship between the state and professional groups is one in which the state selectively favours the interests of certain groups over those of others. Thus those groups who are able to make the most effective contribution to the avoidance of risks, for example fractions of capital, organised labour and professional élites, are granted 'structurally determined privileges' ... the state not only turns to certain groups for the formulation of policies but also for their implementation.
>
> (Cousins 1987: 107–8)

Faced with the scale and complexity of urban industrial society, therefore, the state looks to the technical expertise offered by the professions. This has the additional ideological advantage of enabling the state to present essentially political questions as technical and value-free. Furthermore, state-sponsored professionalisation is a useful device whereby the national state can bypass inept or antagonistic local politicians.

The influence of the professions on the policy process is limited, therefore, by the state's requirement that its experts will operate within explicit or, perhaps more often, tacitly agreed parameters. Professional strength must also rest upon its values and practices corresponding in some measure to public sentiment on an issue. In fact, Wilding argues that in the decades after 1945 public acceptance of professional intervention as an appropriate response to problems of social policy was an important source of legitimacy sustaining the rapid professionalisation of this period (Wilding 1982: 78ff.).

Yet if professional power is restrained by the wider concerns of the state and by the need to retain at least some element of popular acceptance, it is clear that many professions have been able to make their *own* impact upon policy. Wilding offers an extended account of the significance of professional power in the shaping of the British welfare state (Wilding 1982: Chapter 2). This power, he argues, has extended from the highest levels of policy making, to the definition of needs and problems, to power over clients and day-to-day working practices. Most notable was the power of the medical profession in shaping the nature of the National Health Service and ensuring that it developed along quite different lines after 1945 to those envisaged initially by the government. Similarly, although the influence of the teaching profession on educational policy came under pressure in the 1980s, the power of teachers after 1944 was seen in their representation on the Schools Council and in the evidence which teachers' associations have submitted to official committees. Even less well-established professions have also made a significant impact. In social work, for example, Wilding points to the triumph of social work definitions of problems of delinquency in two White Papers in the 1960s and the strong social worker presence on the Seebohm Committee established in 1965 to review the operation of personal social services, leading to the creation of integrated and more powerful social services departments (Wilding 1982: 22).

While the more ideological politics and the growing popular challenge to 'expert' authority in the 1980s brought a weakening of professional power, it is clear that professional groups have had a major voice in most areas of social welfare. Alongside interest corporatism it seems that professions have also been leading players in what Dunleavy has termed 'ideological corporatism', where power flows to those able 'to win a rational argument, to undermine a policy "paradigm" intellectually, to solve specific "technical" problems, to demonstrate a shift in the "intellectual technology" of the policy area' (Dunleavy 1981b: 3).

However, while the mediating influence of professionals upon the development of the welfare state may be accepted as a general principle, it cannot be assumed that this will be of the same significance in every field of policy. As Laffin observes, there are significant variations in the relationship between welfare professions and their respective 'policy communities' and, in the case of public housing, the role in policy development of professional housing managers has been especially peripheral (Laffin 1986: 29 and 31). What are the sources and symptoms of this weakness?

Considering first the *sources* of the marginality of council housing managers, earlier discussion in this book has indicated that, though a response to pressure from a section of the working class and a recognition of its power, the origin and subsequent development of council housing have been shaped powerfully by the wider social, political and economic objectives of the state and the interests of private capital. We have suggested that centrally imposed constraints on policy alternatives were compounded by local pressure in most areas to restrict the scale of council housing and its cost to the ratepayer. Other professions have certainly confronted similar pressures. However, if indeed 'he who defines the issues exercises power' (Laffin 1986: 8), it is clear that housing managers' power has been especially circumscribed. They have been required to operate a service in which the sanctity of private property rights, the need to restrict the particularly high capital costs of council housing to the Exchequer and the ratepayer, and the subordination of public housing to the goal of reproducing labour, both physically and ideologically, have each stood as prior constraints on professional discretion and autonomy.

The opportunities for housing managers to follow other professions in placing their own stamp on policy within overall parameters could have been greater had they been able to draw upon more of the resources used by these groups in establishing their influence. In her analysis of professional power in the welfare state, Cousins draws upon the notion of an occupation's 'indeterminacy–technicality ratio' developed by Jamous and Peloille (1970). 'Indeterminacy' refers to 'aspects of uncertainty in occupational knowledge, that is, the bases of an occupation's mystique, ideology, or sources of legitimation, for instance, non-transferable or esoteric skills such as personal or advocacy skills, or "bedside manner"' (Cousins 1987: 101). 'Technicality', on the other hand, constitutes the extent to which an occupation can claim professional status through its grounding in a systematic body of knowledge which gives rise to a specific competence and expertise. The most influential, prestigious and highly remunerated professions, it can be argued, are those which have a high indeterminacy–technicality ratio. Occupations which rest purely upon a claim to technical competence are vulnerable to routinisation, as their knowledge base is codified and disseminated in the form of specific rules which can be applied by relatively unskilled staff under the supervision of management within a bureaucratic organisation. Nevertheless, even if practitioners are unable to mystify their occupation or deflect close scrutiny of its privileges by aligning its activities with dominant, 'taken-for-granted' social values, the ability to lay claim to a specific sphere of technical knowledge and skill is certainly crucial in securing professional status, even if this position remains provisional and liable to future redefinition. How does housing management stand in relation to these two criteria?

Indeterminacy is partly the product of the secrecy and mystery associated with the antiquity of certain occupations and their role of providing a service for social élites. Hence, practitioners in medicine and law have for centuries derived strength, influence and acceptance as 'gentlemen' and 'status professionals' (Elliott 1972) from their proximity to the rich and powerful. Such association bolsters the mystique of these occupations, which is sustained further by their association with the essentially religious questions of life and death, and guilt, judgement and punishment and by the element of uncertainty which surrounds many if not most of the cases undertaken. In keeping with this 'religious' function it has been common for doctors and lawyers to be judged, in the manner of priests, as much on the basis of *how* they fulfil their duties as in terms of their substantive proficiency.

Housing managers, in contrast, can claim none of these occupational advantages. Their clientele do not include the upper class. Indeed, the progressive residualisation of council housing has ensured that housing managers are serving what some might regard as the decidedly unmysterious marginalised poor. Neither is housing management hallowed by time, being the creation of government legislation in the twentieth century and gaining a substantial presence only after 1945. And the practice of housing management can hold little mystery for a public among which the majority are the 'managers' of their own homes. Problems of rent arrears, leaking roofs or neighbour disputes, and even the more strategic questions of capital finance, rehabilitation programmes and tenant participation seem somehow more calculable and open to wider debate than esoteric medical or legal issues. Finally, far from sheltering under a canopy of dominant social values and beliefs, council housing management is associated with a service which, if only in limited degree, infringes central tenets of prevailing British ideology. The precarious legitimacy of social housing must be a source of occupational weakness for its managers.

If housing management lacks the element of indeterminacy exemplified most clearly in the power and privileges of the traditional professions, therefore, how far can it resort to a specific, systematic technical domain as the basis for a convincing, albeit less secure, claim to occupational autonomy? In fact, a discrete knowledge base for housing managers is likely to remain a chimera. Coalescing in the administration of housing are issues of management, law, economics and finance, design, building, politics, psychology, sociology and social policy. At almost every turn, in addition to their political masters, housing practitioners encounter other professionals in formulating and implementing policy. These competing occupations – founded on more specialist and established skills such as accountancy, surveying or social work – have been reluctant to relinquish control to a usurping group of 'generalists'. The result for many years, as Laffin observes (1986: 107–8), was the reduction of the housing management function to relatively low-level and routine tasks of allocation, rent collection and arrears chasing; hardly a rock on which an imposing professional edifice can be built.

There are many *symptoms* of the structural weakness which afflicts the claims of housing practitioners for acceptance as a distinct profession. Although wider developments in housing policy have produced fluctuations in their status, the history of public sector housing management has been beset by institutional division, operational fragmentation, low levels of training, marginality in policy formulation and limited public esteem.

With reference to the first two of these frailties, the early history of professionalism in public housing was marked by the parallel development of two organisations. The Society of Women Housing Estate Managers stood in the tradition of Octavia Hill and her attempt during the late nineteenth century to activate the principles of '5 per cent philanthropy' whereby, through the intensive management of new housing developments and the instruction of tenants in matters of hygiene and household accountancy, the returns to the investor were to be such as to permit the construction of sound homes for the working class. With women assigned the role of home management, it was deemed appropriate that the task of instructing them should also be that of women, or rather 'ladies' of higher social standing. Women joined the staff of housing associations and other agencies, notably the Church Commissioners, to fulfil this welfare function of managing the tenants, together with door-to-door rent collection and the arranging of repairs and maintenance, while men continued to attend to issues of design, building, and strategic financial control.

At the birth of council housing in 1919, therefore, the Octavia Hill system, with its emphasis on the social as well as the financial and physical dimensions of housing management, stood as a model for councils in administering their new stock. However, as earlier chapters have shown, the first to benefit from this new tenure were not Octavia Hill's poor but comparatively affluent, 'respectable' households of the skilled working class and the lower middle class. Given careful selection procedures, such tenants posed relatively few management problems, so that local authorities were able to avoid the expense of Hill's intensive management style and define their housing role in essentially fiscal and physical terms: the collection of rent and the maintenance and repair of the property (Kemp and Williams 1987: 18–19). A mainly male staff, with professional qualifications, or at least experience, in specialist technical trades and occupations which equipped them to undertake one particular aspect of their council's housing function such as accountancy, surveying, or engineering, was recruited to these tasks. These 'housing officers' were often not based in a housing department but were dispersed among several departments for which housing was merely one (albeit growing) responsibility. Their allegiances were first to these established professions rather than to an all-embracing notion of 'housing management'. By 1935 only 17 per cent of local authorities had appointed housing managers (Laffin 1986: 77) – a situation which persisted in many localities until well into the 1970s.

The institutional reflection of this state of affairs is seen in the Institute of Municipal Estate Managers (later the Institute of Housing), founded in 1931. This organisation was for those officers who had a central responsibility for housing and who had achieved positions of seniority in their local authorities. It operated only as a forum for co-ordinating and communicating best practice in housing management, rather than pressing for a distinct housing qualification and recognition of a separate profession. Until their eventual merger in 1965, the Society of Women Housing Estate Managers – advocating generic housing work with an emphasis upon the perceived welfare needs of tenants – and the Institute, with its predominantly male membership and focus upon housing management as a series of fragmented and essentially physical and financial tasks, continued to offer contrasting models of service delivery in public housing. Of the two, it was the Society's position which offered the greater prospect of the consolidation of housing management as an independent profession. Yet the Institute – which began to change its position on unified housing departments and generic workers in the late 1950s (whilst still eschewing a strong welfare orientation) (Kemp and Williams 1987: 21) – remained the more influential professional body.

Octavia Hill's staff-intensive, high-cost system remained unattractive to councils. With the reaffirmation of council housing as a 'general needs' tenure after 1945, this tradition seemed to offer an unnecessary and outmoded approach. Few women housing managers were appointed by local authorities and, predictably, female staff were frequently assigned 'appropriate' and low-status roles. An early example is found in 1928 when, faced with tenants 'needing to be disciplined in what they ought to do', Bristol Corporation appointed a 'Lady Housing Visitor' on a temporary contract and at a salary well below that of the most junior male staff, her higher qualifications notwithstanding (Dresser 1984: 204).

The post-war decades have seen some consolidation of housing management as a profession. Apart from the merger between the Society and the Institute, the latter established entry by its own examination in 1946 and saw a growth in its membership to 900 by 1950 (Laffin 1986: 81). Although membership remained stable until 1970, subsequent years have seen further growth and by 1992 the Institute of Housing comprised 4,000 members, 900 fellows, and 800 associate members (Institute of Housing 1992a: 7). In part, this expansion reflects the extension of local authorities' role towards a 'comprehensive housing service', embracing the assessment of local housing need, the provision of advisory services, and new responsibilities towards other tenures as espoused by the Cullingworth Report in 1969; the introduction in 1977 of Housing Investment Programmes to regulate capital programmes (Houlihan 1983); and the related general climate favouring the adoption of corporate management in local government and the belated establishment in many localities of housing departments with a diversity of functions. A minority of authorities had no separate housing department in 1965, but after local government reorganisation an Institute of Housing survey indicated that many new departments had been established headed by chief officers, most of whom were members of their authority's corporate management team (Laffin 1986: 90).

However, even at what may come to be regarded as this high water mark of professionalism in public housing management, the Institute of Housing could not lay claim to full control over entry to housing employment or over specifying the credentials necessary for successful housing practice. As early as 1933 the Royal Institution of Chartered Surveyors (RICS) had examined candidates for professional membership on behalf of the Society of Women Housing Estate Managers and, through its General Practice Division, the RICS has continued to offer a housing qualification. Many senior positions in housing departments remain filled by officers with other specialist qualifications. The growth of housing associations and housing aid centres since the 1970s brought the formation of new groups such as the National Federation of Housing Associations, the National Association of Housing Aid Workers and the Housing Centre Trust as alternative housing forums. Furthermore, the move from fragmentation towards integrated housing departments should not be exaggerated. In 1986 the Audit Commission still found it necessary to recommend councils to appoint a chief housing officer responsible for all housing management activities (Audit Commission 1986: 2). The consolidation of functions within a single department now faces a new challenge as central government has sought to reduce the role of local authorities to that of 'enablers' rather than suppliers of housing, to encourage the transfer and sale of stock and to open up housing management to competitive tendering.

In addition to this institutional division and operational fragmentation in housing practice, the ability of housing professionals to influence the direction of public housing policy has been undermined further by the low level of training among housing workers. A study conducted in 1977 indicated that only about 3.5 per cent of housing staff had a professional qualification in housing and only a further 4 per cent held other professional qualifications. Furthermore, training provision was very limited and in many authorities almost non-existent (City University 1977). Subsequently, this position improved, with enrolments on the Institute of Housing's Professional Qualification doubling between 1982 and 1988 and student membership of the Institute rising to over 4,000, bolstered by the increasing numbers of students entering recognised courses in universities. Assisted by government grants made under the Housing and Planning Act of 1986, the Institute also strengthened its training services for a period, although its scale of operation was subsequently curtailed. Nevertheless, it remains the case that throughout most of its sixty-year history council housing has been managed by poorly qualified and trained staff. The Audit Commission noted that of 55,000 local authority housing staff, less than

2,500 were professionally qualified. Demanding estate management roles were still being performed by young, inexperienced and undertrained personnel (Audit Commission 1986: 15). Growing controls on local revenue expenditure brought heavy pressure on training budgets in the early 1990s.

The marginality of housing professionals in policy formulation was illustrated in Chapter 4 by reference to the high-rise era. While Dunleavy's careful reconstruction of the adoption of this policy indicates that *design* professionals constituted a major influence (Dunleavy 1981a), housing *management* was relegated to the role of wrestling with the consequences of policy. Laffin (1986: Chs. 5 and 8) offers a similarly detailed account of the very limited role played by housing officers in national debates on public sector housing management, through bodies such as the Central Housing Advisory Council, Anthony Crosland's Housing Policy Review Panel and, later, the Housing Services Advisory Group. Indeed, his analysis shows that pressure for change on housing management, even the call for a 'comprehensive housing service', emanated from *outside* the profession and encountered much opposition from senior housing officers. While the Institute of Housing was successful in securing some increase in central government support and resources for housing education and training after 1979, it seems clear that Conservative administrations pursued housing professionalism for its *own* purposes, to bypass the influence of Labour councillors in local housing policy. It is, moreover, a professionalism which seems decreasingly likely to establish itself as a distinctive influence on housing policy, for it draws upon more general principles and techniques of commercial property and business management and financial control. The radical restructuring and diminution of public housing of the Thatcher years occurred with little sign that the agenda had been modified by the representations of housing professionals.

Finally, in a nation where a growing proportion of householders are their own housing managers, the lack of mystique or a clearly defined technical core to housing management – together with the strengthening attack on the whole legitimacy of public housing and the growing poverty of those who remain council tenants – are reflected in the relatively low status and public recognition of housing practitioners. In the mid-1970s, Karn observed that

> talented young people looking for promotion are often put off by the ultimate lack of power of housing managers in the authority and, more immediately, by the lower rates of pay and smaller training opportunities accorded to housing trainees as compared with trainees in other departments.
>
> (Karn 1977: 179)

During the mid-1980s, while training opportunities had increased, low pay and poor promotion prospects remained a major source of complaint among housing staff, and many considered that their tasks did not demand their full ability (Centre for Housing Research 1989: 17–20).

The evidence assembled here underlines the failure of a radically alternative model of landlordism to emerge in the public sector. A strong housing profession boasting traditional status, occupational mystique or esoteric technique may have used its role to 'champion the cause of the disadvantaged' (Karn 1977: 178) or, perhaps more realistically, to act as a powerful, self-interested, conservative bulwark against cuts in this welfare sector. But such a profession has never emerged. Faced with declining resources and growing operational problems in the 1980s, the challenge to government policy mounted by housing practitioners was often muted and focused on the detail of change rather than its underlying philosophy. Hence, Sarre and his colleagues remark upon the degree to which housing departments 'accept their difficulties without public protest, and often apparently without realising the difficulties themselves. In effect, they seem to operate at the level of practical rather than discursive consciousness' (Sarre *et al.* 1989: 194).

HOUSING MANAGEMENT IN PRACTICE

We have argued in this chapter that the phrase 'public landlordism' is useful in underlining the limited extent to which British council housing brought a radical departure from the landlord–tenant relations of the private rental market. The preceding two sections have focused upon the two groups sharing the main responsibility for delivering municipal housing services, local government councillors and professional housing officers. Neither group offered the promise of major changes in the terms and experience of housing consumption. They were constrained by wider economic structures and central government policies, restrictive local political pressures and, in the case of officers, secular professional weakness, and guided typically in their exercise of discretion by a combination of various conservative political ideologies and a narrow pragmatism. The remaining task in this chapter is to indicate some of the main consequences of this policy inertia for the actual *practice* of housing management.

Clearly, it is not possible to present here a detailed survey of every aspect of the administration of council housing. The following discussion focuses upon three main areas: tenancy conditions, housing allocation, and general organisational efficiency. An examination of these aspects of council housing management illustrates the extent to which the tenure has deserved the charge of 'public landlordism'. The evidence suggests that council housing management has constituted a service which is defensible in relation to alternative modes of provision, even if it has fallen well short of offering a participatory, socially progressive and organisationally efficient utopia. The discussion will again concentrate on council housing administration in the years preceding the 1980s, before radical changes in government policy provoked a belated attempt to develop new styles of social housing management; these will be explored in Chapter 8.

In terms of tenancy conditions, a forceful description of the typical imbalance in the power relationship between council tenants and their landlords, written from the anarchist Left, was offered by Ward in the mid-1970s:

> Municipal housing is still dominated by its origins in nineteenth-century philanthropic paternalism. The tenant's relationship with his landlord is only a contractual one in the sense that a serf in the middle ages was a party to a contract with the lord of the manor. It is the lords of the municipal manor who call the tune.
>
> (Ward 1974: 14)

This inequality in landlord–tenant relations has been reflected in council tenancy agreements which, until recently, usually amounted to no more than a list of tenants' obligations to their landlord (National Consumer Council 1976; for an example of a typical tenancy agreement in use in a London borough during the 1970s, see Andrews 1979: 303). In contrast, councils made few undertakings and offered limited rights to tenants. Indeed, in one significant respect – security of tenure – the position of public tenants for many years was more vulnerable than that of households with private tenancies. Many tenants also encountered limitations on their freedom in the form of rules concerning alterations of their homes or controls on the right to keep pets, backed by handbooks giving condescending advice on how to undertake housework and rear children.

Local councils showed little inclination to undertake significant reform of their own tenancy agreements. Concerted action by Labour at national level was delayed to the point where the comparison between the controls on tenants could be contrasted in popular debate all too easily with the freedoms (no matter how precarious) of owner-occupiers. Although Labour had drafted a Housing Bill in 1979 with proposals to strengthen tenants' rights, it was the first Thatcher administration which introduced a 'Tenants' Charter' as one element in its Housing Act of 1980. This charter was hardly intended to place public housing on a competitive footing with home ownership. While it established certain individual rights – such as security of tenure, tenancy succession, and the right to sublet and take in lodgers – the Act offered only a limited and indirect strengthening of tenants' collective rights, in the form of the right to consultation and the provision of information.

Of course, the routine application and interpretation of tenancy agreements, as well as their content, have to be considered in judging the management service offered to tenants. It can be argued that social criteria – at least in the more permissive legislative and financial context obtaining before the 1980s – were much more to the fore in the handling by councils of such routine issues as rent arrears, neighbour disputes, evictions, and transfer applications than would have been the case with private landlords. In a comparison of housing management in five European countries, for example, Emms contrasted the greater welfare orientation and 'social slant' of British housing management and education with the stronger prevailing business orientation elsewhere (Emms 1990: 302–3). Also, tenancy agreements or race relations legislation giving councils clear rights of intervention should not be viewed as entirely inconsistent with tenants' interests, for they offer tenants valued protection from the unacceptable behaviour of their neighbours. Nevertheless, the continuing relative powerlessness of tenants has clearly been at odds with their aspirations for involvement in housing management (see Chapter 6). The centrality of tenants' rights to the survival of a reformed public sector has been a key feature of the policy debate, political campaigning, and emerging reforms in housing practice in recent years (see Chapter 8).

Apart from the establishment and administration of tenancy agreements, a further key element in council housing management has been the task of housing allocation. An encounter with an authority's allocation staff and procedures is most people's first experience of municipal housing management, and can therefore be crucial in shaping their long-term view of their landlord, their satisfaction with their home, and their perceptions of their wider housing status.

The rules and practices surrounding the allocation of the housing stock have always been central to distinctions between market housing and 'social' housing. It has certainly been the expectation that need and 'fairness' should be the overriding considerations governing access to public housing, and local authorities have justified their policies in these terms. In practice, however, the intrusion of other criteria into housing allocation is now a matter of long-standing record. Both entry into the tenure and, as the form and quality of the stock have diversified, transfers into the better dwellings seem to have been governed not only by considerations of social need but by a set of quasi-market processes which match particular kinds of households to 'appropriate' kinds of home in accordance with other principles. For example, in a major report on council housing administration, the Cullingworth Committee expressed surprise concerning some housing authorities who took up a moralistic attitude towards applicants: the underlying philosophy seemed to be that council tenancies were to be given only to those who 'deserved' them and that the 'most deserving' should get the best houses . . . . Moral rectitude, social conformity, clean living, and a clean rent book on occasion seemed to be essential qualifications for eligibility.

(Central Housing Advisory Committee 1969: 33)

The Committee's surprise, unless it is rhetorical, is itself remarkable for, even by the late 1960s, the use of local discretion to discriminate between applicants was a matter of long-standing experience. The kind of detailed councillor intervention mentioned earlier was displaced in most localities by the use of seemingly precise, 'scientific' points schemes, or by date-order systems with priority categories for certain homeless people, the elderly, medical cases and other vulnerable groups. Yet these developments did not prevent the wider spatial segregation by class, race and household type in British towns and cities being reproduced in the public sector (see, for example, Gray in Merrett 1979: 213ff; Reade 1982; Henderson and Karn 1987).

In explaining the development of this quasi-market within a bureaucratically administered public housing stock, however, the limited autonomy of council housing management identified earlier in the chapter is underlined. Housing allocation occurs within a context framed powerfully by the past. Previous chapters have shown that British council housing is highly differentiated in quality, reflecting interrelated fluctuations in subsidies, designs and standards, and the overall status of the public housing sector. It forms a fairly well-defined hierarchy of desirability in the perceptions of both applicants and established tenants. A continuing constraint structuring housing allocation, therefore, is the excess in the demand for the better council dwellings over their supply. The pressure on housing officers intensified considerably during the 1980s, as many of the most popular houses were removed from the stock through Right to Buy sales. The virtual cessation of new building, combined with restrictions on modernisation and renovation programmes, increased the premium attaching to the best homes. Economic restructuring, the sponsorship of home ownership and the residualisation of public housing have also heightened competition and conflict over council house allocation and transfers as existing residents, often struggling themselves with the consequences of local economic decline, have resisted the arrival of less 'respectable' neighbours. For all these reasons, the allocation process hardly occurs on terms of housing managers' own choosing.

Of course, such considerations must not lead to a neglect of the part

played by local housing staff and politicians in establishing formal allocation policies and related departmental operating procedures. In fact, as
exemplified in the context of racial inequalities in public housing, there has
been widespread inertia by local authorities in ensuring that social
priorities outweigh immediate expedience in allocation. On the basis of
both its own inquiries and studies in many other localities, one research
team has observed that

> In view of the imperatives of the 1976 Race Relations Act, the recom-
> mendations from government inquiries and independent researchers,
> and interventions and exhortations of the Commission for Racial
> Equality, it is surprising how persistent many local authorities have been
> in denying the existence of racial bias in their housing departments, or
> in doing anything about it. Although there is evidence that things are
> changing . . . it has often been left to independent researchers to attempt
> to assess the impact of council policy on ethnic segregation and dis-
> advantage. The findings of some of these researchers have been met
> with a vitriolic response and a blind acceptance of the status quo by the
> very institutions investigated.
>
> (Sarre *et al.* 1989: 193)

This passivity, reflected in widespread reluctance or negligence in establishing racial monitoring in allocation, effective staff training programmes,
standard assessment procedures, or effective liaison with ethnic minority
communities, could be taken as a sign of an active affirmation of racial
inequality by individual housing staff. The urban managerialist perspective
provoked numerous studies exploring the extent of discrimination in the
actions of housing personnel. Such research tended to concentrate on junior
staff, notably housing visitors, and the values and perceptions directing
their use of discretion in grading applicants and steering their choice of
housing. While these studies yielded important insights into the
mechanisms of allocation, however, they offered only a partial illumination
of the forces driving the process. As Henderson and Karn (1987: 18) have
remarked, an exclusive focus upon the racially prejudiced behaviour of
individuals fails to explain why those who are not prejudiced engage in
discriminatory behaviour, or why discriminatory outcomes persist when
staff change or even when formal procedures are revised.

These considerations force us to focus again on the context of council
housing management. Henderson and Karn argue that 'all forms of discrimination . . . need to be understood in relation to the source of their
reproductive dynamics, the fundamentally inegalitarian British social
structure' (Henderson and Karn 1987: xxii). Drawing upon their empirical
research in Birmingham, these authors contend that structural influences

are at the heart of council housing allocation, shaping the actions of individual officers and councillors.

Here it is important to recognise that allocation in a context of scarcity *requires* discrimination. In understanding the discrimination involved in housing allocation, knowledge of a local authority's formal policies is insufficient. Officially, the criteria governing housing access may be those of technically determined social need. In informal practice, however, the immediate pressures confronting housing officers, including the applications of many households who in formal terms are equally qualified for a particular letting, oblige them to engage in a 'creative adaption' of the rules. The exercise of this discretion takes the form of 'culturally sanctioned, rational responses to struggles over scarce resources' (Wellman 1977: 4 – quoted in Henderson and Karn 1987: 18). In their role as 'managers of scarcity', therefore, housing officers utilise socially dominant distinctions so that not only race, but also class and gender-based discriminatory ideologies and practices 'articulate both within the structure of housing departments and within the consciousness of housing officers such that they are able to adversely influence the housing allocations which particular sorts of applicants receive' (Henderson and Karn 1987: 19).

Both Henderson and Karn's work and the research carried out by Sarre and his colleagues in Bedford indicate how this wider context of class, race and gender-based inequalities influences the detailed practice of housing allocation through the grading (formal or informal) of housekeeping standards, the notions of 'appropriateness' which guide advice to applicants and the discretion of lettings officers, and the stereotyping of households' preferences and expectations of housing type and location (Sarre *et al.* 1989: 184–94).

The absence of a strongly developed and distinctive professional ideology – emphasising housing as a social right and the legitimacy of non-market, socially undiscriminating criteria of access – simply confirms the power of prevailing definitions of gender roles, 'deserving' and 'undeserving' working-class households, and racial status to direct housing allocation. Indeed, to pursue any other than a 'rational' course is often to invite the displeasure of ward councillors and 'respectable' tenants. Moreover, housing staff are more likely to secure career advancement through achieving rapid allocations, minimising empty properties, reducing rent arrears, containing disputes between neighbours, and reducing, through segregation, the risks of racial conflict, particularly given current enthusiasm for performance indicators. To adopt a less pragmatic, more progressive view of the social role of council housing, let alone a more forthright advocacy of social equality, is to court powerful opposition and reduced personal material prospects.

All this highlights an acute dilemma facing council housing managers. Equality demands that public housing is administered according to distinctive 'social' criteria. But steps towards this goal can make public housing less attractive to more affluent white households, so confirming its status as a residual tenure for the poor and stigmatised (Henderson and Karn 1984: 126–7; Phillips 1985). In fact, recent official concern has been concentrated less upon council housing as a vehicle for social equality and more upon its efficiency and effectiveness in operational terms. It is to this issue that we turn to complete our review of housing management in practice.

We noted earlier how for many years central government's control over local authorities' housing operations was confined largely to issues of design, numerical construction targets and Exchequer capital commitments. One result of this official preoccupation with issues of housing production was that, during the decades of the tenure's expansion, there was very little research into the quality of council housing management. By the time that a series of major studies was published in the 1980s the practice of local housing management was already changing significantly, in response to the profound fiscal, ideological and legislative challenges confronting the public sector. It is now possible to derive valuable insights into the general efficiency and effectiveness of council housing management from the recent past.

Important studies of the organisation and performance of local authority housing management include those by the Audit Commission, notably the report *Managing the Crisis in Council Housing* (Audit Commission 1986); reports commissioned by the Department of the Environment (Kirby *et al.* 1987; Centre for Housing Research 1989; Emms 1990); and research financed by the Joseph Rowntree Foundation (Walsh and Spencer 1990; Cole *et al.* 1991).

The tone of these reports varies. For example, although it is an independent body, it can be argued that the Audit Commission is a creation of central government, with which it shares a common perspective on the degree and causes of the problems facing public housing (Malpass and Murie 1987: 163). Hence, the Commission identifies a 'crisis of serious proportions' in council housing and highlights the low standard of housing management which gave 'cause for serious concern' in a number of local authorities (Audit Commission 1986). The Glasgow University report does not headline poor local authority management. Noting the government's desire to transfer the managerial function from local authorities to other agencies, this inquiry indicates that, in a comparison between local authority and housing association management, 'no single organisational type is free from criticism or is dominated by effective providers' (Centre for Housing Research 1989). The report presents 'a more complex view of both problems and solutions than is commonly advanced in discussions of these policy areas in Britain' (Centre for Housing Research 1989).

However, although the balance and emphasis of these reports may differ, important common conclusions emerge. First, there were many examples of good local authority housing management. Even the recommendations of the Audit Commission were based substantially on the good practice in many localities uncovered during the inquiry (Audit Commission 1986). Second, however, it is clear that the quality of council housing management varies significantly from place to place. The Glasgow University inquiry found, even within the sub-categories of large and small authorities, considerable differences in managerial performance (Centre for Housing Research 1989). If it is possible to identify good local authority landlords who compare favourably with the better housing associations, therefore, it is also possible to point to other councils whose practices conform more to the caricature of local authorities as inefficient and unresponsive bureaucracies. What are the recurring criticisms of council housing management emerging from these studies?

While organisational type or structure have not been revealed as decisive determinants of managerial effectiveness (Centre for Housing Research 1989: 130), the fragmentation of housing management functions between different local authority departments still compromises service quality through inconveniencing tenants, reducing managerial accountability and increasing problems of co-ordination. The Audit Commission also highlighted the lack of control exerted by housing departments over charges levied within authorities for central services such as personnel, legal advice, computer facilities, payroll administration, and maintenance of open spaces on estates. It found that inefficiencies in service departments were being passed on to the Housing Revenue Account (Audit Commission 1986). In larger authorities the organisational problems have been more often those of co-ordination within a single housing department. In particular, it is still common for a rigid division to exist between technical staff responsible for repairs, and management staff (Walsh and Spencer 1990). Until the 1980s, large centralised departments confronted the public with daunting problems of accessibility, communication and accountability (Emms 1990: 50–2).

Another object of criticism in council housing management is the frequent exercise of local political discretion in the past to use the valuable advantages of historic cost accounting and rent pooling procedures to set unduly low rents, which restricted management and maintenance resources available to housing managers (Audit Commission 1986: 58; Centre for Housing Research 1989: 108 and 129). Only a minority of councils raised rents to increase their management spending towards the much higher norm for housing associations.

But a key finding in the Glasgow University study was that successful housing management – as defined by various indicators of economy, efficiency, effectiveness and consumer response – did not appear to be related in a clear way to management expenditure, organisational type or structure, or even to the difficulty of the context managed. Rather 'what matters most is the will to manage efficiently and effectively . . . . In remaking social housing, government could learn from the lessons of industrial policy. Performance is largely a function of managerial conduct rather than industrial structure' (Centre for Housing Research 1989: 130).

This judgement directs attention to the actual operating procedures of local authority housing management. Here, common areas of criticism are the lack of performance monitoring and performance targets, notably in the crucial area of repairs services; inadequate access to good management information and underdevelopment of appropriate information technology (Walsh and Spencer 1990); poor communications within housing departments; and inadequate liaison with tenants, with participation initiatives neglected until the challenge to public housing in the 1980s brought a belated response by many authorities. Management research underlines the demanding nature of council housing administration and it is clear that this task has been met all too often by poorly trained, inadequately paid and resourced staff who, as suggested earlier in the chapter, experience limited autonomy and scope for initiative in their work. The importance of strong senior management, and the vital role of area or neighbourhood managers, is a recurrent theme in this research (Cole *et al.* 1991).

The evidence certainly points to important deficiencies prevailing in council housing management in Britain, and it is possible to identify cases of inefficient and ineffective local housing administration. However, it is also the case that many councils have operated a much better housing service and that significant advances have been achieved in more recent years. Certainly, the national variation in council housing management belies the political rhetoric which has advanced a blanket condemnation of council housing as an indelibly flawed enterprise. Some councils have achieved significant service improvements with a minimal increase in resources. Further advances could be secured with appropriate material support, and this future potential is explored in Chapter 8.

This review of the quality of everyday council housing management underlines the conflicting pressures confronting local housing administration identified in the earlier discussion of housing allocation. Just as there is a tension between the 'social' criteria of public housing and demands for financial and operational efficiency in allocating the stock, so recent research upholds the principle both of local democracy and of the right of 'managers to manage' as making good past weaknesses in municipal housing services (see, for example, the Audit Commission 1986: 80). Similarly, the narrow financial measures of economy and efficiency, which may flow from greater managerial autonomy, have to be weighed against the increased effectiveness and democratic legitimacy which can stem from the costly and time-consuming process of tenant participation.

CONCLUSION

During recent years several local authorities have been organising events to celebrate one hundred years of municipal housing in their locality. Reviewing the material assembled in this chapter, the conclusion must be that some recognition of the achievements of many local housing services is in order and, as was stressed in the second Inquiry into British Housing chaired by the Duke of Edinburgh, it is by no means clear that a future reliance on alternative landlords will yield automatic improvements in service quality (Inquiry into British Housing 1991: 38).

Yet it is hard to escape the conclusion that – in comparison with council housing production and design – both the practice of housing management and the political debate surrounding it have been afflicted for decades by a deep-rooted torpor. It is almost as though the sheer effort of producing the stock exhausted the imagination of even the tenure's staunchest advocates. Such vision as did exist was restricted by the particular influences of Fabian and labourist ideas which encouraged an accommodation of council housing management within prevailing notions of class distinction, the legitimacy of racial segregation, the greater relative 'deservingness' of particular households, and the right of political leaders and technical 'experts' to make detailed decisions on other people's behalf. As seen earlier in the chapter, a host of factors prevented the numerically large housing management profession from consolidating as an effective defender of public housing, or as a force for its progressive redefinition. The result was a form of housing consumption which conformed too much to the epithet of 'public landlordism'. It was a service of uneven, sometimes poor and oppressive, quality in which the conflicting demands of social justice, political democracy, user empowerment and managerial efficiency remained unresolved.

However, our review of housing management in practice has indicated that the legacy of the past is not so negative as to make fruitless the current search for reform. It would be fanciful to suppose that council housing management could emerge quickly as a sleeping beauty after so many years of neglect. For a start, the defects of British public housing cannot be attributed simply to the failures of its management. This management is itself affected by wider processes of economic and social restructuring, which ensure that the re-establishment of the tenure cannot be achieved by management reform alone. Nevertheless, there are sufficient examples of current good and improving practice to sustain the belief that imagination and innovation could make council housing more than competitive as a form of housing for a significant section of the population.

On the basis of academic literature and official research, we have concluded that council housing, although embattled, is in principle defensible and capable of reform. However, this judgement would be premature if it is not checked against the experience and testimony of a further, crucial group of witnesses – council tenants. If the users of the service have no confidence in its quality and potential compared with alternatives, then any hope in a future for council housing would be misconceived. It is therefore to the tenants' response to council housing that we now turn.

6 Tenant experiences and responses

The 'outsider's' view of council housing as discussed in the preceding chapters of this book could be developed using a generally extensive and detailed literature. An exploration of users' views, the construction of an 'insider's' account of British public housing, involves working with much more scattered evidence.

This imbalance of perspective is scarcely surprising. The confidence and domination of producer interests in council housing has been such that, until recently, tenant voices have rarely been sought. This has both reflected and compounded the wider economic, political and cultural subordination of working-class people, including most council tenants. Also, as Saunders has observed, very few academic commentators have been able to write of council housing with insight born from first-hand experiences of life in local authority housing (Saunders 1990: 4). It can be argued that this detachment was reinforced during the 1970s and most of the 1980s by the retreat of the earlier 'community studies' tradition in British sociology and the ascendancy of structuralist perspectives in urban studies. Sometimes the result of the biographical gulf between council tenants and most academics has been a spectacular misreading of tenants' experience of their homes and their likely response to changing circumstances. We shall also find a further reason for the lack of documentation of tenants' impressions of their homes in the nature of the tenants' movement itself which, although it may be the subject of a rich (albeit very unresearched) oral history, has left few written records. Analysts writing from the perspective of the New Right are likely to be as prone to the misrepresentations of an outsider's perspective as representatives of the academic Left, although this is not a matter pursued by Saunders. Certainly there has been an interesting coincidence in the views of the Marxist Left and New Right concerning council housing. Exponents of both standpoints have tended to operate on the assumption that everybody, including tenants, 'knows' that public housing is poorly designed, inefficiently managed, and oppressive. The allocation of research funds has served generally to leave many conventional assumptions unexplored, reflecting the theoretical, financial and technical preoccupations of researchers, politicians and professionals. Housing 'knowledge', therefore, has also reflected the distribution of economic, political and cultural power (Kemeny 1988).

However, the challenge posed by successive Thatcher administrations to the nature and scale of council housing stimulated a belated and welcome interest in the views of the 'consumers' of state housing. In addition to studies commissioned by central government and other agencies, the 1980s brought a welter of 'customer-orientated' surveys by local authorities faced with a challenge to their survival as major landlords. By the early 1990s, therefore, it had become more possible to explore tenants' views of their housing by combining a review of this accumulating survey material with an examination of existing research on the mobilisation of council tenants as a political force, together with reference to ethnographical research which is showing signs of a welcome revival (Franklin 1990).

Earlier in this book we described the fluctuating history of state housing in Britain, the uneven amenity of the dwellings on offer, and the tenure's diverse consumers. In view of this variation, it might therefore be expected that the response of tenants to their housing will be marked by a corresponding diversity. In the following discussion the themes of protest, resignation and contentment are used as a typology through which to explore the divergent and often complex response of council tenants to their housing situations.

PROPHECIES OF PROTEST

One possible reaction by council tenants to the housing service would be to mobilise collectively, whether in the form of militant direct action or through vigorous campaigning and lobbying. Indeed, for many commentators on the Left, this is anticipated as the dominant reaction to the financial and management regimes and the use-values of state housing. Such a political mobilisation of tenants is seen from this perspective as a predictable corollary of life in housing built as a grudging response to capital's need for a reproduced, controlled labour force.

Some have therefore seen tenant protest as carrying significant potential in contributing to the transformation of capitalist social and economic relations (for example, see Moorhouse *et al.* 1972). The most influential academic analysis framing an assessment of the possible impact of 'urban' protest in spheres such as housing in recent years is found in the work of Castells. Lowe provides a detailed account of the developments and major changes which occurred in Castells' understanding of urban political mobilisation between the early 1970s and early 1980s (Lowe 1986: Chs. 1 and 2). He identifies three stages in Castells' thinking, corresponding broadly with the publication of three of the latter's major texts (Castells 1977, 1978, 1983).

For all the major revisions and frank recantations presented in Castells' more recent work, a continuing theme in his writings is the potentially crucial significance of 'urban social movements' as agents of major social change. Castells' early work rested upon a largely functionalist Marxist understanding of the state which we outlined in Chapter 1. He identified the city as an arena of 'collective consumption', the place where the necessary but unprofitable business of reproducing the labour force is undertaken by the state through the provision of public services. In these terms, therefore, British council housing is a key form of collective consumption. Castells argued that the increasing cost of collective consumption obliges the state to raise its expenditure to the point where a public fiscal crisis forces cuts in services which may be met by strong working-class resistance. This resistance is the more likely because the state's involvement in service provision politicises their availability and delivery. Crucial to the emergence of an urban social movement capable of a significant challenge to prevailing class relations is a vanguard socialist party to link protest over service cuts to the growing workplace conflicts of late capitalism. Such a catalyst can serve to transform a latent 'social base' into an effective 'social force' for change. According to this analysis, council estates in Britain could be identified as promising bases of change.

Castells' later work involves a progressive departure from his initial structural Marxism. By the mid-1970s he was not linking urban protest exclusively to working-class interests. He now argued that cuts in state services also affected the middle class who, indeed, are often the principal beneficiaries of public expenditure. People's interests as *consumers* creates the potential for cross-class alliances to oppose cuts in health, education, housing and other services. Broad mobilisation of this kind opens the possibility of a democratic road to socialism and a 'gradualist infiltration of the state apparatus' (Lowe 1986: 25), with an important contribution being made by professionals within state institutions. This focus on modes of consumption as the basis for politics is a theme developed by British non-Marxist writers such as Dunleavy (1980) and Saunders (1984a, 1986 and 1990). Finally, in *The City and the Grassroots* (1983) Castells moves still further from his original structural class theory to stress the active role of people as conscious subjects in enacting change and the way in which the nature of people's response to their circumstances may vary in the light of different historical and local experiences and according to other sources of identity such as ethnicity, gender, nationalism and religion. Modern cities, he argues, are arenas in which battles are fought for cultural identity, local (often neighbourhood) self-government, or consumption interests.

Through all these changes in his detailed position, therefore, Castells adheres to the view that protest is likely to be a major and growing response of urban populations to their experience of state services. It will emerge from our subsequent discussion that his work supplies a graphic illustration of the gulf that can develop between the perceptions of urban researchers and urban residents. However, Castells has stimulated a debate and critical research which has shed some important light on the factors influencing housing consumers in their response to their situation. In the boldness of a prediction such as the following, 'We are willing to make the historical and theoretical wager that there will be a significant development of urban social movements as a means of changing social relations, and this will arise from urban contradictions' (Castells 1978: 126–7), he threw down a challenge which has provoked others to assess the likelihood of his winning his bet in a British context.

Certainly, as Lowe observes, council estates might appear to constitute a clear and relatively homogeneous social base which under certain circumstances could be expected to mobilise to defend collective interests or to press for change. Frequently, council estates have also formed spatially discrete 'communities' of working-class households with residents sharing a common consumption sector location and shared experiences of housing management (Lowe 1986: 82–4).

The long-term constraints on municipal housing as a form of collective consumption, culminating in the 1980s with strong upward pressure on rents together with tightly controlled budgets for repair, modernisation and Housing Benefit, might seem a context ripe for emergence of a mass 'urban social movement' as predicted by Castells. The following section explores the extent of protest by council tenants, and the reasons for the scale and intensity of their mobilisation falling far short of such academic prophecies.

PROTEST AND QUIESCENCE

It is clear, even from the limited historical documentation available, that protest by public sector tenants in Britain should not simply be dismissed as insignificant. This discussion will include references to several episodes of well-supported tenant action. Such activity has not been entirely without success and it is important to recognise the possibility that

> despite the supposed insignificance of housing consumption actions, even of a collective nature, they do have a cumulative effect on state

intervention; taken singularly they may usually be unimportant, but taken together they may constitute a formative context and pressure on a national state.

(Dickens *et al.* 1985: 206)

One period of intense tenant campaigning occurred in the years surrounding the Housing Finance Act of 1972. Although unsuccessful in its immediate aims of preventing major rent increases, this mobilisation can be identified as symptomatic of a wider strength and confidence in working-class organisation which played a major part in the eventual defeat of Heath's Conservative administration (Hague 1990: 247–8). Furthermore, the success of the mass campaign by tenants against the transfer of local authority stock into other hands after the Housing Act of 1988, just as many had assumed that effective grassroots support for council housing had finally dissipated, must be underlined (see, for example, Woodward 1991). Further reference will be made below to this more recent awakening of collective action (see p. 161).

However, in comparison with an apocalyptic scenario in which tenants act as the crack troops in an urban social revolution, it must be said that what has been termed the 'tenants' movement' in Britain has been typically limited, localised, occasional and defensive. In fact, the examples of mass tenant revolt merely tend to highlight those prerequisites for mobilisation which are so often absent. The following discussion, therefore, will focus more on those factors which inhibit tenant protest.

Using Castells' contributions as a framework, the limited extent of protest as a response by council tenants to their housing experiences can be interpreted by reference to several interrelated themes: the weak and weakening links between workplace conflicts and consumption struggles; the declining association between social class and housing consumption; the fragmented nature of council housing as a 'social base' for political action; the impact of working-class cultures and consciousness on political mobilisation; the lack of resources (psychological, political and material) in many situations to sustain successful tenant activity; the limited extent to which council housing is truly a *collective* form of housing consumption; the success of state agencies in containing or shaping tenant activity; and the availability of other options for tenants seeking an improvement in their housing.

First, Castells' early hopes that consumption struggles could be linked with class-based workplace conflicts have shown few signs of fulfilment in relation to British council housing. Certainly, from a Marxist standpoint, such a 'dual contradiction' – with all its potential for socialist trans-formation – has sometimes moved tantalisingly into view. In Chapter 2 we showed how the most celebrated tenants' action of all, by private tenants in Glasgow during the First World War, drew crucially upon the wartime industrial strength backing the rent strike and upon the active collaboration of a range of labour organisations. Similar substantial support from the labour movement for battles against rent increases occurred in Greater London in 1968 (Moorhouse *et al*. 1972: 142) and in the new town of Crawley in the early 1950s (Dickens *et al*. 1985: 225–9).

However, such 'occupational communities', marked by a close association between people's home and workplace relations, developed only in some localities. The accelerated economic restructuring and contraction of traditional manufacturing during the 1970s and 1980s saw their decline even in areas of former strength. This has been a major factor weakening the links between consumption and production conflicts. A further obstacle has been the long-standing reformist 'economism' of the British labour movement (Giddens 1973: 205–7), with its focus on wage bargaining in the productive sphere rather than the defence of the social wage in the sphere of consumption (Cockburn 1977: 168; Saunders 1979: 133–6). Attempts were made by the Communist Party to engage in 'consciousness-raising' and to connect housing conflicts to wider class struggle – for example through its involvement in the National Association of Tenants and Residents from 1948 to the 1970s, and more directly through its intervention in a major housing conflict in Sheffield in the late 1960s (Lowe 1986: 90–5). However, such intervention generally proved unsuccessful and caused division within the tenants' ranks.

Second, the practical difficulties of co-ordinating political action by workers and tenants have been heightened in recent decades by the diminishing association between social class and housing tenure. Even if collective consumption issues such as housing remained largely marginal to the immediate practical agenda of the trade union movement after the Second World War, there was at least widespread acceptance by the representatives of organised labour of the role of municipal housing in furthering their members' interests. This association between class and consumption sector interests in housing has since weakened markedly as, by the census of 1981, 60 per cent of skilled manual workers and 40 per cent of semi-skilled workers had become home owners (Hamnett 1984) – a trend which strengthened during the 1980s and early 1990s, particularly as the result of the sale of council houses. With the growing importance of white-collar unions with still higher proportions of owner-occupiers, the search for a linkage between the labour and the tenants' movements has become increasingly forlorn. Many workers are no longer council tenants, and those who remain in the public sector are increasingly those in poorly paid, non-unionised occupations, or are unemployed or retired and dependent on benefits rather than wages.

Third, the debate surrounding Castells' work leads us from a consideration of the relationships between tenants and wider working-class politics to an assessment of the relationships between council tenants themselves. To what extent do the tenants of public housing constitute a 'social base' with the potential for forming a 'social force' for change? This is a field in which Castells has attracted particular criticism. As noted above, many council estates may appear to constitute an homogeneous working class, territorially bounded, consumption sector-defined social base. Given structural contradictions in service provision and the 'magic wand of organisation' (Pickvance 1977: 179), Castells' early work would suggest a clear promise of grassroots action. However, it is important to consider the extent to which council estates are indeed homogeneous and to explore their social structure, the social consciousness and values of their residents, and the organisational means to initiate and sustain action (Pickvance 1977).

As indicated by our earlier account of the fluctuating subsidy arrangements, amenity standards and dominant definitions of the role of council housing, significant variations occur *between* estates in each locality. This tends to fragment the unity of tenants as a social base founded on a distinct consumption sector, with estates competing with each other for resources and subsidy. While past attempts by local authorities to introduce differential rent schemes – in inter-war Leeds, for example (Finnigan 1984), or Sheffield in the late 1960s (Lowe 1986: 94ff.) – have been the catalyst for tenant mobilisation, such conflicts have also exposed divisions within tenant ranks. They have reflected the unevenness of the housing stock and subdivisions in local working-class communities. In her analysis of the mass campaign by tenants in Tower Hamlets against the imposition of a Housing Action Trust in 1988 and 1989, Woodward notes the continuing risk of borough-wide divisions along racial or broader ideological lines (Woodward 1991: 49 and 53). This seems to be a major source of the difficulty long experienced by tenant activists in securing successful federations of tenant associations in British cities. The typical operation of the allocations and transfer system described in Chapter 5 has often sharpened such inter-estate rivalry.

The status differences in the working class, which are in some measure reflected in status differences between council estates, can also produce divisions *within* individual schemes. To the perceived status distinction between 'respectable' and 'rough' households can be added further divisions which may confront attempts to develop collective responses to housing issues in particular neighbourhoods. An early relative homogeneity of population in public housing schemes in the post-war years has given way to growing variation within neighbourhoods. Even allowing for the spatial segregation of black and white households in local authority housing, ethnic and racial diversity has become a characteristic of more council estates, as more black households have entered the public sector (Brown 1984: Ch. 5). Increased unemployment and economic restructuring since the 1970s have produced a greater general variation in employment status and diversity in occupations, and council estates are now housing an increasing proportion of the economically marginalised. Furthermore, greater differentiation is found in forms of household structure in the public sector, notably the increase in one-parent and elderly households. These distinctions, together with gender differences, can be the basis for variations in experience, perception and response to housing and also become sources of mistrust and disagreement which fragment collective action (see Morris and Winn 1990 for a review of the changing class, race, gender and household mix of council housing).

Fourth, however, the propensity of tenants to mobilise cannot be deduced simply from a survey of their demographic characteristics. Pickvance (1977: 176) criticises Marxist studies of urban protest for relying upon this taxonomic approach and stresses the importance of studying the dynamics of neighbourhood social structures and processes and the nature of tenants' social consciousness. Drawing upon the earlier British community studies literature, Lowe indicates the informality of working-class neighbourhood organisation and suggests that 'one of the main problems facing new local movements is precisely how to penetrate or harness established networks of associational activity, which are often informal and relatively unstructured' (Lowe 1986: 64). In 'getting by', lower income households of varying ethnicity have long tended to turn first to informal co-operation with kin and, perhaps, neighbours. Wider local co-operation tends not to occur unless problems arise which cannot be resolved through everyday social networks. This resistance to formal organisation in many working-class cultures is reflected in the main characteristics of the tenants' movement. Hence, mobilisation has tended to be a fitful, pragmatic counter to immediate local problems which require a defensive response, rather than a sustained national or even locality-wide challenge to the wider economic and political context of council housing backed by a strong, permanent bureaucratic structure.

To the extent that attempts have been made to bring wider political perspectives and organisational expertise to the pursuit of housing campaigns, we have seen already that the result can be a damaging split in the tenants' ranks. This tension is seen partly along lines of gender. From Clydeside in 1915 to the present, owing to their centrality to neighbourhood social relations and their particularly intense experience of the dwelling and the estate as domestic managers, women have played a key role in sudden, widely supported, largely undocumented protests. Discussion with tenant activists confirms that, in recent years, women have again been predominant in supplying the initial impetus to the formation of most new tenants' associations and campaigns. However, with the establishment of formal committee and organisational procedures, it is men with experience of trade union affairs or involvement in formal party politics who have often acceded to key posts and introduced an approach which is at odds with the more direct, focused and informal strategy characteristic of female activists. Lowe's research of tenant mobilisation in Sheffield gives some empirical confirmation of this tendency (Lowe 1986: 113–14).

This detachment of tenant protest from established political institutions and processes, and its typical defensive character, is reflected also in the organisational life-cycle of many tenants' associations. A common pattern is for associations to be formed in response to a particular threat or grievance, but then either to vanish as the action is won or lost, or to concentrate increasingly on co-ordinating a programme of social activities for their members. The salience of tenants' associations – either as campaigning movements or as a focus of local social and cultural events – is likely to vary according to the presence and richness of alternative associational life in the vicinity. For example, social identity and consciousness may be established and shaped not so much through housing experiences as through ethnicity (Pickvance 1977: 178–80) or through involvement in other voluntary and workplace associations, recreational activities, or through church membership. Of course, these alternative sources of consciousness and objects of commitment can often themselves mobilise to defend their members' interests and conduct campaigns against housing policies or conditions. However, if there is a rich variety of other organisational options, it is not easy to retain a view of a homogeneous and inert social base of council tenants simply awaiting the arrival of structural contradictions in the urban system and of a single umbrella organisation before taking united mass action.

Fifth, it is important to highlight what should be the rather obvious issue of resources. In non-material terms, tenant campaigns must draw upon reserves of mutual trust, time, confidence and political knowledge and contacts. The examples of the success and skill of tenants during the 1980s in forming effective federations to inject a tenants' voice into the housing management of some local authorities, in forming housing co-operatives (MacDonald 1986), and in resisting the declaration of Housing Action Trusts in their original form, all underline the willingness and ability of tenants to take action, particularly when their latent skills are realised by suitable training support services. In Woodward's terms, 'tenants should not be seen as a faceless, marginalised underclass, or as second-class citizens. They should be recognised as active citizens prepared to fight for their housing rights' (Woodward 1991: 55). However, the 'hidden injuries of class' (Sennett and Cobb 1976) and the toll which they extract in the form of fatalism, resignation, distrust of neighbours, alienation from formal organisations and public authorities and lack of confidence should not be understated. Moreover, compared with middle-class pressure groups, empirical studies suggest that tenants frequently lack the important insider contacts and first-hand experience of the internal workings of bureaucracy so useful in maximising the chances of campaign success (see, for example, Saunders 1979: Chs. 6 and 7).

The material resources available to organisations representing an increasingly poor population are inevitably limited. It is widely recognised that a major barrier to the co-ordination of a national tenants' movement has been the lack of adequate finance. The National Tenants Organisation (NTO), founded in the 1970s, was hampered severely when financial support from the National Consumer Council came to an end (Wolmar 1991), being unable to afford its own premises or appoint even a single full-time worker. The National Tenants' and Residents' Association (NTRF) established in 1989 'to promote and protect public housing and tenants' rights in the face of hostile legislation' (TPAS Newsletter, April 1990) soon achieved affiliations from over forty tenants' organisations. However, this body too is liable to financial stringency, as those local authorities willing to support the tenants' movement confine their commitment to a local, rather than national, level.

In fact, even support for local activity is highly restricted. Local authority finance for federations of tenants' associations, either through direct grants or through administering a levy on tenants' own rents, was confined in the early 1990s to a limited number of large urban authorities such as Manchester, Kirklees, Newcastle, Sheffield, Leicester and several inner London boroughs. At neighbourhood level, material backing for individual tenants' associations has been directed mainly to the provision of halls for social events. Research conducted at Glasgow University for the Institute of Housing and TPAS used a nation-wide survey to examine the effectiveness of tenant participation and found that 'the levels of assistance provided to tenants' groups was very low and did not match the apparent commitment of councils and housing associations to tenant participation' (Institute of Housing/Tenants' Participation Advisory Service 1989: 54–5). Moreover, the empowerment of tenants often has to depend on local or national governmental funding, and any campaign faces the familiar problems of all who seek simultaneously to rely upon state institutions and confront them. The £3.25 million available to tenants' groups from central government in 1990–1 under section 16 of the Housing and

Planning Act of 1986, for example, was at once a promising development but also one designed to channel tenant activity into state-approved alternatives to council housing.

The preceding points in our discussion have all carried an empirical emphasis, indicating the practical obstacles confronting Castells' prediction concerning urban political mobilisation in the context of British council housing. Further insights into tenants' responses to council housing can be gained by reference to one of his key theoretical concepts, 'collective consumption'.

There appears to be a major difficulty in applying this concept to British public housing. The problem is expressed succinctly by Saunders in his remark that, even though council housing may constitute, in Castells' terms, an example of 'collective consumption' in that it is an item of consumption where provision has been supported by the state, the acute politicisation of housing and mass action does not occur because the dwellings are 'consumed individually' (Saunders 1979: 123). As we showed in Chapter 5, for example, the balance of power in tenancy agreements between landlord and tenant has traditionally been very one-sided. In the case of the most drastic action of a rent strike, therefore, the tenant has been much more vulnerable than the striking industrial worker because

> there is a somewhat parlous but nevertheless established place for industrial strikes in law . . . . Rent strikes are vulnerable because ultimately they depend on individuals in their own homes breaking tenancy agreements. The threat of eviction is a card that local authorities are quick to play.
>
> (Lowe 1986: 110–12)

Similarly, writers have long noted the manner in which bureaucratic methods of council housing allocation operate to reduce tenants to individuals in a 'queue' in competition with each other (Lambert *et al.* 1978: Ch. 3).

Several recent developments in public sector housing have served further to 'individualise' the experience of tenants. First, the large-scale sale of dwellings to sitting tenants in the 1980s was perceived by many as offering an individual route to a better housing deal. Second, the continuing shift away from general housing subsidies to means-tested support for individual households further differentiated the experiences of neighbouring households (Hills 1991). With so many tenants being in receipt of Housing Benefit paid directly to their landlord by the Department of Social Security, the rent strike was also effectively removed as a potential campaign strategy. The ring-fencing of local authority housing revenue accounts in the Local Government and Housing Act of 1989 tends to pit tenants against each other, as the subsidy of some tenants, or the toleration of their arrears, can only be achieved through rent increases for others. All these factors represent further obstacles to locality-wide or national mass protest. The limited rights conferred by the Tenants' Charter provisions of the 1980 Housing Act and those contained in the Tenants' Guarantee of the Citizen's Charter in 1991 are largely confined to giving individuals rights to information, consultation and redress in cases of poor management.

This leads to a final obstacle to protest as a response by council tenants to their housing experience. The extent and subsequent course of grassroots tenants' mobilisation is conditioned also by the response of local and, increasingly, national governmental institutions. The ahistorical, structuralist nature of Castells' early work not only neglected tenants' consciousness and their creative, often unexpected, response to their situation. It also ignored major national and local variations in political systems, institutions and cultures and the conscious strategies to cope with protest which can be selected by politicians and state personnel. Certainly, the oligarchic nature of most local authorities in Britain, many of which were for many years in continuous single-party control, has insulated councils from electoral pressures (Dunleavy 1980: 138) and this can serve in certain circumstances to provoke extra-electoral collective action. However, such political unassailability also means that councils can often afford to ride or resist protest, depicting it as irresponsible or undemocratic. Local variations are important here. In some localities council tenants constitute small minorities whose demands for extra resources strike a discordant note in environments where the ideology of private property ownership is overwhelmingly dominant, and where councils have been elected with a mandate to protect the value of private property, minimise local taxation, and contain expenditure on subsidising tenants (Saunders 1979: Ch 7). Conversely, Lowe found that tenants in Sheffield in 1968 largely failed to secure their immediate objectives, but their withdrawal of support from the Labour Party, and the latter's ensuing electoral defeat, secured a redefined and generally more advantageous relationship between tenants and the council (Lowe 1986: 106).

These contrasting examples raise the question, therefore, as to whether measurable success by tenants can be achieved, as implied in Castells' original position, only through recourse to the drastic collective action of an 'urban social movement'. It is clearly the case that the absorption of tenant activists into local party structures, the participation of tenant representatives in housing advisory committees, the provision of a social centre to dissipate the energy of a management committee of tenant leaders, or the exercise of preferential treatment to protest leaders, as in the case at Beckton in east London in 1970 (Dunleavy 1977: 196), can all be construed as carrying the potential to contain and 'incorporate' more troublesome tenant activity. Yet changes which fall far short of a revolution but which still bring worthwhile gains to tenants can often be won by institutional means such as lobbying, electoral pressure, the cultivation of insider contacts, professional advocacy, petitions and committee representation. Thus, 'the mobilisation of the social base is only one way in which urban effects are produced' (Pickvance 1976: 211). Certainly, council tenants confront particular difficulties in utilising informal networks compared with more middle-class groups. Nevertheless, tenants can at times find state institutions responsive to demands for more than token changes. In the conflict over the privatisation of council housing after 1980, for example, both central government and large Labour local authorities sought to sponsor tenant participation for their own reasons. In pursuing wider objectives, state institutions may find it in their interests to make quite important concessions to tenants' interests. This is likely to be most important in localities where particular economic and cultural factors combine to produce a 'radical region' in which local government (and even central government where it wishes to court tenant support, as in the case of Housing Action Trusts) becomes responsive to normally subordinate interests (Duncan and Goodwin 1988: 71ff.).

This section has emphasised the obstacles to the development of mass collective action by council tenants to redefine the economic conditions, political relations, and ideological meanings surrounding their tenure. These obstacles have been missed or underestimated in many 'outsider' analyses developed by social scientists who have made little attempt to bridge the gap between their own experience and that of working-class households. Nevertheless, council tenants remain a latent social base which, in particular circumstances and with basic material resources and effective leadership, can become an active political force. This is most likely in situations where either central government policies or factors specific to a locality or estate serve to 're-collectivise' the experience of individual households. We have seen that this occurred at the time when the Housing Finance Act of 1972 brought a nationwide threat of substantial rent increases. We have also seen that the late 1980s brought a marked resurgence in tenant mobilisation, as central government extended its housing strategy from the 'individualising' measures of Right to Buy and the replacement of general subsidies by means-tested Housing Benefit, to the attempted transfer of entire estates from council control. Here, tenants encountered a perceived common threat. Moreover, the acceleration in the centralisation of housing policy in the 1980s made them more disposed to direct their opposition towards Whitehall rather than simply continuing to blame 'the council' for service deficiencies. Further tenant activity has arisen in response to design failures in public housing which have blighted the lives of whole communities. Local tenants' associations have linked with single-issue groups such as the Anti-Dampness Campaign, the National Asbestos Campaign, the Systems Building and National Tower Block Campaign, and the National Tower Block Network. Although 'direct action' has rarely been the dominant strategy of these organisations, their protests can be judged in many cases to have brought important policy responses.

However, an exclusive focus on protest is to remain wholly within a problematic which has dominated past academic debate and confines us to a restricted agenda which neglects an important possibility. It is certainly the case that quiescence or 'non-protest' among council tenants can be interpreted as born partly of resignation and fatalism in the face of all the barriers to action and to the experiences of powerlessness reviewed above. A major problem for tenant activists indeed may often be the 'sullen and passive indifference' identified by Seabrook (quoted in Chapter 4, p. 92). However, limited tenant mobilisation could also be interpreted as signalling widespread *contentment* with council housing. This is an alternative which receives fairly cursory treatment by most Marxist and New Right commentators. It is important not to lapse into a pluralist complacency which views satisfaction or a low 'intensity of preference' as a virtually sufficient explanation of political non-action (Lukes 1974: 16ff.). Yet it is an interpretation which must be explored, given what we have seen in earlier chapters of the high use-value of much public housing, the reasonable management of much of the stock and, at least until recent years, its security and favourable rent levels compared with other housing options. This task involves an examination of more diverse sources through which a tenant voice can be heard more directly, if incompletely and with some distortions.

RESIGNATION OR CONTENTMENT?

We can assess council tenants' experiences and evaluations of their homes and estates by an examination of both what they say about their housing circumstances and what they do when the opportunity to act arises. The conclusion emerging from such a review must be that the response of tenants mirrors the diversity of council housing which we have emphasised throughout our earlier discussion. In particular, a clear disparity emerges between the conventional wisdom, consolidated powerfully during the 1980s and early 1990s, concerning the failure of council housing, and the perception of the tenure held by many of its consumers.

Galbraith has written of the key influence upon the policy process of an 'institutional truth' which 'serves the needs and purposes of the large and socially pervasive institutions that increasingly dominate modern life' (Galbraith 1989, cited in McCrory 1990: 49). The insistence on the failure and unpopularity of council housing – a verdict which accords with the economic and political priorities of government and with the material interests of building societies, housing exchange professionals and private construction companies – has become established as a prime example of 'institutional truth' in contemporary Britain. To argue this is not to patronise tenants and other householders as dupes, the passive victims of a 'false consciousness'. Rather, the spell of such 'knowledge' is cast most strongly *within* the institutional network of housing production and consumption, where it influences research priorities, the identification of policy 'solutions' and the allocation of investment and subsidies. Hence, the constant stereotypical portrayal of council housing as a 'problem tenure' becomes a self-fulfilling prophecy, as users and potential users of council housing are confronted with powerful material and ideological reasons for doubting the desirability of this form of housing consumption. Dominant institutional definitions in setting an ideological and material framework for the perception and evaluation of council housing are a crucial consideration when we consider tenants' experiences of their homes.

At the beginning of this chapter it was noted that a tenants' voice has rarely been allowed to intrude into housing debates. To the extent that tenants have been able to speak at all, it has tended to be a voice heard through the particular amplifier of a housing research which has been heavily reliant on state funding and committed to a Fabian 'social administration and policy-oriented perspective' (Kemeny 1988: 215) in which the social survey constitutes a dominant method of inquiry. In attempting to piece together an account of tenants' views, therefore, we are confronted with a dearth of studies which adopt other stances. While we shall draw on a few available sources which utilise less structured, more qualitative techniques, or at least combine them with survey research, we are obliged to place a review of survey evidence on tenants' assessments of council housing at the centre of our discussion.

The use of surveys by governmental and other large organisations to measure consumer 'housing satisfaction', or to probe for housing preferences and future aspirations, has been the subject of fierce criticism (see, for example, Donnelly 1980 and Lipman and Harris 1980b). These criticisms have been reviewed and assessed elsewhere (Furbey and Goodchild 1986a). Stated briefly, in the quest for hard and apparently precise measurement, housing consumer surveys frequently oversimplify the relationship between respondents and their housing. Even where information is gathered concerning householders' occupation, gender, tenure, race, previous residence and other personal characteristics and experiences, there remains a clear danger that the correlation of respondents' views on housing with such a taxonomy will fall far short of furnishing an adequate account by understating 'the emergent, innovational and problematic character of everyday life by imposing a deterministic "grid" on it' (Cicourel 1964: 113). It is clear that the 'findings' of many tenant surveys have to be interpreted with great caution. On one hand, feelings of general housing dissatisfaction may be repressed in a society in which housing is a badge of identity and a key source of social status. Conversely, expressions of tenure preference are likely to be informed by the prevailing balance of official ideological and material support for different tenures.

The following discussion of the evidence on tenants' experiences of council housing combines several elements in an attempt to make some advance on the simplistic presentation of housing consumer surveys which have become so common. First, our discussion will report survey research which has invited tenants to express not only their view of the general virtues of their homes (which may elicit repressed responses), but also their appraisals of their council landlords and detailed aspects of their homes and tenancy and neighbourhood relations (where they may be more prepared to be critical). Second, the complexity of people's responses to formal survey questions is related to the picture of their experiences and evaluation of their housing which emerges from the less structured, more open-ended forms of inquiry. Lastly, the distinction between housing tenure preferences and housing satisfaction is stressed.

Turning to this evidence, our argument – that the dominant 'truth' concerning council housing is an outsiders' stereotype failing to capture the complexity and range of tenants' experiences – is given some support by a national survey of voters in England and Wales conducted by MORI for the Audit Commission in 1986. Satisfaction with council housing was expressed by only 34 per cent of respondents (although 46 per cent felt unable to express a view). Among the *users* of the housing service, however, 61 per cent expressed satisfaction with council housing (MORI 1986: 9–22, cited in Gyford *et al*. 1989: 238–42). An NOP survey for the Widdecombe Committee Inquiry into the Conduct of Local Authority Business in 1986 identified a similar difference of perception between users and non-users of public housing (cited in Gyford *et al*. 1989: 239). The clear majority of tenants expressing a positive assessment of local authority housing services in these national surveys confirms the conclusion of the Glasgow University research team in their major report for the Department of the Environment, that there is 'something less than a crisis in social housing management' (Centre for Housing Research 1989: 104). This study, drawing on a survey of 139 English local authorities (albeit with an under-representation of inner-London councils), revealed 67 per cent of council tenants as satisfied with their housing services (Centre for Housing Research 1989: 124). In a study for the Building Societies Association in 1989, fewer than 10 per cent of council tenants expressed dissatisfaction with their housing (BMRB 1989, cited in Forrest and Murie 1990a: 625).

In general, local authorities have been lamentably slow to monitor their tenants' views. One of the earlier surveys was of over 1,000 tenants in Bexley in 1981, where only 7 per cent of respondents expressed dissatisfaction with their homes (Quirk 1982: 200) – a very low proportion even in response to a question on general housing satisfaction. Later years brought a spate of such studies, prompted by the 'Tenants' Choice' provision of the 1988 Housing Act. Again, these confirmed a much more positive assessment of council housing by its users than the prevailing image of a tenure in crisis would lead us to predict. For example, a study by Salford University for Calderdale District Council found 87 per cent of respondents to be satisfied with their homes, with 58 per cent who were very satisfied; and 82 per cent who were satisfied with their neighbourhood, with 50 per cent who were very satisfied. Research for Leeds City Council by Leeds Polytechnic found 78 per cent of respondents satisfied with the council's housing management service, 66 per cent with its repairs service, and 60 per cent with its improvement work (source: TPAS Library records).

Within this overall frame, however, there is a complexity in tenants' detailed perceptions which highlights the danger of a simplistic interpretation of survey evidence. Any assessment of a future for council housing must be based upon a recognition of the very real complaints which many tenants express. Contentment with public housing varies according to which aspects of the management service or physical design are in focus, according to locality, and even according to seemingly minor distinctions in particular housing schemes.

Although most council tenants have regularly expressed satisfaction in surveys with their housing services, therefore, nearly one-third register dissatisfaction (see, for example, MORI 1986). In some studies a more negative picture seems to emerge. For example, in Saunders' 'three towns survey' 65 per cent of council tenants said the council was 'unresponsive' (Saunders 1990: 93), whilst in Lesley Andrews' earlier study of a large and diverse, mainly flatted, estate in inner London, nearly half those tenants reporting contact with the housing department in the preceding year felt 'poorly treated' (Andrews 1979: 86). Whilst we have seen that 67 per cent of council tenants expressed general satisfaction with their landlord in the Glasgow University survey, the proportion of satisfied housing association tenants was as high as 80 per cent. As noted in Chapter 5, such a disparity in average managerial performance must be partly attributed to the generally lower level of management resources available to local authority housing managers compared with their housing association counterparts. Certainly there is widespread awareness among council tenants that their landlords are under-resourced (Forrest and Murie 1990a: 625). Yet it is clear that a significant number of tenants do have negative perceptions of their housing and their landlord. Moreover, average 'satisfaction levels' for a locality can mask variations in enthusiasm, even within individual estates and between neighbouring households. The social differences between estates, differences in amenity standards and design and variations in management quality reported in earlier chapters all influence tenants in their often highly perceptive and subtle assessment of their housing.

Which factors predominate in the development of positive and negative assessments of council housing by tenants? The available evidence suggests that for most tenants the problems stem from the management rather than from the physical amenity and design of their homes. Thus, in a national survey of Great Britain conducted by Gallup for the National Consumer Council in 1988 of 929 council tenants, respondents were asked to identify the worst thing about being a council tenant. Thirty-nine per cent could think of nothing at all – a high proportion in the context of state housing policy in the 1980s. Clearly, the most important issue for respondents was that of housing repairs, with 21 per cent complaining of an inefficient repairs service. Ten per cent complained of undesirable neighbours. When asked to state the advantages of council housing, 37 per cent could think of none (compared with 54 per cent in Saunders' survey – Saunders 1990: 89), 37 per cent mentioned the fact that repairs were carried out by the landlord and were not a matter of worry for the tenant, 11 per cent referred to the peace of mind and security of being a council tenant, 9 per cent mentioned the reasonable level of the rents, and 6 per cent the helpfulness and support of the council in responding to problems (Gallup 1988).

The Glasgow University study moves beyond its assessment of general satisfaction to an exploration of tenant perceptions of specific aspects of the management of social rented housing (Centre for Housing Research 1989: Part 7). The study identified some particular areas of recurring complaint. The picture is initially reassuring, in that most respondents report housing officials as being easy to contact and individually friendly. However, when asked whether their landlord was 'caring' the picture was less encouraging. The proportion of tenants feeling that their landlord did not care about their well-being ranged from one in five for small councils to one in three for large councils, although there was significant variation within these categories (Centre for Housing Research 1989: 93). The demeanour of individual staff is clearly very important to tenants, and Andrews found that many of the complaints expressed by respondents in her survey 'concern the manner of treatment and for those who had an unfavourable experience in this regard that appeared to rankle more than any complaint about the effectiveness or efficiency of the service received' (Andrews 1979: 87). The importance of 'personal contact with friendly, understanding housing staff' also emerged as a crucial factor governing tenant perceptions in another major study of the quality of housing management (Walsh and Spencer 1990). This report identified an approachable staff as much more important for tenants than an accessible housing office.

Of course, an indifferent attitude tends to coincide with an inefficient service, to produce personal impressions such as these:

> Not only do they not do it, they don't listen to you either, when you try to explain. It's not just the repairs that go by the wayside, it's your feelings, your opinions as well, it just doesn't matter. You can't talk to people at —— and you can tell they're not listening and they couldn't care less. And they put the 'phone down and you can hear absolutely nothing.
>
> I stood at the desk and she said 'Can I help you?' and I said 'It's about repairs' and she didn't move off her seat. She didn't even turn round, it was as if I wasn't there, she was talking to her dictating machine – 'Oh, what's the number?' and she wrote it down on a bit of paper. 'We'll get somebody down.' I could have been anybody – she didn't know who I was. She didn't even see me.
>
> (Centre for Housing Research 1989: 94)

The sense of alienation and powerlessness which flows from such encounters may occur even where front-line officials are more sympathetic because contact with the particular officer with the authority and the knowledge to resolve a problem proves elusive. One tenant reports getting

> as far as the receptionist and then it comes to a blind full stop, and I'm sure she must have a waste paper bin that big, with scraps of paper in that she's written with complaints and names and addresses down, because they never get anywhere, never.
>
> (Centre for Housing Research 1989: 91)

Such experiences underline the need for staff flexibility and the importance of breaking down rigid divisions between the various functions of housing management.

Respondents consulted in the Glasgow University study remained generally unimpressed by the extent of effective tenant participation in housing management decisions. By the end of the 1980s local authorities had begun to strengthen their tenant liaison practices and, although the Local Government and Housing Act of 1989 proscribed voting rights for tenants on full housing committees and their advisory sub-committees, some councils were using various means to involve tenants in decision-making (Institute of Housing/Tenants Participation Advisory Service 1989: Ch. 3). However, only 20 per cent of the 1,252 tenants interviewed in the Glasgow survey believed that their landlord always or usually consulted them on important issues, and only 50 per cent thought their landlord took heed of their views even after consultation (Centre for Housing Research 1989: 92). Informal discussions with tenants underlined these experiences of marginality:

> Information was often confined to rent increases and was frequently regarded as unintelligible. Tenants resented the lack of consultation and where it did take place it was confined to modernisation or new-build proposals. Tenants wanted more consultation, through formal consultation procedures on management issues relating to repairs, allocations and rent-setting.
>
> (Centre for Housing Research 1989: 93)

While most tenants did not seek full control of their housing and looked to landlord action to improve their housing circumstances (Centre for Housing Research 1989: 92), they did seek greater consultation and involvement. By neglecting such links with the consumers of their service, council landlords restrict their contact with tenants largely to dealings with households over problems such as rent arrears, neighbourhood disputes and urgent allocation requests. This can foster an underestimation of tenants' ability to contribute to the improvement of housing management, and a lack of awareness of the main criticisms and priorities for change held by the majority of tenants who rarely visit the office.

Clearly, many housing authorities seem unaware of tenant priorities. The Glasgow management survey found that 30 per cent of tenants of large councils and 23 per cent of tenants of small councils felt they received poor value for their rent and, although many recognised centrally imposed resource constraints as a significant handicap for their landlords, many were critical of the efficiency and mix of the services offered. Fifty-seven per cent of respondents wanted the provision of more or better services, particularly relating to repairs, improvement, and enhanced management of public spaces. Conversely, 41 per cent expressed criticism of services, such as particular environmental works which they considered to be wasteful or doomed to failure, or of inefficiencies in repairs co-ordination (Centre for Housing Research 1989: 98).

Nearly a quarter of tenants were prepared to pay more rent for improvements in services. Tenants most satisfied with their landlord reflected their confidence in being more likely to pay more for better services, especially among those with higher incomes. It is likely that the transformation of the tenure from one for the relatively affluent to one catering disproportionately for Britain's poor has left those with higher incomes who remain in the public sector with an unfulfilled desire to improve their housing status.

Most tenant dissatisfaction relates to issues of council housing management. However, it is important not to neglect user criticism of the inadequacies and inappropriateness of the physical design and amenity of many council houses discussed in Chapter 4, or the contribution of these failures to the erosion of support for the public house building programme. There certainly is a widespread desire for a house with a garden – especially in England, where flat-dwelling has long been less common than in other European countries including Scotland. Such a preference was expressed by 66 per cent of Andrews' respondents in her study of a mainly flatted estate (Andrews 1979: 44). However, Andrews also discovered that most people 'expressed themselves well pleased with their own flats' (1979: 45). The main criticisms were not of the flats themselves but of the estate outside the dwelling. For many, the visual appearance of the estate was uninspiring, having an 'institutional' feeling. But most importantly, it was the poverty of the public areas, with their poor landscaping, inadequate caretaking and vandalism which attracted the most adverse and widespread negative comments, along with references to the intrusions into privacy caused by noise (Andrews 1979: 45–6).

Confirming the discussion in Chapter 4, therefore, it is often the visual symbolism and appearance of council estates, rather than the functionality and amenity of the homes themselves, which stir negative experiences and responses in tenants. Evidence of the relative importance to tenants of the external image projected by their neighbourhood was found in interviews with over 400 residents in four estates composed of houses with gardens completed during the 1970s by Sheffield City Council in inner areas of the city (Furbey and Goodchild 1986b). Two of these schemes were built to the Parker Morris standards mandatory at the time. The remaining developments, however, were built using a special dispensation from the Secretary of State to 'low-cost' standards, involving some compromises in Parker Morris specifications. While these compromises in space standards and internal amenities, notably the inferior heating systems, elicited negative comments from tenants, the 'low-cost' schemes evoked much more favourable responses than a strict architectural functionalism would lead us to expect. While the more architecturally idiosyncratic of the two Parker Morris estates provoked remarks such as 'looks like the Gestapo built it', the 'low-cost' development composed of unremarkable semi-detached houses which were only a little smaller than Parker Morris standards was particularly well received. However, a major lesson to be drawn from the Sheffield survey was the high level of contentment with modern low-rise public sector schemes, even ones built to high residential densities, if they incorporate the basic lessons derived from earlier, less successful episodes in council housing history.

This review of consumers' experiences of the management and physical amenity of council housing indicates the ambivalence of many tenants towards their dwellings and neighbourhoods and the variation in perceptions between individuals. This is well captured in Tony Parker's valuable and unobtrusive study of the people of 'Providence' (Parker 1983) – an estate in inner London composed of tower blocks, medium-rise flats, maisonettes and prefabs which, according to 'institutional truth', could be expected to elicit overwhelmingly negative reactions. Although some residents are unreserved and forthright in their criticisms (see, for example the comments of Audrey Gold quoted in Chapter 4 (p. 92)), Parker constructs an initial sketch of Providence through a series of less dramatic impressions.

First, he records the comments of an estate caretaker:

> Used to be a nice place: used to be, I'll say that. Oh yes, when I came to work here seven years ago it used to be quite a nice place. But now, nowadays . . . bloody hell! . . . But there's still nice parts though too, you know, still some very nice parts . . . . In one word? If you asked me to sum up the estate for you in one word what'd I say? Well, I don't think I know, not really, it's very hard isn't it, just one word? But what I'd say is '*mixed*'. That's the word I'd use.
>
> (Parker 1983: 11–13, emphasis added)

Parker then puts this verdict to a series of Providence residents who, while they interpret the word in differing ways, all accept 'mixed' as a good adjective to describe their estate and its people.

In Parker's ensuing record of the impressions of the tenants of Providence regarding life in their district, the 'mixedness' of the architecture and the people of the estate is paralleled by the mixed assessment of the area which emerges from the varying accounts. Hence, even in the case of high-rise flats, while for Audrey Gold the isolation and loneliness of life as a mother on the sixteenth floor of a tower block is 'like living in hell' (Parker 1983: 54), for Linda Norris, expecting her baby in a fourteenth-floor flat, the move to Providence has reconstructed her life, saved her marriage and given her a 'real home': a place to paint and decorate with pride, a place where

> All your gloomy thoughts go out of your head, you start living and enjoying life again and being thankful for what you've got. I'm not just

thankful; I do enjoy being here, really enjoy it. I'm not a very religious person, so I say being up here is the nearest to heaven I'll ever get.

(Parker 1983: 23)

Clearly, such different assessments must be related to varying personal circumstances and experiences. Andrews, who used her training as a social anthropologist to combine survey research with less formal and interventionist techniques to study a broadly similar estate to Parker's in inner London, found that contentment varied according to age, life-cycle stage, gender, race, past housing history and length of present residence. In general, however, she concludes cautiously that 'since few express extremely positive or negative views, it may be suggested that most respondents are moderately pleased with their overall housing situation' (Andrews 1979: 44).

The complex, socially-mediated response uncovered in this review of tenants' *satisfaction* with council housing stands in sharp contrast with the conclusions which have been drawn by some commentators from surveys of consumers' tenure *preferences* (Forrest and Murie 1990a). A series of studies by the British Market Research Bureau (summarised by Coles 1989) revealed a high and rising general preference for owner-occupation. By 1989, 81 per cent of respondents expressed a preference to be in owner-occupation in two years' time, compared with 12 per cent preferring council renting (BMRB 1989). Such data have been central in endorsing far-ranging academic critiques of council housing, notably that by Saunders (1990). Combining these surveys with his own empirical evidence of tenants' experiences of local authority housing departments as unresponsive and council housing as oppressive, Saunders argues for home ownership as a popular tenure, marked by its ability to offer the freedom and autonomy which council housing inevitably denies.

Responding to Saunders' assertion of the inherent undesirability and, in the final analysis, immunity to reform of council housing, Forrest and Murie (1990a) argue that evidence on tenure preferences must be balanced by evidence on housing satisfaction. Hence, the same BMRB survey which identified such a strong overall preference for owner-occupation found fewer than 10 per cent of council tenants expressing dissatisfaction with their housing. It seems that 'the strength of expressed tenure preferences does not mirror expressed dissatisfaction with tenures' (Forrest and Murie 1990a: 623). Moreover, in explaining the growth in preference for owner-occupation, Forrest and Murie argue that decisions concerning house purchase are based on 'actual circumstances and hard practical judgements rather than being influenced by more abstract or instinctive factors' (Forrest and Murie 1990a: 623). In a context of energetic state sponsorship of owner-occupation, booming house prices, large discounts on council house prices, rising public sector rents, stagnation in municipal building programmes, and growing disrepair in the council stock, respondents to preference surveys in the 1980s based their replies on a pragmatic assessment of the tenure in which they were most likely to secure a home offering financial advantages, affirmation of their social status and good physical amenity given the prevailing circumstances. In fact, amongst council tenants, even the evidence on preferences is more equivocal. In the BMRB survey more tenants (48 per cent as against 47 per cent) expressed a desire to be renting from the council than to be home owners in two years' time (BMRB 1989: 14, cited in Forrest and Murie 1990a: 620).

This leads to the final point in this chapter. The preceding discussion has explored what tenants *say* about their council housing. It is important also to consider what tenants actually *do* when the chance to offer a practical verdict on public housing arises. After all, surveys can be construed by respondents as inviting them to express their housing choice given *ideal* circumstances, particularly the possession of secure, well-paid employment. The *actual* choices taken by households are shaped crucially by the realities of housing supply and their own fortunes.

One opportunity for choice presented itself with the introduction of the mandatory Right to Buy in the 1980 Housing Act. During the 1980s one-and-a-half million public sector dwellings were bought by their occupants. Saunders argues that this movement cannot be seen simply as a 'coerced exchange' (Dunleavy 1986: 138), with people obliged to make private provision in the face of a decline in public provision (Saunders 1990: 103ff.). Certainly, for some tenants the attraction of owner-occupation has lain in the release from the constraints of one-sided tenancy agreements and inefficient or unresponsive management. However, it is not clear that this exodus is to be viewed as an historical inevitability produced by ineluctable deficiencies in public housing. Faced with an exceptional deal, the relatively affluent households which form the majority exerting the Right to Buy have certainly voted with their feet, but their votes have been cast against an already strongly residualised, increasingly centralised, unmodernised tenure which was not resourced or managed to meet their changing aspirations. Indeed, Saunders himself cites research by Madigan in Glasgow which found that although most low income buyers saw owner-occupation as 'overwhelmingly advantageous', 59 per cent of them would have been content to rent initially, had a good-quality council house been available (Madigan 1988: 61). The percentage is likely to be even higher among those tenants who have not already committed themselves to purchase.

Even if it was dissatisfaction with council housing management which prompted some tenants to buy their homes, for many others the right to buy highly prized homes of solid construction and high amenity at such a favourable price was simply a bargain not to be missed. As suggested in Chapter 4, their willingness to purchase can be read partly as a testimony to the high standards of their public sector homes. Many tenants had the financial means to exit the tenure before the advent of Right to Buy, but did not do so.

A further opportunity for tenants to register their verdict on council housing and to act upon their preferences was presented by the 'Tenants' Choice' provisions of the Housing Act of 1988 whereby tenants (other than those in sheltered housing or others excluded from the Right to Buy) were given the right to choose an alternative landlord. In practice, the response by tenants (or by prospective landlords, who could also initiate a transfer) was negligible. The main impact of Tenants' Choice was to persuade some local authorities to use the provisions of the 1986 Housing and Planning Act to seek a 'voluntary transfer' of their entire housing stock to new landlords, usually housing associations, often as a defensive measure to prevent the fragmentation of social housing in their localities. Such transfers were frequently given heavy backing by Conservative councils. In many early ballots tenants voted decisively to remain with their local authorities, often mounting impressive campaigns to counteract glossy promotions advocating transfer. Other councils were obliged to abandon transfer plans after opinion surveys indicated tenant resistance and satisfaction with present services. Research conducted for the Department of the Environment by the British Market Research Bureau in the spring of 1988 involving group discussions with tenants in eight local authority areas gave an early indication of the lack of enthusiasm for transfer among tenants (Duncan and Greaves 1989). By the end of 1991 there had been eighteen successful transfers, almost all in small southern English authorities, while attempted transfers had been unsuccessful or abandoned in twenty-four other localities (*Public Housing News*, November 1991: 4–5).

Initially, the proportion of transfers blocked by tenants was very high. It was only after the financial implications of the Local Government and Housing Act of 1989 became more apparent, with their indications of a further erosion in the relative quality of public housing, that more ballots produced majorities in favour of stock transfer. Similarly, the provision for the establishment of Housing Action Trusts in the 1988 Act elicited a strong negative reaction and an impressive mobilisation to block the establishment of all such bodies until, in 1991, tenants in Hull and Waltham Forest were able to secure government guarantees on such key issues as future rent levels and the option to return to local authority control. Increasingly, votes by tenants in favour of transfers away from local authorities via the Tenants' Choice, voluntary transfer or HAT routes have to be seen as substantially a 'coerced exchange', a negative manoeuvre by tenants to secure such government resources as are available and to prevent their overall welfare being reduced. Such votes hardly amount to an active rejection of the principle or past experience of council housing, or a positive endorsement of alternative landlords. It therefore seems that the 'popularity of Right to Buy was confused with the unpopularity of council housing' (Forrest and Murie 1990b: 41).

CONCLUSION

The response of tenants to council housing mirrors in many ways the design and management strengths and weaknesses of the tenure described in Chapters 4 and 5. There is certainly discontent, which sometimes wells into more vehement protest. The power of producer interests and the lack of resources available to tenants also produce fatalism and resignation. However, there is also evidence of genuine contentment, despite the long-standing flaws in council housing provision and management, the imbalance of power between landlords and tenants, the under-investment in repairs and modernisation, and the tensions caused by the concentration of the poor, the deprived and the marginalised in the remaining stock. The issues which most frustrate tenants – the approachability of housing staff, the quality of neighbourhood office management, the efficiency of the repairs service, and the upkeep of the neighbourhood environment – are all matters which can be addressed with imagination and determination and at relatively little cost.

Unlike such sectors as health and education, where there are powerful middle-class voices raised to defend service standards, council tenants have a hard battle to make their voice heard. Official and academic commentators may find it difficult or inconvenient to accept, but for many tenants their houses are truly homes. If the collective biography and full range of personal experiences and circumstances permit household members to share love, affection and happiness with each other, with kin, and with neighbours, council houses offering good design, amenity and management can indeed be 'homes' which give pride and security. The distribution of the psychological and emotional benefits of 'home' are not necessarily related to differences in tenure. Rather, '"home" undergoes a transformation in meaning based upon personal experiences rather than socio-political taxonomies' (Gurney 1990: 29).

The accounts of many tenant campaigns testify to the pride of community and sense of possession, both individual and collective, which many feel towards their homes and neighbourhoods. These qualities have been too often overlooked in the blanket ideological and academic criticisms of council housing in Britain. The most fitting last words in this chapter therefore go to Marion Golding, active in a campaign to avoid the privatisation of her estate in Hounslow:

> I still remember the day I got the letter asking me to come and view this place: I was physically sick with relief. When I got the key I remember thinking: this is it, *a home at last*, after nineteen years of battling. I thought, I'm here to stay; the only way I'll leave it is feet first. It still makes me cry now when I remember it. It's hard to describe – I never thought I'd get *a brand new house that I could make a real home of* . . . . I was one of the first tenants here . . . now it's a smashing community . . . . To have to now fight again for a home, and this time for something that was *already ours* . . . it's been hard.
>
> (Dibblin 1989: 44, emphases added)

Part III

Council housing in crisis

7   The impact of Thatcherism

We have argued that the 'failure' of state housing in Britain has been caused by contingent factors – such as the dominance of private property rights, its vulnerable financial basis, and its mode of delivery – rather than any inherent shortcomings as a form of provision. Mass state housing was flawed in its original conception and then undermined further by economic pressures, political compromises and successive government policies. However, in the sixty years after the First World War, these weaknesses did not diminish the scale or importance of direct public provision in the British housing market. The reverse was the case. The growth of council housing continued over this period until it served nearly one-third of households in Britain by 1979.

State housing had grown from a negligible role to providing over six million dwellings. Yet this expansion should be placed in perspective. Unlike health or education, the public sector in housing still only provided for a minority of the population. In the same period owner-occupation had expanded more sharply still, and enjoyed a much more privileged status in financial, political and social terms as the 'natural' housing tenure in Britain. The development of council housing was not the triumphant march forward of a service driven by wholehearted public support, or the product of bold political visions for meeting housing needs. The expansion conveyed more about the failures of private renting, the pragmatic interventionism of governments seeking political stability and the skewed system of housing subsidy. The growth of council housing was achieved less by a dramatic flourish than an uncertain passage through a quagmire of ill-conceived policies, wavering public commitment and contradictory financial strategies.

The expansion of state housing seemed a classic illustration of what critics had termed the 'ratchet effect' of public sector growth (Brittan 1977). In this analysis, the development of welfare services said little about the persistence of social need or the failure of the market, and far more about increasing public expectations and government fears of damaging electoral prospects through containing state provision. In the post-war period local authorities had assumed ever greater responsibility for directly meeting housing needs in their communities, and each new building programme or redevelopment scheme represented further expansion of this role.

From 1979, of course, this ratchet effect was reversed with a vengeance. Council housing was sharply reduced. By the end of the third term of the Conservative Government, well over one million local authority dwellings had been sold under the Right to Buy, new construction had virtually ceased and the transfer of council estates to other landlords had become a reality. This policy transformation was without precedent in the development of the modern British welfare state. In other social services the scope of welfare service provision had been narrowed, the trend· of expansion checked and levels of subsidy cut back, but from 1979 to 1992 all the core services retained their basic shape. The panoply of privatisation measures introduced by the Thatcher Government had been confined to nationalised industries – such as steel – or utilities – such as British Telecom – rather than welfare services. Council housing was the exception.

In the 'golden age of the welfare state' (Gough 1979) in the 1950s and 1960s, any attempt to cut back public provision so radically would have been deemed to be electoral suicide. Yet the transformation of state housing under the Thatcher Governments had been achieved without dramatic public outcry, and, if anything, had attracted rather than lost votes for the government. True, the dismantling of public provision had been heavily criticised by many of the housing *cognoscenti* and provoked negative comments in the housing press. Independent reports from various sources had also cast a nervous eye on the imbalance in the housing market and the decline in capital investment (for example, Inquiry into British Housing 1986, 1991; Royal Institution of Chartered Surveyors 1987, 1991). In the mass media, critical analysis of housing policy was confined to the occasional exposé of the rising tide of homelessness (often prefaced by grainy prints of *Cathy Come Home* as a melancholy reminder of housing protest's finest hour). When they were allowed into the picture, council tenants themselves were either portrayed as helpless victims or nascent Thatcherites buying their homes and fitting new front doors with carefree abandon. The sharp reduction of public housing did not, then, reap any whirlwind of political dissent: indeed, the other main parties soon had to accommodate themselves to dropping their outright opposition to the sale of council homes.

The third successive election victory of Margaret Thatcher in 1987 seemed to offer the opportunity for the complete 'privatisation' of a state service; a dramatic step which seemed more likely to produce a splutter of resentment than a cacophony of criticism. The selective radicalism of

Thatcherism could settle comfortably on the remnants of council housing, sweep them up without delay and then move on to the tougher areas of education and health. This self-confidence, however, was soon to give way to unexpected uncertainty and caution.

The change of direction towards state housing provision, from sixty years of fitful expansion to thirteen years of steady disintegration, was a remarkable process which has not been given close enough attention in the housing policy literature. We have already commented on the vulnerable nature of public support for a service weakened by market priorities, poor management and lack of finance; yet waning public faith during the 1960s and 1970s in itself did not lay the ground for such a forthright assault on the principles, values and practice of state housing provision. That transformation was the real achievement of the Thatcher Governments from 1979 until 1990.

In this chapter, we are therefore concerned with the questions which arise out of this policy change. How was the transformation of public housing provision achieved? What were the political, economic and social consequences of this policy? In Chapter 8 we will examine the way in which attempts have been made to improve the management and financing of state housing in the face of growing criticisms. This leads us to consider the growing reaction against the housing strategy of the Conservative Government which emerged towards the end of the 1980s. In the Conclusion, we bring the main strands of our argument together and look to the future, suggesting that the commitment to the privatisation of rented housing overreached itself. There may still be an opportunity to reformulate a strategy for social housing in Britain during the 1990s which will accord with public preferences, economic change and deep-rooted social values, even if it is highly unlikely that council housing *per se* will survive.

THE RISE OF THE NEW RIGHT

The Thatcher Governments professed an open allegiance to the ideas of the New Right in developing their social and economic strategy. A decisive alternative was advanced to the post-war orthodoxy of Keynesian economics and Beveridgian/Fabian social policy. The strategy of dismantling council housing, and counterposing it to a vibrant image of wholesome home ownership, therefore fulfilled a crucial function in the New Right's broader political project towards the welfare state. A weakening of public provision was not to be achieved by a fundamental transformation across the board of all state services. It was more feasible politically for the government to break the fabric of state welfare at its weakest point and then make inroads into more hallowed areas of service provision.

The dismantling of a relatively unpopular service – council housing – demonstrated that radical incursions could be made into the heart of public provision without disastrous electoral consequences. Indeed, it showed that votes could be won (at a price) by such a policy. The attack on state housing therefore foreshadowed a more fundamental reappraisal of other services – first, social security, and then health and education. It posed a challenge to the conventional wisdom of the post-war settlement by demolishing the weakest pillar of a welfare state which, despite criticisms, still commanded broad public support (Mishra 1984; Taylor-Gooby 1985, 1988).

The first thirty years of the post-war welfare state are sometimes assumed to have been marked by an implacable ideological consensus, suddenly punctured by the New Right's critique. This analysis does an injustice to some of the critical debates about the aims and objectives of state welfare in Britain during this period; notably, the argument between Richard Titmuss and the Institute of Economic Affairs (Titmuss 1968; IEA 1961). Their debates about the respective roles of the market and the state in the provision of health care, for example, hardly suggest a blind un-thinking adherence to the Beveridgian welfare state. Yet these arguments rarely percolated into the mainstream of political debate. Conservative politicians were free in their criticisms of bureaucratic excess and mal-administration, but often stopped short of denouncing the underlying principles of state welfare. During the 1960s, politicians such as Enoch Powell or, in less refined tones, Rhodes Boyson, were aware of the work of the IEA, Milton Friedman and Friedrich von Hayek – but these were fairly marginal influences in the Conservative Party and their analysis of state provision was hardly seen as vote-winning material. The brief flourish of such ideas in the 'Selsdon' period of the Heath Government (1970–2) was soon abandoned, mainly for perceived risks of political unpopularity and the potential for social conflict (Gamble 1974).

There was, then, little that was 'new' about the New Right's critique of state welfare taken up by the Thatcher Governments. Its philosophy was little more than a revamped version of some very familiar themes: the glories of the market, the dead hand of the state, the value of individual enterprise, the sovereignty of the consumer. Yet it nonetheless emerged from the shadows as the most potent ideological force of the era.

The change of fortunes for New Right ideas, of course, sprang directly from the difficulties encountered by the prevailing Keynesian orthodoxy during the early and mid-1970s. The apparent certainties of sustained economic growth – which had carried before it Beveridge, the National Health Service, comprehensive education, the development of personal social services – started to falter. The nostrums of the New Right therefore offered a clear way through the cul-de-sac of a mixed economy sagging

under the weight of growing expectations, political confusion, and contradictory popular attitudes about levels of taxation and state provision. Public
opinion at this time did not represent a revolt against the basic principles of
social welfare, but more a calculated appraisal of its benefits set against
competing attractions of higher wages, lower taxes and reduced inflation.
The New Right did not offer the only self-contained critique of state
welfare – the Marxist analysis of the failings of the mixed economy and
Fabian social policy thrived in the academic literature, if not as an electoral
influence (see, for example, Gough 1979, Ginsburg 1979, Lee and Raban
1988). Yet the New Right reaped the reward of public discontent, partly by
having its monetarist prescriptions adopted by the Callaghan Government
from 1976 onwards and partly by having a representative strategically
placed on the political scene – as Leader of the Opposition.

The election of Margaret Thatcher to the leadership of the Conservative
Party in 1975 provided an opportunity for the ideas of the New Right to
gain a wider hearing on the political stage. If at this stage Thatcher was far
from a convincing monetarist her political instincts at least favoured
striking a different note to the post-1972 corporatism of Edward Heath. The
New Right's critique of prevailing economic wisdom was then grasped as
a means of promoting a change of direction within the Conservative Party.
From 1976 onwards the Labour Government had adopted an economic
strategy best described as uncomfortable monetarism, replete with cuts in
previously precious areas of social expenditure. This programme undoubtedly smoothed the way for a more full-blooded version from April 1979
onwards.

From 1979 the New Right 'seized the intellectual initiative' (Deakin
1987) just as surely as Thatcherism became the dominant force in British
politics. The two developed in tandem. But one should not mistake this
symbiotic relationship for an assumption that Thatcherism was the perfect
practical embodiment of New Right ideas. An understanding of the gap
between the two is crucial in order to understand the way in which the
Thatcher Governments' housing policy developed from 1979 onwards, and
its relationship with the wider programme of restructuring welfare.

There are two primary difficulties with the assumed equivalence of New
Right 'theory' and Thatcherite 'practice'. First, it assumes the existence of
an internally consistent, unified New Right ideology, rather than a jumble
of ideas, presuppositions, values and analytical techniques. This is not the
place to chart every tributary in the New Right stream of thought, but two
different perspectives at least should be identified. Levitas, among others,
has referred to these aspects as neo-liberal and neo-conservative
approaches (Levitas 1986). Very crudely, neo-liberals provided a market-
orientated thrust and have focused attention on economic strategies, while

neo-conservatives concentrated on political priorities and moral guidelines, normally of an authoritarian flavour.

There is another reason why we should be wary in linking Thatcherite social policies directly to New Right principles. Several commentators have pointed to the strong populist and pragmatic aspect to the Thatcher Governments, once the rhetoric is stripped away (Gamble 1988; Jessop *et al.* 1988; Marquand 1988; Marsh and Rhodes 1992). In fact, the ideas of the New Right received a selective application by the Thatcher Governments, with an eye more to political arithmetic than every nuance in Hayek's writings. The modification of the values of the New Right in practice can be clearly seen in Thatcher's housing strategy. The pragmatic quality of Thatcherism, for example, caused it to focus its attack on council housing during the first two terms, rather than on more entrenched state services. The populist aspect preserved mortgage interest relief virtually intact, despite its spiralling cost and its role as a distorting influence on the operation of the housing market. In consequence, Thatcher Governments regularly distanced themselves from the requirements of New Right orthodoxy for reasons of political expedience.

The differential emphasis given to the canons of New Right thought by the Thatcher Government helps to explain why state housing was initially singled out as the service requiring the most radical treatment.

Several writers have provided comprehensive overviews of the New Right's approach to the welfare state (George and Wilding 1985; Bosanquet 1983; Clarke *et al.* 1987; Hills 1990). Our intention is not to go over the same ground, but to summarise the essential characteristics of the approach. Several key themes can be identified: the celebration of the market as the basis of both economic order and economic change; the shortcomings of state provision; the burden of public expenditure; the value of consumer choice; and the importance of individual responsibility and enterprise.

The market is at the heart of New Right thought – in housing policy and social welfare as in every other area of social, political and economic life. It is therefore not surprising that, in Gamble's words, 'All New Right theorists seek the reassertion and extension of market principles in areas where social democracy has encroached and set limits to the market or suspended it altogether' (Gamble 1986: 50). And nowhere had 'social democracy' encroached further in Britain than in the development of the post-war infrastructure of the welfare state.

The costs and benefits associated with different products, services or courses of action are revealed in the price mechanism. Prices show the true costs of welfare, rather than concealing them through indiscriminate subsidies or universal benefits. In the market, the cost of failing to meet consumer preferences is extinction. The balance of opportunities and the consequences of failure provide a continuous commitment to developing new products or improving existing goods and services for the benefit of the consumer. The case against a service like council housing, therefore, flows out of this analysis. The cost of council housing to the consumer does not reflect market pricing; there is no competition to supply the product; there is consequently no incentive to improve the service or to respond to consumer preferences. Shielded from the rigours of market pressures, the provision of state housing will inevitably stagnate.

The application of market principles to social welfare therefore involves a shift to private provision in which consumers pay the cost directly rather than through subsidy or taxation, support for voluntary rather than statutory welfare, and the development of diverse systems, goods or services on offer to the consumer, such as private pension schemes, medical schemes, private schools, and so on. The long-term dynamics of the market ensure the wider spread of welfare provision, consumer choice and social progress. In the past, these aims had been thwarted by the short-term political calculation, bureaucratic inertia and wrong-headed benevolence which characterise state regulation and intervention.

Just as the market is the repository of progressive and liberating influences in our society for the New Right, the state is the source of all the forces of darkness. The origins of the post-war welfare state were couched in terms of the need to limit the inequalities produced by the market, redistribute resources in favour of the poor and guarantee a minimum level of provision for those in need. To the New Right, the Fabian vision of the welfare state was little more than an expensive exercise in self-delusion. While there are distinct differences between the neo-liberal and neo-conservative view, both approaches condemn state welfare as a pernicious failure. The inability of the welfare state to provide a more equal society was a case in point. To the New Right, attempts to achieve equality of outcome would inevitably founder. In a mixed economy, those efforts would be constantly undone by the dynamics of a market seeking to break free from bureaucratic constraint. The only alternative was totalitarian state control, but even here the bid to achieve equal rewards was chimerical. The state would never lay claim to the omniscience required for a rational and socially just distribution of resources – needs and demands change too quickly for bureaucratic categorisation. In any case, different people would have very different ideas about who was most in need. Public policies to promote social equality would therefore fail, undermine incentives or require undue coercion (Robbins 1977). The post-war welfare state was found guilty on all three counts. This line of argument struck a chord with a wider sense of public disappointment about the impact of the welfare state. Research inquiries seemed to show that, if anything, state provision achieved regressive, rather than progressive, redistribution of resources (Le Grand 1982; Le Grand and Goodwin 1987).

A second element in the New Right critique was that the welfare state had become too cumbersome and too detached from its consumers. The expanding scale of state provision was used as a barometer by the Right of bureaucratic and professional self-interest, political timidity in appeasing voters, interest group pleading and empire building. It had nothing to do with unmet social need. The consequence was a system spinning out of control, impervious to consumer needs and sheltered from the rigours of political scrutiny or private competition. Far from being a weapon with which to fight Beveridge's famous Five Giants – Want, Disease, Ignorance, Idleness and Squalor – the welfare state had become a bloated, expensive and ineffectual institution.

The third, and perhaps most effective, aspect to the New Right's critique was that the welfare state was becoming too expensive. There were two main strands to the argument. The first suggested that public expenditure spelt economic decline, by sucking resources out of the wealth creating sector and 'crowding out' private investment (Heald 1983: Ch. 1). The second line of argument claimed that the costs of public spending had been concealed and the benefits overstated. Social expenditure had not redistributed resources in favour of the poor. From the mid-1970s, both these approaches began to penetrate mainstream debates about the future of state welfare.

The costs and benefits of public expenditure received close scrutiny from the New Right. The expansion of state welfare had been sustained through a fiscal illusion: partly through inadequate information and partly through manipulation, voters had not been made fully aware of the real costs of expenditure. The benefits, on the other hand, were visible and tangible – new schools, hospitals, welfare payments, and so on. Services seemed free because the costs fell upon an abstraction – the community – rather than on an individual at the time he or she used the service (Brittan 1983: Ch. 1). It was, however, becoming easier for the New Right to remove the veils from the fiscal illusion, as issues of distribution and taxation entered the political foreground. Furthermore, evidence began to mount that social expenditure did not result in a more equal distribution of resources. In medical care, transport subsidies and student grants, for example, middle-class people benefited more than the working class (Le Grand 1982), thereby confirming public scepticism about the direction of welfare spending (Taylor-Gooby 1985).

The post-war welfare state was therefore portrayed as an 'uncontrollable monster with an insatiable appetite for tax finance and incestuous administrators' (Seldon 1981). The New Right's prescriptions were de- signed to slay the monster, set the taxpayer free and invigorate the faltering private market. Future expenditure, regarded throughout most of the post- war period as a benign instrument for securing the goals of social policy and the final guarantor against the return of economic depressions, had changed sides: from being an essential part of the solution, it had now become 'part of the problem' (Deakin 1987: 72).

To the New Right, the value of state welfare to the public arose directly from its monopoly position in the supply of certain goods and services. Much of this critique rested on an idealisation of the market form, but the frustration of choice and accountability under the state undoubtedly struck a chord. Consumers have some notional redress under a market system if they receive a poor service – to take their custom elsewhere. Supplicants for state welfare merely had to endure a mediocre and uniform system which did not have to heed its customers.

Consumer choice was also extolled by the New Right through the rationing of demand under market systems of welfare – ensuring that only people who really wanted the service would use it, as they were paying for it directly. By providing a health service free at the point of use, for example, the state had merely opened the floodgates of demand, making it impossible to distinguish between genuine and false need, between urgent requests for help and flippant inquiries. In consequence, a 'rough justice' model of rationing was usually adopted – such as queuing – as the expan- sion of state services could not keep pace with spiralling demand. Under the market system, prices would rise to reflect intensity of demand – the queue would be replaced by the ability to buy.

Finally, the costs of the British welfare state could not only be measured in terms of rising taxes, longer queues and poorer services. There was a moral cost to pay as well. To the New Right, state provision was irredeem- ably paternalist. Professionals, bureaucrats and politicians took decisions on behalf of other people. This created a syndrome of dependency, sapped individual enterprise and reduced the incentive to provide for one's own welfare. The state operated as a kind of surrogate family, which undermined a genuine sense of responsibility. 'The provision of direct social services is regarded by many as something that the family should undertake. When the state provides these services, there is serious concern that families feel morally justified in abandoning their responsibilities to the State' (Minford 1984: 60).

Although blessed with benign intentions, in practice state welfare was morally corrosive, by undermining the family and replacing it with an impersonal, ineffective and costly system of care which reduced people to a state of abject dependence. As Harris put it,

A welfare state is necessarily paternalistic, fails to respect individuals as thinking and choosing agents, and rests upon the use of illegitimate coercion whereby resources are stolen from those entitled to keep them and persons are prevented from realising their own values in their own way. Quite independently of its practical failings, the welfare state is morally bankrupt.

(Harris 1987: 8)

The proportion of social needs which merited state help was relatively small. For example, the neo-liberal Right acknowledged the case for state support for mentally handicapped adults without parents. It would be difficult to sustain a case for individual responsibility and self-help here. Single mothers, on the other hand, presented a different proposition. They had created the situation for themselves: if the state stepped in, this was simply subsidising the breakup of family values and relationships. Wherever possible, individuals should retain the right to make provision for themselves. Reliance on the state merely undermined altruism, as people felt that 'the government would help' and that personal support was unnecessary.

THE NEW RIGHT AND STATE HOUSING

The New Right critique of post-war state welfare provision dealt the decisive ideological blow against council housing during the 1980s. The case for market-based forms of provision may have lacked conviction to the public in certain areas of welfare, such as health and education. But the attack on the dead hand of the state was far more persuasive when applied to housing provision. Council housing seemed to be the perfect symbol for the failings of the public sector: unpopular, socially stigmatising, incompetently managed and oblivious to consumer preferences. The summary by Black and Stafford was typical: 'Housing segregation, immobility of tenants and rising rent arrears have become the products of a succession of ill-founded past decisions in the name of social engineering, planning, development and civic blunders' (Black and Stafford 1988: 101). As the New Right grew more confident in its assertion of market principles, the cumulative weaknesses of state housing were eagerly exposed, and contrasted with the vitality of the private sector.

If the New Right's assessment of state education and health provision was occasionally tempered by an awareness of their relative popularity and universality, no such difficulties restrained the onslaught on state housing, as critics such as Henney were quick to point out: 'Compared to the NHS, council housing is no jewel in the crown of the welfare state for, whereas

74 per cent of the population at large think that the former is good value, a mere 42 per cent think the same of council housing' (Henney 1985: 12). The market solution could be advanced without pausing for thought or elaborate justification.

It is perhaps for this reason that New Right analysis of council housing can only be found in scattered works and essays. With some exceptions (Gray 1968; Pennance 1969; Minford *et al.* 1987), the work of the Institute of Economic Affairs, for example, has been directed towards health and education (Harris and Seldon 1987). The focus of the New Right analysis of the British housing market was also rather imbalanced. There appears to be an inverse relationship between the size of housing tenure and the importance assigned to it by the New Right. The small and declining private rented sector, for example, has still been given pride of place, in order to demonstrate the damage of state regulation and control. The much larger owner-occupied sector, on the other hand, has generally received cursory treatment. The extent of indirect public subsidy to support owner-occupation is perhaps a little too embarrassing. The attacks on wasteful expenditure have generally been reserved for local authority housing sub-sidies rather than mortgage interest relief (see, for example, Minford *et al.* 1987: 120). Debates about council housing have therefore been pursued in the context of a distorted model of the wider housing market itself.

The New Right's critique of state housing shifted ground from 1979 onwards, to reflect wider policy changes. The amount of direct central government subsidy to council housing, for example, fell dramatically in the first term of the Thatcher Government. The arguments about com-parative subsidies to different tenures therefore gave way to new criticisms about the design, ownership, management and control of council housing (Coleman 1985: Henney 1985). The aspects of *housing in use* which we considered in Part II have been increasingly acknowledged in the New Right's critique, raising various questions about management, participation and social processes. This shift of emphasis has also been reflected in the changing mythology of the New Right: the ubiquitous pampered council tenant of the past was duly replaced by the oppressed, stigmatised and ignored consumer. The New Right's appraisal of state housing thereby incorporated a more qualitative perspective, as the judgement of the right-wing think tank, the Adam Smith Institute, illustrates: 'the public sector has become inefficient, wasteful and costly, has discouraged mobility and has allowed no place for consumer preferences to determine its supply' (Adam Smith Institute 1983: 153).

Let us examine this claim in more detail. The allegation of *inefficiency* covered the financing, management and allocation of council housing. Access was governed by a dubious, vague and politically impregnated criterion – housing need. The system failed because it was impervious to the interaction of supply and demand. Applicants on the waiting or transfer list could do nothing themselves to increase their chances of getting a property. They just had to wait. Their only decision was whether to hold out for their main preference or, if they lost patience, to accept a less desirable dwelling.

When demand for council housing exceeded supply, rationing was essential and the dead hand of bureaucracy held sway. The result was stagnation. Households had little incentive to move, causing the inefficient use of the available stock. (The elderly widow 'under-occupying' her three-bedroomed council house was a recurrent nightmare for many New Right protagonists.) Despite excess demand, in some areas unpopular properties could remain empty, but rents would be little different from those charged for the most desirable properties in the council's stock. The inertia of the allocation system explained the paradox that long waiting lists and difficult-to-let properties could coexist in a local area.

For the New Right, the council stock was inefficiently managed because there were no incentives for staff to keep down arrears levels, reduce the number of void properties or speed up the lettings period. Any loss of revenue to the Housing Department in the past could be met by subsidies from the rates, or by reducing long-term commitments – such as programmed maintenance. Ultimately, the costs of inefficient practice were borne by the tenants rather than the staff. Yet the housing officer had not been held accountable to the tenants for delays, poor decisions, lack of expertise or unprofessional conduct. Mistakes had been concealed by the sheer scale of the local authority housing service. Staff were rarely sacked for bad practice, and rarely rewarded adequately for performing well. Decisions were usually made in any case on the basis of short-term political calculation rather than any notion of providing tenants with value for money. 'Incentives, rewards, penalties scarcely exist. Targets are subjects for discussion, not action. Part-time councillors, few of whom know much about housing development are supposed, in their ignorance, to control huge operations' (Henney 1985: 20). In this environment, why should anyone bother about efficiency?

The charge that council housing is *wasteful and costly* stemmed from its protection from market processes. In previous chapters we have argued that, from the outset, council housing was riddled with market-orientated assumptions, which shaped its financial base and management approach. The New Right perspective took the opposite view. Market mechanisms had not been prominent enough. Costs had not been properly controlled. Vast sums of money had been frittered away on wrong-headed schemes. The history of council housing was seen as a classic example of how the best laid plans of politicians to interfere with market processes would, sooner or later, go astray.

The New Right's criticism of wasteful expenditure ranged widely. The level of public expenditure devoted to council housing was seen as irrelevant to the actual extent of housing need (Anderson and Marsland 1983). Local authorities were in fact able to cut back on spending without affecting the condition of their stock to any noticeable degree (Prentice 1983). Public housing maintenance and development were often carried out by the councils' direct labour organisations – which were considered inflexible and inefficient, shielded from competitive pressure and organised so that 'the preservation of jobs is generally placed ahead of customer satisfaction in priority' (Hoppe 1983: 16).

Traditional 'bricks and mortar' subsidies were criticised by New Right analysts as indiscriminate, distorting the operation of the entire housing market. The New Right favoured cash supplements targeted at 'genuinely poor' households: in housing as in other social services. In this manner, customers could make their own decisions about priorities. The absence of adequate pricing mechanisms in council housing had also encouraged waste. Housing costs are a major part of household expenditure and therefore it was essential that the price of housing conveyed information about supply and demand, consumer preferences and expectations. These objectives were thwarted by the way in which council housing has been financed.

Council rents had been set at a level which related neither to actual property costs nor the ability to pay. The system of rent-pooling on the basis of historic cost had spread the burden across the local authority sector. This cross-subsidy was anathema to New Right principles of individualising costs and benefits, making it clear that 'you get what you pay for'. In practice, the range of rents was too compressed. It did not reflect the wide variation in demand for popular and unpopular dwellings. The lack of adequate price signals therefore induced inefficient management, poor maintenance, a second-rate service and many frustrated tenants. (For a fuller discussion, see Audit Commission 1986.)

The effects of council housing on *discouraging mobility* figured strongly in New Right critiques. Market forces provided the pressure to promote sufficient mobility for a rapidly changing labour market. Subsidised state housing was a trap. In 1987, Minford and his colleagues calculated that the level of unemployment in Britain could be reduced by 2 per cent if measures were taken to free the housing market from state regulation and control. They went on to claim that the lack of mobility – especially among unskilled workers – was costing the country £7,500 million a year (at 1986 prices). The existence of a large, stagnant public housing sector was the chief culprit.

New Right advocates such as Minford often appeared to assume a direct relationship between the degree of immobility and the size of the council sector. Lack of immobility was the inevitable consequence of a tenure predicated on political interference, bureaucratic control and subsidised rents. Minford therefore quoted with approval Mackay's pungent view that in Scotland, where council housing is the majority tenure, the 'obsession with cheap public sector housing may come close second to the Berlin Wall as the most formidable obstacle to geographical mobility yet devised by man' (Mackay quoted in Minford *et al.* 1987: 109–10). Little did he know at the time of writing that the Berlin Wall would prove the less durable of the two.

Minford's analysis rested on empirical data which showed that council tenants were less likely to move in search of work than were owner-occupiers or private tenants. Hughes and McCormick, for example, studied the relationship between housing tenure, personal characteristics and inter-regional migration and found that council tenants were less likely to undertake an inter-regional move, regardless of their level of education, age or occupation. They concluded that 'differences in the probability of migration between owner-occupiers, council tenants and private unfurnished tenants are caused by the way in which the housing market operates' (Hughes and McCormick 1981: 935–6). Other studies tended to support this view (Johnson *et al.* 1974; OPCS 1983; Champion *et al.* 1986).

The policy recommendations of Minford and his colleagues were, however, more contentious. The proposals included imposing a limit on state benefits, calculated as a proportion of previous net income. Unemployed tenants would not then be protected from the effects of council rent increases, and this would act as a spur to mobility. This strategy would be supplemented by the deregulation of rents and the phasing out of security of tenure in the private sector. The link between a large state sector in the housing market and the lack of labour mobility in Britain was a more palatable analysis for the Thatcher Government than one which directed attention at the high level of owner-occupation as a constraint on mobility – particularly at times of growing regional differences in house prices. The mobility factor prompted the government to attempt to 'free up' the rented sector, by encouraging competition to municipal landlords, developing housing associations and relaxing controls on the private rented sector. 'Footloose' labour would thus find a toehold in the rented property market which had previously been denied by council housing allocation procedures.

The final element of the New Right analysis concentrated on the *denial of consumer choice* in state housing. The critique penetrated the lack of accountability and responsiveness at the heart of council housing. The design and management of council housing had been dominated by professional and bureaucratic self-interest, impervious to consumer preferences. Notional accountability was provided through the local political system. The reality was that local councillors acted to ensure their re-election, by keeping rent levels unrealistically low, judiciously siting new developments and allocating houses to their friends. For the New Right, the level of public disenchantment with council housing was easy to understand.

The stultifying effects of many traditional housing management practices were considered in Chapter 5. As a result, the New Right's analysis extended increasingly into the consumer experience of council housing. It was not difficult to list examples of negative and patronising practices, or lack of consultation in design or rehabilitation by local authorities (Robinson 1983). The attack therefore moved away from a concern with structures and housing form towards a consideration of housing processes – in Turner's phrase, from housing as a noun to housing as a verb. The experience of state provision was, of course, dismal on both counts.

Council housing may have improved standards – as we argued in Chapter 4 – but, for most of those in the New Right, this was to miss the point. It had failed to connect with personal aspirations and preferences. 'Except in the narrowest sense, people are no more likely to regard the most palatial of local authority houses as meeting their housing desires than the most menial and unhealthy of slums from which they might have been rehoused' (Robinson 1983: 80). The fatal combination of centralised decision-making, professional arrogance, political patronage and managerial weakness – which typified municipal landlordism – ruled out opportunities for genuine tenant involvement. The traditions of housing management ran counter to core New Right values of freedom, choice, self-actualisation and achievement. 'The very essence of home is the ability to personalise structures, to humanise concrete and brick and to mould their immediate physical environment to their satisfaction. All this council housing prevents' (Robinson 1983: 86). Policy solutions lay in the dual strategy of extending home ownership and creating self-governing tenant bodies.

Poor management and lack of accountability were central to Alex Henney's short but influential critique of council housing, outlined in his pamphlet *Trust the Tenant* (1985). He identified the failure of public housing as stemming from problems of landlordism on a mass scale, and the departure from the responsiveness of market processes. Henney proposed the establishment on council estates of Housing Management Trusts, covering 500 to 2,000 dwellings. The Trusts would be run by a management board of nine representatives – five elected by tenants. The Trusts would take control of council property, manage and renovate dwellings, appoint and dismiss staff and allocate 75 per cent of the properties.

Henney claimed that this system would introduce greater accountability, reduce bureaucracy and increase choice. Many of these ideas were to find favour when the government attempted to diversify rented housing in the late 1980s.

There was widespread agreement among New Right theorists on the failings of a virtual public sector monopoly in rented accommodation. Views differed on the extent to which local authorities should maintain a residual housing role. However, the thrust of the New Right analysis was clear – to decimate council housing and ensure the triumph of market-based alternatives.

TURNING THE TIDE: THATCHERISM 1979–87

While the New Right put forward its ideas for restructuring state welfare with growing confidence and certainty, the actual record of the first two Thatcher administrations fell well short of such a radical overhaul. Peter Riddell summarised the strategy as containing 'far-reaching rhetoric and cautious practice' (Riddell 1983: 112). Instead of rolling back the frontiers of the welfare state, the government's programme made only limited and selective incursions.

It is not our purpose here to review the social policies introduced during the first two terms of the Thatcher Government (see, for example, Gamble 1988; Skidelsky 1988; Kavanagh 1987; Walker and Walker 1987). We wish instead to concentrate on our claim that state housing has, throughout, been located uneasily in the infrastructure of British welfare provision. Housing policies from 1979 to 1987 were to give a dramatic illustration of this distinctive position of public sector housing. While other core welfare services retained their basic shape, the weaknesses of state housing were readily exploited. The lessons of this strategy prepared the ground for the more fundamental welfare reforms proposed by the third Thatcher administration, in which it was intended that the gap between rhetoric and practice could be closed.

The Thatcher Governments' social strategy was largely shaped by the priority given to economic objectives of controlling inflation, cutting back taxes and reducing public expenditure. The government's first White Paper on Public Expenditure began with the statement: 'Public expenditure is at the heart of Britain's economic difficulties' (HMSO 1979: 1). Whereas the previous Labour Government had been compelled to reduce spending, the Thatcher administration made a virtue out of this strategy, and willingly embraced retrenchment (Flynn 1988). In the event, the programme turned out rather differently. Rather than a wholehearted reduction in expenditure levels, a more pragmatic, selective and uneven strategy prevailed. Over the period, the level of public expenditure actually increased, although there was significant redistribution across different services.

It is difficult to measure changes in expenditure levels during the period. The management and presentation of statistics – particularly the move from 'volume' figures to 'cash' figures from 1982 onwards – masked underlying trends. Allowances also need to be made for cost and wage inflation, effects on the standards of service and increases in fees and charges. However, Robinson (1986) suggested that, overall, total social expenditure actually increased by more than 11 per cent between 1979 and 1985. The changing internal composition of this spending, however, bears closer study.

Expenditure on social security and health over this period increased sharply (by 36 per cent and 24 per cent respectively), education spending increased more modestly (6 per cent), while housing expenditure was *cut* dramatically – by 55 per cent (Hills 1987: 89). This is a telling indication of the way in which the most vulnerable state service – in terms of public support – bore the brunt of the government's economic strategy. Of course, one should not read these expenditure trends as reflecting precisely the government's priorities. Spending patterns are difficult for central government to control or predetermine. (For a fuller discussion, see Levitt and Joyce 1987, Heald 1983.) These problems were compounded during this period, as many of these services were run by local authorities pursuing quite different priorities. The first Thatcher Government failed to keep the lid on expenditure, and the second eventually fared little better. Public expenditure White Papers after 1979 began with an apology, rather than a confident assertion about reducing public spending.

The government did not lack determination in its efforts to contain expenditure: financial pressure was the main weapon used to restructure welfare provision. The government's major priority was to control local authorities defying central control by increasing local resources through rate increases. A complex panoply of targets, penalties and controls was therefore introduced. The Thatcher Governments fought shy of redefining the scope or structure of public provision, preferring to control, whenever possible, through resource constraints. In every area except housing, it failed.

Politically, the government reaped few benefits from this unintended generosity to the welfare state. John Hills reviewed the government's spending record during the first two terms and suggested that the relatively constant level of spending was 'the accidental result of the collision between exploding *needs* for services as the economy has dived into recession and the government's attempts to cut back levels of provision in selected areas' (Hills 1987: 89). For this reason, increased spending exacerbated inequalities and increased poverty rather than improved service standards. The evidence was damning, although not politically fatal. Piachaud (1987), for example, estimated that about one million more men, one million more women and one million more children were living at or below the official poverty line (Supplementary Benefit level) in 1987 when compared to 1978.

To the New Right, the case against public expenditure was its impact on levels of taxation, and the consequences for enterprise and risk-taking. Ever pragmatic, the Thatcher Government eventually managed, in its first eight years, to achieve one goal – reducing direct taxation – while failing to achieve another – reducing public expenditure. The gap was only bridged by asset sales and North Sea Oil revenues. It could not last.

We saw earlier in this chapter that the New Right critique of state welfare extended beyond issues of cost. The lack of market discipline rendered such services wasteful and inefficient. Here again, the attack of the Thatcher Government was sporadic, with the noise much greater than the substance. There were occasional glimpses of radical measures more in keeping with the strictures of the New Right, but these were often shelved, modified, thwarted or discarded.

The essence of the Thatcher Government's approach from 1979 to 1987 was to contain spending, impose greater control over local authority spending and provide tax cuts through politically painless measures wherever possible. The task of restructuring state welfare proved to be a longer-term project than initially envisaged in 1979. The most urgent priorities had been to loosen public expectations about state provision, weaken morale in the public sector, face down pockets of opposition and puncture the principles of state welfare. This was an ambitious and concerted strategy – but it was not the reconceptualisation of the role of the welfare state that the advocates of the New Right had hoped for. Thus, the final White Paper on public expenditure produced by the second cost-conscious Thatcher Government in 1986 increased the target for future expenditure by £4.7 billion.

Of course, the overall objective of the welfare strategy remained as before, even if the political calculations had been underestimated. In Deakin's words, 'the welfare state had merely been reprieved, not acquitted' (Deakin 1987: 118). It was only after eight years of 'softening up' that far-reaching reforms were envisaged by the Conservatives in such central aspects as the funding of local government, education and health. The Thatcher Government remained nervous about the political and electoral impact of its welfare strategy and the proposals to reform the National Health Service were, in particular, advanced *sotto voce*.

Only one public service is exempt from this analysis of the Thatcher Government's record during its first two terms – housing. In 1977, the Labour Government's detailed Housing Policy Review had been heralded as a fundamental reappraisal of housing finance, subsidy and tenure. In the event, little changed: the uneasy role of state provision in a predominantly private market continued (Lansley 1979). This reprieve was short-lived. In housing, as in no other service, the rhetorical flourish of the first two Thatcher Governments was matched by sweeping policy change, amounting to a redefinition of the roles of the public and private sectors. As we have seen, officially defined public housing expenditure was cut by more than half from 1978–9 to 1986–7, although this was partly mitigated by an increase in housing benefit spending, signalling a shift from 'bricks and mortar' to personal subsidies.

The most important element of the far-reaching housing programme was the vote-winning potential of the keynote of the strategy, the sale of council houses, described as 'one of the most successful and symbolic of all the government's policies' (Gamble 1988: 138). Yet the Right to Buy was simply the most prominent aspect of a wider housing programme during this period.

The thrust of the government's housing policy from 1979 to 1987 can be simply summarised: the reduction of council stock, the expansion of owner-occupation, the decrease in capital spending by, and housing subsidies to, local authorities, and the maintenance of mortgage tax relief. Subsidiary policies included attempts to stem the decline in the private rented sector and continued support for housing associations. This amounted to a wide-ranging programme of *privatisation*. Privatisation however can take on a number of different dimensions – the private provision of services, the reduction of public subsidies and expenditure, or the removal of regulatory measures for private services (Flynn 1988; LeGrand and Robinson 1984). The government's housing strategy in this period managed to move ahead on each of these fronts. It reduced state provision, by limiting new building programmes and encouraging council house sales; it reduced subsidies to council tenants while enhancing tax expenditures to owner-occupiers; and it reduced state regulation by re-laxing controls on rents in the private sector. For once, the frontiers of the state really were being pushed back, or at least reshaped.

The heart of the Thatcherite strategy was the legislation enabling local authority tenants to buy their properties. The 1980 Housing Act gave tenants the right to purchase, on a sliding discount, after a minimum three-year period. The Housing and Building Control Act 1984 reduced the qualifying period to two years and raised the maximum discount to purchasers from 50 per cent to 60 per cent. The discount was raised still further to 70 per cent for flat dwellers in 1986.

During the first two terms of the Thatcher Government over one million properties were sold by local authorities and new towns under the legislation – a massive transfer for a stock of under six million. In practice, the sale of properties had a very uneven impact – houses rather than flats were sold, in prosperous rather than depressed areas, to middle-aged tenants with adult children rather than pensioners or the young, to skilled working-class people rather than those dependent on benefits (Williams *et al.* 1986). But by any standards the policy represented a major shift in wealth from the state to individual households and a most significant change in the tenure patterns of the British housing market.

The justification for council house sales was advanced, typically, with both positive support and negative comment. Government ministers queued up to extol the virtues of freedom, choice and property ownership bestowed by the policy, while condemning local authority inefficiency in investment, management and maintenance. Local authorities took the blame for increasing disrepair in the stock, dereliction and vandalism in estates.

Yet the rhetoric was propelled forward by significant financial inducements for any tenants who still remained to be convinced. As the government withdrew subsidies to local authorities, sharp increases in council rents resulted, especially between 1981 and 1983. Subsidies to council tenants were cut by 31 per cent in the first six years of the Thatcher Government, compared to an increase in subsidies to owner-occupiers of 212 per cent. For many tenants, rent increases were cushioned by housing benefit – but even here, housing proved the most vulnerable element in the system. In the first four years after its introduction in 1983, seven changes to the calculation of benefit effectively removed one million households from eligibility. The Social Security Act 1986 then reduced housing benefit expenditure by a further £450 million (Bennett 1987).

The shifting scale of discounts and subsidies to different sectors prompted Christine Whitehead to comment: 'it is extremely difficult to avoid the conclusion that owner-occupation is being stimulated for ideological rather than economic or financial reasons' (Whitehead 1984: 128). Yet the popularity of this slice of Thatcherite ideology was undeniable and, after a little angst, the Labour Party eventually withdrew its opposition to the policy of council house sales.

The effects of this approach by the Thatcher Government rapidly intensified the trend to the *residualisation* of council housing. Residualisation refers to the shrinking size of the tenure, the concentration of social and economic disadvantage on council estates and the political marginalisation of council tenants (Forrest and Murie 1983: Clapham and MacLennan 1983; Malpass and Murie 1990; Malpass 1990). The strategy of council house sales increased social polarisation and segregation, as well as reducing choice for those who remained in the sector (Hamnett 1984; Willmott and Murie 1988). The state sector was, more than ever, associated with failure.

We noted earlier that the Thatcher Government's wider strategy to restructure state welfare foundered during the first two terms for a variety of economic and political reasons. In housing, the attempt to reorganise provision through financial pressures, indirect subsidy and legislative control was much more successful. Why the difference? As our account so far has shown, council housing has always been a minority tenure: its principles at odds with dominant private market values, its practice unconvincing as an alternative mode of provision. The fragmentation of the sector marginalised support for council housing still further, exacerbating difficulties for those still in the sector and increasing the pressure to exit and seek solutions through the private market (Saunders 1986). During the Thatcher years, public support for state welfare generally remained a constant, if contradictory and ambivalent, feature on the political landscape (Jowell *et al.* 1986; Edgell and Duke 1983). For council housing, however, support ebbed away, until the majority of the population favoured a policy of unrestricted council house sales (Bosanquet 1987). As Flynn suggested: 'For the privatised majority in housing and welfare there is little to be gained by a reversal of current policies: for the residual minority, political acquiescence may be a pragmatic response to the coercion of circumstances and difficulties of everyday life' (Flynn 1988: 309).

A change of focus in the Thatcher Government's strategy became increasingly apparent during the second term, prompted by the growing realisation that owner-occupation could only be expanded to a certain limit. Right to Buy rates started to slacken and the new incentives were not achieving great success. Furthermore, growing regional differences in house prices indicated that even the magic of the owner-occupied sector had its weaknesses, notably in terms of labour mobility. A significant minority would still require rented accommodation, but control of this sector needed to be wrested from local authorities.

The government's critique of council housing began to penetrate more deeply into issues of management and control, as well as ownership. As the then Housing Minister, John Patten, wrote in 1987:

> I want us to increasingly think in terms of transferring ownership of estates or parts of estates in small units to others – including the tenants themselves – who will be in closer touch with the needs and aspirations of individual tenants . . . there will be a substantial number, perhaps more than three million, who will not want to or will not be able to exercise the Right to Buy. But continuing as a tenant should not mean 'being a pawn in the hands of bureaucratic management'.
>
> (Patten 1987)

The criticisms of inefficient large-scale municipal landlordism were significantly stepped up. Since 1979, the government had argued that local authority housing management must be radically improved. The Department of the Environment set up the Priority Estates Project – demonstration projects of localised, small-scale management encouraging tenant involvement on difficult-to-let estates (Power 1982, 1987). The intriguing aspect of the government's strategy was the way in which these issues were subsequently blended into an overriding strategy of privatisation. The government set up the Urban Housing Renewal Unit (later renamed Estate Action) to 'topslice' housing investment expenditure for local authorities to spend on earmarked schemes. The approval process often included direct encouragement for 'partnership' arrangements with the private sector (Urban Housing Renewal Unit 1986). Local authorities would pay the price if they turned down the prospect of additional funding.

Finally, the strategy to improve management was coupled with a new vision of selective tenant control, through co-operatives or trusts. Those remaining in the public sector were increasingly portrayed as hapless victims of uncaring, inefficient bureaucrats, trapped in difficult-to-let estates of poor design. The government would now set these tenants free as well – not just through the Right to Buy, but through a change of landlord. This approach set the tone for the third term in office after the election victory of 1987.

This synopsis of certain key aspects to the housing programme of the first two Thatcher administrations shows that many of the ideas of the New Right considered earlier in this chapter closely informed the introduction of new policy measures. Council housing was assailed on all sides – its rents, capital programmes, relationship with tenants, management practices, its barely existent maintenance and repair programmes. Support for owner-occupation was effectively portrayed in terms of extending freedom of choice. The government took an increasingly interventionist stance. The 'freedom' to change from council landlordism was slowly becoming a compulsion. The need to check radical sentiments for electoral reasons was not present, as it was in health or education policy. If the broader social welfare programme of the Thatcher Government had failed to realise the New Right vision of a strong market and a residualised state, its housing policies at least showed the way forward. It had apparently shaped an agenda for the 1990s.

1987–90: EXTENDING CHOICE IN RENTED HOUSING?

The experience of the first two terms of the Thatcher Government increasingly demonstrated the limitations of a housing strategy reliant almost entirely on the expansion of a single tenure – owner-occupation – as a means of strengthening market ideas and principles. Choice had been associated with a move out of the clutches of the state – in council housing – and into the warmer embrace of home-ownership. The Right to Buy was the vehicle through which this choice was expressed. The 1987 election victory, which ushered in the third consecutive term of Conservative administration, was the high water mark of Thatcherism – and the start of an even sharper hostility than before towards local government provision and the extension of privatisation into the core areas of the welfare state: in addition to council housing and social security, state health and education provision became objects of increasing attention.

It was during this period that the government published a White Paper, *Housing* (HMSO: 1987), which expressed in bold and unequivocal terms its self-confidence in transforming the rented sector by introducing greater consumer choice, while maintaining the expansion of owner-occupation. This prompted two pieces of legislation – the 1988 Housing Act and the 1989 Local Government and Housing Act – which gave expression on the statute book to these policy objectives.

The primary aim of the legislation was to transform the role of local authorities in the rented sector – by replacing their landlord function with a more strategic, co-ordinating or enabling role. It was also an implicit recognition that the sale of council houses would not, of itself, lead to the extinction of the public sector. Instead, many of the remaining four million households in council housing were to be offered the alternative of transferring to another landlord. The government pinned its hopes on reviving private sector renting, which was now little more than a rump in the housing market, and extending the role of housing associations. The attraction of housing associations lay in their independence from local political control and dependence on direct central government support – a more acceptable form of public landlordism. The revival of the private rented sector was to be achieved through liberalising controls on rents in the sector, and strengthening the landlord's control over contracts with tenants through the development of new 'assured' and 'assured shorthold' tenures.

Central government was also to intervene selectively as a landlord – by the creation of Housing Action Trusts, which would take control over municipal estates and 'parcel up' sections of the estate for direct control by other landlords or through sale. The Trusts would act as demonstration projects for central government to show local authorities how large-scale municipal estates might be broken up and more diverse forms of ownership and control introduced.

Finally, the government supported the extension of tenant involvement and control through the development of housing co-operatives. However, there was not any specific funding set aside at this juncture to develop these organisations – their growth relied more on general government exhortation.

These measures did not, however, achieve the objectives intended by the government. Council tenants remained loyal to local authorities when faced with the choice of moving to another landlord. Tenants were particularly concerned about losing their security of tenure, and increasing rent levels in the future. Many of the younger and more prosperous households had already moved out of the sector as a result of buying their council homes, prompted by the financial incentive of discounts on the sale price. Elderly tenants were less convinced about such advantages, and preferred to stay with the landlord to whom they had paid rent for perhaps forty or fifty years. In this way, very few transfers of council stock took place under the Tenants Choice legislation; and the proposals to transfer ownership to Housing Action Trusts were rejected in tenant ballots in all of the six schemes launched in the first experimental phase of the programme.

The revival of the private rented sector also fell short of expectations. Initially, potential private landlords received no financial incentive to invest more heavily in the sector. In 1988, the government introduced a programme giving tax relief to institutions investing in rented companies for a period of at least five years, through an initiative known as the Business Expansion Scheme. This had a limited impact, and the production of new dwellings for rent was mainly confined to the more prosperous areas in the South of England and to younger, socially mobile tenants. The rents charged on new properties were often out of the reach of poorer tenants (Crook and Kemp 1991).

The expansion of housing associations, to take the place of municipal landlords, was rendered vulnerable by their reliance on loans from the private sector. The degree of public subsidy required to produce 'affordable' rents (defined as rents within the reach of low income households in low paid employment) was greater than the government – and especially the Treasury – had wanted. Many housing association representatives were concerned that the organisations would not be able to fulfil their traditional role of meeting housing need – especially among single people and the elderly – due to pressure on rent levels and housing rehabilitation programmes. To some extent, these fears have been realised. Average earnings in Britain increased by 31 per cent between 1988 and 1991, although the incomes of new housing association tenants increased by only 20 per cent. In the same period, housing association rents increased by 81 per cent (NFHA 1992).

Finally, even the expansion of home ownership began to falter in the late 1980s. At first, government legislation led to an increase in the sale of council houses, with tenants growing uncertain about their future under municipal landlords. However, the extension of owner-occupation was thwarted by a sharp increase in interest rates – the result of an explicit economic strategy to reduce the reliance on consumer credit and to bring down the rate of inflation. As the costs of mortgage loans began to spiral upwards – from under 10 per cent in July 1988 to 15.4 per cent by February 1990 – the financial advantages of home ownership started to appear more fragile than at any time since 1979.

One sign of the lack of affordable rented housing was the increase in the rates of officially recorded homelessness across Britain towards the end of the decade. Media coverage tended to concentrate on those people 'sleeping rough' in the streets, especially in London. However, this was merely the sharpest manifestation of an underlying trend in which poorer households were becoming displaced in the housing market, and where income support for housing costs fell well short of comprehensive and effective coverage.

By 1990, the triumphalist tones of the Thatcher Governments' attempt to effect a second 'housing revolution' by the transformation of the rented sector had given way to a more measured assessment. Some of the vulnerabilities of the housing strategy had been revealed – its dependence on high levels of owner-occupation, the susceptibility of housing policy to peaks and troughs in the economic cycle, the persistence of poverty and evidence of growing inequality in incomes, the difficulties facing poor households when costs increased sharply, and the absence of a regional strategy to balance inequalities between local housing markets and assist in labour mobility. In particular, the desire to finish off council housing altogether during the third term of Thatcherism was not achieved.

Opposition political parties' housing programmes did not, however, offer a dramatic alternative to the priorities of the government. Official reports, such as the Duke of Edinburgh's Inquiry into British Housing, highlighted the dislocations prompted by different forms of subsidy to households: tax relief for owner-occupiers, as against income subsidies for tenants. The former was less easily controlled than the latter, and proposals were put forward to provide a general housing allowance for poorer households in *all* tenures. However, this suggestion did not gain widespread acceptance among political parties, nervous about the political sensitivities of affecting the livelihood of the 70 per cent of the population who now owned their homes. Despite the lack of a clearly articulated alternative housing strategy, the problems of the government's wholehearted commitment to privatisation were now coming under increasingly critical scrutiny.

HOUSING POLICY AFTER THATCHER: CONSOLIDATION AND RETRENCHMENT

The election of John Major as Prime Minister in November 1990 represented a degree of continuity with those policies pursued under the Thatcher administration. Yet there was a more conciliatory emphasis, and a less ideological tone, in the social and economic policies pursued by Major's first government. This was as evident in housing as in other arenas of public policy.

The government introduced a degree of modest interventionism into the housing market. At the end of 1991, £100 million was redirected from the investment budget to assist housing associations – working with local authorities – to provide temporary accommodation for the homeless in south-east England. The sacred policy of tax relief to home owners was breached, through the removal of additional relief to higher rate tax payers, and more heretical constraints were still under consideration. The rules over the transfer of municipal housing to Housing Action Trusts were relaxed and £50 million was invested in just one estate as the first project, with the full agreement of the Labour-controlled local authority. Grants to increase tenant participation and the development of housing co-operatives were also maintained.

The biggest challenge facing the Major Government, however, was the collapse of the private housing market, in the light of continuing high interest rates, economic recession and growing unemployment. House transactions fell to their lowest level for more than a decade and the slump in housebuilding was matched by a similar trend in the commercial property market as business confidence fell sharply. As the number of house repossessions due to mortgage default increased dramatically, the government struck a deal with major building societies to stem the tide, through the development of 'mortgage rescue' schemes to prevent the eviction of beleaguered home owners. The hallowed policy of Right to Buy was unchanged, though its impact diminished as the attractions of owner-occupation started to wear thin.

Some indication of the changing emphasis of government strategy could be gleaned from the manifesto published prior to the 1992 General Election (Conservative Party 1992). The housing proposals were concerned with issues of regulation and detail rather than with the broad sweep of policies launched during the previous campaign. Housing was rarely raised as an issue in the 1992 election – either by the Conservatives or the opposition parties – though the growth in homelessness and the difficulties facing home owners did occasionally feature in public debates.

The election of the Conservatives for a fourth consecutive term of office led to a more cautious strategy of privatisation as the central feature of the housing programme. The further extension of owner-occupation to more marginal groups in the population was seen to depend less on any specific housing legislation than on the overall success of the government in bringing down the level of interest rates and encouraging greater stability in the housing market.

Nevertheless, one aspect in which the tradition of the previous Thatcher administrations could prevail concerned the diminution of council housing. In particular, the financial controls by central government over local authority housing expenditure introduced in 1989 would be able to take effect. The pressure on both capital and revenue spending prompted a growing number of local authorities to consider transferring their entire stock to other landlords. Between December 1988 and April 1991, sixteen councils, mainly in the South of England, successfully transferred their stock to housing associations – representing 76,000 dwellings at a gross transfer price of nearly £650 million (Newton 1991).

Many local authorities were attracted by the prospect of transfer, having determined that several more years of financial pressure on budgets, the gradual loss of housing stock, and complaints about high rents and poor service would undermine any lingering attractions of municipal land-lordism. In principle, the government initially welcomed the transfer of stock to housing associations, although it placed a limitation on the total number which could be transferred so that mass landlordism was not simply reproduced in another sector. The key question remained whether housing associations – much smaller organisations as a rule – would be willing or able to take on these responsibilities. In 1992, renewed concerns were expressed by the Treasury about the financial terms of such transfers and the leakage from the asset base. It also threatened to swamp the loans market, and thereby make finance more expensive for housing associations to develop their own programmes. A more likely scenario was the development of 'trickle' transfers, in which council property is transferred to housing association ownership as and when it becomes vacant. This strategy would avoid disrupting existing tenants, and would constitute a steadier process than the abrupt transfer of the entire stock. At the time of writing, the government has moved to regulate the process of transfer still further: yet another exit route out of council housing had fallen short of its expectations.

The second arm to the further reduction of the municipal role in the housing market was the privatisation of council housing management. The Major Government introduced compulsory competitive tendering of man-agement of local authority stock: depending on the response, it is likely to result eventually in a wider range of companies managing the stock and further to erode the control of local councils. The principle of moving to a more diverse network of social landlords, coupled with the slow but steady development of housing co-operatives, has received broad support. In the housing profession, however, there have been concerns about the maintenance of standards, the increased costs of a more competitive environment due to the loss of economies of scale, and the absence of democratic accountability for the 'new' landlords. Nevertheless, it seems increasingly certain that the combination of financial pressures, stock transfers and diversification of management will bring to an end the era of municipal landlordism in Britain. What still remains more difficult to predict is the time scale over which this process will occur – council housing having received countless premature obituaries in the past – and whether the future strategic housing role envisaged for local authorities will carry substance, or merely prove to be chimerical.

CONCLUSION

The dominance of Thatcherism during the 1980s was critical in advancing the decline of council housing. While government practice diverged significantly from the ideological hallmark of New Right thinking in many social policy arenas, rhetoric and reality were closely aligned in the government's strategy to state housing. The vicissitudes of public intervention and the attractions of the market could be readily identified. The policy was not just taken forward by reductions in expenditure and subsidy: crucially, this policy was coupled with a critique of the *quality* of provision: its management, its design and the potential for user involvement. This attack accorded with the day-to-day experience of many council tenants dealing with unresponsive or ineffective landlords. It made plausible the more fundamental challenge posed by Thatcherism to the nature of public provision, in a way that parallel attacks on the running of, for example, local schools or hospitals did not.

Yet the triumph of Thatcherism in reducing council housing to rubble was not as complete as it had appeared, for example after the Conservatives' third successive election victory in 1987. Subsequent events revealed unsuspected degrees of loyalty among council tenants to their landlords – no doubt prompted by fears about the alternative. Government policies also misjudged, time and again, the capacity and interest of the private sector to adopt a more diverse role in the housing market. Building societies, to take just one example, never demonstrated much interest in taking on a prominent landlord role (Cole and Wheeler 1986). As the economic 'miracle' of the mid-1980s evaporated, council tenants remained too poor – and the market became too volatile – for them to play the role assigned for them at

the peak of Margaret Thatcher's ascendancy: as ex-addicts who had kicked
the drug of state dependency in return for an altogether healthier life-style
as an owner-occupier, private tenant or co-operative member.

The fortunes of the Conservative Governments' enthusiasm for privatisation have ebbed and flowed in line with the movement of the domestic
economy from slump to growth and back to recession during the 1980s and
early 1990s. The Thatcher Government's support for 'privatisation' in
housing was, initially, narrowly conceived – it related only to the expansion
of owner-occupation. Only as a second stage did it embrace a wider
dimension, including the development of a non-municipalised rented sector
and the private management of council housing estates. The devotion to
home ownership was a constant feature, although its expansion was bought
at a cost. The Thatcher Governments' financial support for the housing
system was extensive throughout, but it shifted from visible public subsidy
to more concealed tax expenditures. Recent experience suggests that the
direct encouragement for economically marginal groups to become home
owners was a risky enterprise – but the government really had nowhere else
to go in pushing ahead with market-orientated policies in the absence of a
buoyant private rented sector.

The government undoubtedly achieved considerable success in
reducing municipal housing, though again it was bought at a price. The
value of discounts to tenants buying their council houses under the Right to
Buy was estimated in 1988–9 as totalling £2,700 million (Forrest *et al.*
1990: 162). The extent to which local authorities are going to take on an
'enabling' rather than a direct provision role in housing markets remains
open to doubt. Without explicit co-ordination and forward planning, it is
quite likely that the more variegated rented system of the future will lack
coherence and fail to achieve genuine diversity in meeting a complex range
of housing needs.

In order to achieve its programme, a large number of policy instruments
were introduced by the Thatcher administrations, with varying degrees of
effectiveness. Many have run into difficulties at the stage of implementation as Peter Malpass has noted: 'housing policy since 1979 has been a
curious mixture of unyielding ideological commitment and the appearance
of being made up in an almost casual, reactive way' (Malpass 1993).

Many commentators have noted that the Conservatives' housing
strategy has been skewed; in effect a policy obsessed with housing tenure,
rather than the broader shape of the housing system. This has been an
enduring feature of post-war government policy in Britain, but it has never
been as sharply revealed as in the period since 1979. The government has
only intervened indirectly in the supply side of the housing market, for
example. The deregulation of the banking system in 1980, and new powers

granted to building societies in 1986, prompted a process of major restructuring among these institutions – competition to provide home loans became more intense, just at the time that they also became more expensive. But the government has studiously avoided any estimates of housebuilding targets, relying on creating an appropriate climate for housing investment rather than dictating the level of activity. This caused renewed concern in the wake of the economic slump in the late 1980s. The Institute of Housing, for example, argued for the government to stimulate production so that an additional 120,000 affordable homes to rent are provided annually in Britain (Institute of Housing 1992b). The government remains unlikely to heed such calls. Conservative administrations since 1979 have also shown little interest in developing planning strategies for housing, or in making inroads into the extent of housing disrepair. It remains to be seen how the 'market will provide' in a way which sustains a more balanced system in the housing market.

What has been the impact of eleven years of Thatcher government and the paler, more emollient version of the Thatcherite housing programme since, under John Major? While there are few who will mourn the replacement of two monolithic 'blocks' of housing provision in Britain by a more diverse network of agencies, there has been growing recognition that the pursuit of privatisation has not necessarily brought beneficial results. Critics have pointed to the growing polarisation of the housing system, between an owner-occupied sector catering for the affluent majority and a rented sector serving an 'underclass' of poor, unemployed, elderly, ethnic or social minority households. Political calculations have encouraged the government to focus on maintaining a buoyant home ownership sector and exploiting a two-thirds/one-third division in its housing programme. This trend has prompted one observer, Mark Kleinman, to conclude that it is becoming increasingly meaningless to refer to a single housing policy being pursued by the government: instead, a twin-track strategy has emerged.

> For the majority of the population, their interests are served by the state intervening to ensure continuity and reasonable market conditions. This means providing a legal framework for the enforcement of contracts; ensuring the supply of finance; supplying output to some degree, especially counter-cyclically; providing a land-use planning framework; maintaining affordability through subsidies, especially to owner-occupiers; and, perhaps most importantly, ensuring steady economic growth and relatively full employment.
>
> Other aspects of housing policy, e.g. homelessness, social housing provision and renovation, means-tested allowances, etc., are provided to a minority of the population, a minority which is increasingly

segregated or at least differentiated from the majority geographically, ethnically or in terms of household type. Whatever the formal appearance, such policies and their associated expenditure are consented to by the majority, not as a type of collective provision but as a form of altruism (helping the poor); or as an insurance payment, against riot, theft or social disaster; or as socially necessary expenditure (because low-paid but essential workers need to live somewhere).

(Kleinman 1991: 5)

In this way the development of a more market-orientated housing strategy in Britain – the hallmark of Thatcherite policy – had a differential, if predictable, impact – liberalising a congealed system while reinforcing entrenched social and economic divisions. It would, however, be misleading to suggest that the consistent attacks on public housing since 1979 passed without response. Many local authorities refused to heed the death knell sounded for its housing stock once Margaret Thatcher achieved power. Instead, they sought to develop more sensitive and effective management methods, to sustain investment, improve the stock and extend tenant choice. It may have been an unequal battle, but any account of policies towards council housing during the 1980s and early 1990s which rested solely on the intentions, successes and failures of central government would be one-sided indeed. It was also a period when local authorities fought, against the odds, for the very survival of the principle and practice of locally accountable public housing. We consider some of these initiatives in Chapter 8.

8   Rescuing council housing?

In Chapter 3 we traced the steady post-war retreat from the glimpse of a genuinely universalistic public housing sector provided by the 1945–50 Labour Government. Forty years on, it had become axiomatic that council housing in Britain was doomed to an increasingly residual role in the housing market. The only issues for debate were the likely pace of this decline and whether its demise should be an occasion for rejoicing or regret. The ideological assault and financial constraints on state housing were intensified, with each new piece of legislation bringing a further turn of the screw. This trend culminated in the 1989 Local Government and Housing Act, which vested immense potential power in the hands of central government (or, more specifically, the Secretary of State), providing all the necessary financial levers to drive council housing out of business. The Act also closed any loopholes which recalcitrant councils could use to wriggle out of financial controls. The Act seemed to mark the final chapter in the hundred years of council housing legislation.

The consequences of this strategy were clearly inscribed in the housing market of the early 1990s – the shifting balance of subsidies away from local authorities, the growing concentration of council tenants dependent on Housing Benefit, the virtual cessation of new building by local authorities and, above all, the transfer of nearly one-and-a-half million households from the public to the private sector during the previous decade.

The clarity of purpose and remorseless intent of government housing policy fed the view that council housing was past the point of no return. It was suffering from a terminal condition, and the only difference between the major political parties was the amount of respect to be shown at its funeral. It follows from this analysis that any belated attempts to reform council housing would seem to be irrevocably flawed, for any one of several reasons – a misunderstanding of the dynamics behind changing tenure patterns, perhaps, or a misreading of consumer attitudes, or simply an ignorance of political reality. Support for either the principles or the practice of state housing could be dismissed as a kind of quaint romanticism, harking back to a long-gone period when a council tenancy was a symbol of hope and aspiration rather than despair and failure.

It is important to establish that these assumptions about the dismal future for council housing have not been confined to inveterate free market policy-makers or academics glorying in the success of privatisation. They have covered a wide spectrum of opinion. Peter Saunders, for example, shed few tears about its decline:

> council housing is unpopular – few young households want to enter it, and many of those already in the sector would like to get out of it. It is a system which strengthens the power of service producers while disabling and stigmatising the consumers who are dependent upon them . . . . British council housing is a system which encourages political patronage and bureaucratic caprice. Consumers must take what they are given for they are deprived of the power of exit. Where people have no alternative suppliers, they have no choice and no power.
>
> (Saunders 1990: 356)

Writers more predisposed to take a positive view, such as David Clapham, nevertheless concluded with a similar prognosis, having first developed a fundamental critique of the tenure. To Clapham, council housing was beyond reform because of the inherently unequal power relationship between producer and consumer which was structured into the core of municipal landlordism (Clapham 1989a). Different future strategies have been advocated – Saunders, for example, opted for a reformed housing voucher system, while Clapham favoured the phased transfer of council stock to tenant management co-operatives – but the common ground has been clear enough: local authorities should cease to have any responsibility for owning or managing housing stock as soon as possible.

In this chapter we wish to question the assumptions behind this view, even if we share a pessimistic appraisal of the future of council housing. Our evaluation of the historical development of the tenure challenges the belief that council housing has been an unremitting failure. Our analysis of its role and impact invites a more ambivalent judgement about its past value and future worth – especially, as Chapter 6 showed, if we listen to accounts from tenants themselves. Certainly, local authority housing management has often veered from the paternalist to the punitive, the stock has been poorly maintained, dreadful design mistakes have been made, and the service has hardly been suffused with far-sighted political vision at the local level. However, a closer examination of design and amenity standards, consumer views about the service and changing priorities in housing management produces a more complex and diverse picture.

Many council tenants have simply not expressed an overwhelming desire to leave the local authority sector. Of course, a high proportion of these tenants are only marginal operators in the market place – many are poor, or elderly, or both. This helps to explain the apparent reluctance of many council tenants to accept the 'exit' options so readily provided by Conservative Governments since 1979. We certainly do not seek to portray council tenants as virtuous believers in the principles of public housing, heroically withstanding the blandishments of home ownership or private renting against all the odds. But we feel it is even more misleading to characterise all tenants as miserable serfs, groaning under the yoke of council landlordism. Most tenants, we suspect, have been more interested in keeping their security of tenure while getting a better service for their rent than in leaping to join a co-operative or contributing to overheated prescriptions about the transformation of housing tenure in Britain.

In this chapter we wish to redress the balance, and assess some of the recent attempts to reform council housing, drawing on the experience of various local authority initiatives since 1979. We will also reflect on proposals for national housing reform to restructure state housing while retaining it as a significant sector of the rented market in Britain. In so doing, we want to move beyond simply providing an unending list of defects in the tenure, so that the only successful policy remedies are seen as those which push tenants into other sectors of the housing system – whether they want to go there or not. We wish to assess the potential for, and constraints on, more constructive strategies towards council housing. Before analysing the opportunities for reforming, rather than destroying state housing, however, we need to outline how the criticisms of the tenure took such a firm hold over housing policy debates during the 1980s.

MASSAGING THE MYTHS ABOUT COUNCIL HOUSING

One of the central achievements of the Conservative Governments since 1979 was to consolidate the move from referring to a crisis *of* council housing to a crisis *in* council housing. The focus thus moved away from the general problems confronting this tenure: meeting the growing extent of homelessness in particular localities, dealing with the financial constraints on investment, the decline in new building activity, the lack of long-term maintenance, and so on. Many of these problems had their origin in trends and pressures 'external' to the sector, such as general policies towards public expenditure, or wider economic and demographic trends, affecting household dissolution and mobility rates. Instead, government housing policies during the 1980s and early 1990s simply assumed that local authorities were *uniquely* poor as landlords, that the 'crisis' had been of their own making: a result of their inefficient practices, their lack of responsiveness to consumers or their monopoly position in the rented housing market in many local areas. In other words, local authorities were accused of *causing* the crisis they were struggling to confront.

This change of emphasis became particularly important from 1986 onwards, because this signalled a change in the direction of government housing strategy. As we saw in Chapter 7, there was a growing realisation by the Conservatives that wholesale home ownership was not the universal panacea for the British housing market; that 100 per cent owner-occupation might have ominous consequences for labour mobility, for example, in a period of sharp differentials between regional house prices. At the 1986 Conservative Party Conference, the then Housing Minister, John Patten, unveiled a new phrase for the government's housing strategy – audaciously borrowing a term from the Labour Party's own policies – by introducing the 'right to rent'. The term implied that the values of 'freedom' and 'choice' – which had been so successfully linked to the Right to Buy – would now be extended to the rented sector itself.

This change of emphasis in government policy at the end of the second term of the Thatcher Government acknowledged that a changing housing market required an alternative to owning for a significant minority of households; what was unacceptable was that local authorities should continue as majority landlords in this rented sector. The 'right to rent' passed from party rhetoric to legislative embodiment in the 1988 Housing Act. Rented housing was to be freed of debilitating constraints; and council tenants were to be encouraged, or even forced, to change their landlord.

In order to legitimise this strategy, it was essential for the government to gloss over those aspects of council housing dependent, at least in part, on central government action, such as the overall level of investment, the use of receipts from council house sales, or the comparative balance of housing tenure subsidies. Instead, attention turned to the failure of local authorities to carry out their responsibilities as landlords – especially in their management and maintenance functions. The failure of council housing, in short, was down to the inadequacies of local authorities – and as the bulk of state housing was run by Labour-controlled councils, they provided an ever more tempting target in the period of triumphalist Thatcher Government.

We can illustrate this process by considering one of the more positive initiatives directed by central government towards the public housing sector during the 1980s: how to improve the 'problem' council estate. The Priority Estates Project (PEP) was launched by the Department of the Environment in 1979, aiming to 'experiment in, and publicise, ways of improving living conditions on run-down council estates which are difficult to let' (Power 1982: 1).

The project exhorted local authorities to adopt a strategy comprising a localised management and maintenance presence, tenant involvement, interdepartmental co-ordination, modernisation and, of course, council house sales. From this basic recipe, local authorities were encouraged – through promotional literature, seminars and videos – to devise their own blend, according to the characteristics of their estates and the preferences of tenants. The PEP started with three pilot programmes, in Lambeth, Hackney and Bolton. After 1982, its influence extended to an advocacy role for a large number of councils seeking to uplift their 'sink' estates.

The difficult-to-let issue had come to light during the 1970s, as the situation of sheer housing shortage gave way to more complex questions of allocation and control. The single-minded pursuit of new building in the post-war era was now superseded, as years of neglect in maintaining inter-war estates and the design disasters of system building and high-rise coalesced, producing unpopular housing estates in many local authority areas. The nature of these estates also reflected the changing social com-position of council tenants from the late 1960s onwards, as well as wider trends in area deprivation, social and economic disadvantage as the post-war economic boom faded. In the face of this complex interplay of factors, however, the PEP tended to emphasise only one element – poor management.

It is not our purpose here to assess the impact of the Priority Estates Project (for a fuller analysis, see Power 1987). As we will show later, many of the key ideas behind the strategy were taken up in a more wholehearted way by local authorities seeking to regenerate their housing service during the 1980s. But one of the main implications of the PEP strategy was that the ills of council housing could be laid at the door of the councils themselves – the problem estate was simply the sharpest manifestation of insensitive bureaucratic management, a lack of tenant involvement, poor interdepart-mental communication and a lousy repairs service. Central government, meanwhile, evaded responsibility. In the words of the Housing Minister in 1982, 'in many, perhaps most, difficult-to-let estates the central challenge is as much one of management as of expenditure' (DoE 1982: 1). In short, local authorities were to blame for conditions on the estate – and central government support would be limited to cost-free solutions, encourage-ment and advice.

The Priority Estates Project is just one example of the means by which the failure of council housing as a tenure has been underlined and the blame largely attached to the poor operation of local authorities as landlords. We referred to these assumptions as constituting an 'institutional truth' in Chapter 6, as a self-fulfilling prophecy meeting dominant material, political and professional interests. From the mid-1980s, this 'truth' needed to be confirmed ever more vehemently, as the government sought to show that local authority housing was an obviously inferior option not just to owner-occupation, but to other forms of renting as well, whether through the private sector, housing associations or tenant co-operatives. The 'truth' required sustenance and embellishment, and research was duly launched to examine the comparative effectiveness of these rented options for tenants. The findings, however, provided a less convincing indictment of local authority housing management than the government might have hoped.

An apparent vindication of the government's assumptions about housing management in local authorities was provided by the Audit Commission's influential study in 1986. Their national survey underlined poor management performance according to the criteria of 'economy', 'efficiency' and 'effectiveness'. The report painted a picture of local authorities charging rents which were too low to meet the demands of stock maintenance, offering a fragmented form of service delivery to consumers, weighted too heavily towards middle management, hijacked by local councillor intervention, neglecting training needs and providing insufficient incentives to attract a higher calibre of senior staff (Audit Commission 1986). However the Audit Commission's work, which only concerned local government provision, lacked a comparative dimension. For the case against council housing to be argued strongly, it was equally necessary to convince tenants that alternative landlords would offer a higher quality service: that transferring out of council control would provide a better deal.

The other options for renting therefore came under renewed scrutiny from 1987 onwards. The spectre of Rachman still overshadowed attempts to resurrect the private landlord – despite policies to burnish its image and to provide indirect financial support. The extension of assured tenancies, and the introduction of assured shorthold tenancies in the 1988 Housing Act, was thus buttressed by tax relief on investment through the Business Expansion Scheme (BES) introduced in the 1988 Finance Act. Yet subsequent research by Crook and Kemp (1991) suggested that four-fifths of the number of homes could have been built if the public cost of BES (in tax not claimed by the government) had been directed instead to housing associations.

Tenant co-operatives constituted another alternative to local authority renting and they received both financial and rhetorical support from the government accordingly. The provision of section 16 grants (under the 1986 Housing and Building Control Act) to fund tenant-led initiatives, and the accolade granted to various initiatives in Glasgow, London and Liverpool have illustrated this commitment. However, the number of properties owned and managed by co-operatives remained, in relative terms, extremely small, and dramatic expansion remained an unlikely prospect.

Housing associations therefore became the most politically attractive option to the government for council tenants wishing to become landlords. They had an image of being locally based, offering sensitive management, well-equipped to meet 'special' housing needs, and award-winning designs in new build and rehabilitation schemes. There were two further attractions. Rather than being run by local councillors, management committees comprised volunteers, often with a beguiling combination of charitable and entrepreneurial backgrounds, rather than past involvement in municipal socialism. Furthermore, the 1988 Housing Act forced housing associations to rely more heavily on private sector loan finance than before; and public subsidy could be channelled directly through the Housing Corporation, rather than becoming entangled in the politically sensitive morass of central–local government relations and financial controls. The Adam Smith Institute has expressed these advantages clearly enough in the midst of an onslaught on council housing. Housing associations, it claimed,

> have been more responsive to tenants' desires than have local authorities
> .... They have done well in catering for groups in society with special
> needs and in restoring older property, often in the declining city centres.
> They avoid the social stigma attaching to council house estates and their
> rents cannot be manipulated to buy votes in local elections.
>
> (Adam Smith Institute 1983: 57)

The assumed superiority of housing associations was put to the test in the large-scale research programme undertaken by Glasgow University for the Department of the Environment in 1985–7. As we saw in Chapter 5, the research found that intra-tenure differences were so large that any overall judgement as to which were the better landlords would have been invalid. Effectiveness varied according to size and task, as the following summary makes clear:

> Housing associations were the most effective at repairing and, more
> marginally, letting. Councils performed better in aspects of rent collec-
> tion and arrears .... In each tenure sector, small organisational units
> were more effective than the large. The converse relationship applied to
> economy in securing resources. Associations were more expensive than
> councils, and small organisations had higher purchase costs than large
> scale producers of services.
>
> (Centre for Housing Research 1989: 12)

The overall verdict did not, therefore, amount to a damning indictment of poor management in the local authority sector. The myth of the unique failings of council housing services was confounded by empirical in-vestigation. This evidence reflected two trends in particular. First, the government's ability to provide 'exit' options for council tenants was being thwarted by the problems of encouraging 'entry' into other sectors of the rented housing market. Second, it paid testimony to some of the changes in the organisation of service delivery by local authorities during the 1980s – no doubt prompted by the threats contained in government policy – to enhance quality and to shore up defences against the tide of legislation, subsidy reduction and investment ceilings designed to render council housing obsolete. Housing management in local authorities was being reformed from within – and the pay-off for the councils was a more tenacious degree of support from tenants than had once been assumed.

In the following section, we will examine one of the key features in this process of reform: the decentralisation of local authority housing services. Decentralisation offered continuing hope that council housing could endure as a tenure, not just in the hostile climate of the 1980s, but in the future, as a central element in a rapidly changing rented housing market. The MacLennan study found, *inter alia*, that decentralised provision was generally more effective than centralised service provision (Centre for Housing Research 1989: 7). We will therefore analyse the contribution of the decentralisation bandwagon which ran through many local councils during the 1980s, and assess the extent to which it secured more effective and responsive housing services.

REORGANISING COUNCIL HOUSING – DECENTRALISATION

We have suggested that government criticisms of local authority housing management became more virulent during the 1980s, partly to deflect attention from more structural problems facing the sector. But local authorities were not wholly passive victims in the face of this assault. Labour-controlled councils in particular devised strategies to regain a measure of support for their services. Programmes of decentralisation came to the fore as a growing number of councils set up networks of offices on estates or in neighbourhoods in order to establish a more responsive and convenient service for their tenants. Decentralisation rapidly became an article of faith for local authorities seeking to withstand central government pressure, in the hope that tenants would rush to the defence of their housing service just as surely as if their local schools or health services were under attack. By the late 1980s, decentralisation had become a key strategy for many local authorities attempting to ensure survival of council housing in their area.

The wave of interest in housing decentralisation is generally traced back to the decision by Walsall Metropolitan Borough Council in 1981 to set up an ambitious network of thirty-two neighbourhood offices and to abandon a Town Hall-based service (Mainwaring 1987; Seabrook 1984). Drawing on strong political direction and a clear management strategy, the programme was launched as an antidote to the excesses of rigid, bureaucratic hierarchies which characterised most metropolitan housing departments. However, decentralisation seemed to offer more than an administrative rearrangement of deckchairs on the Titanic of council housing. It incorporated a political vision of community involvement and regeneration as well as a critique of the prevailing mode of public service delivery, steeped in the top-down Fabian tradition (see Chapter 5). Decentralisation was an unstable distillation of ideas culled from various sources – community action, local estate-based initiatives, changing management paradigms and, in many areas, the political impact of the 'New Urban Left' (Gyford 1985). The 'ripple effect' of the Walsall experiment was considerable, as more and more local authorities took up decentralisation as a means of improving services and as a riposte to central government criticisms and controls. As the heat of central–local relations grew fiercer during the 1980s, initiatives such as decentralisation became invested with an ever growing range of political and managerial aspirations as the view took hold that local authority services in general, and housing services in particular, would be strengthened as a result (Stoker 1987).

The impact of decentralisation merits analysis, therefore, as a policy in its own right and as an emblem of the strengths and limitations of reforming council housing from within the ever tighter constraints developed by central government policy. Decentralisation covered a wide range of objectives and addressed many of the key weaknesses in council housing management we referred to in Chapter 5. These included: i) the problem of scale – breaking down mass landlordism into a more responsive, local and personalised service; ii) the problem of structure – in which hierarchies were replaced by more dispersed forms of control; iii) the narrow functional range of housing management – whereby neighbourhood provision would offer a more comprehensive span of services; iv) restricted patterns of communications – encouraging more open relationships between different tiers of housing staff and between front-line staff and consumers; v) the fragmentation of housing practice – replacing specialised division of labour with more generic practice; vi) 'top-down' decision-making styles – replaced by a commitment to neighbourhood participation and involvement (Cole *et al.* 1991).

So how far did decentralisation prove to be a successful strategy for local authorities by spanning such a wide spectrum of interest? Decentralisation may have been something of a fashion, but it had tangible consequences in council housing services across the country, as offices were opened, staff recruited, departments reorganised and budgets allocated with varying degrees of ambition and acclaim. However, the way in which the success of decentralisation was gauged changed perceptibly. Most of the early initiatives were propelled by the overriding desire to create a more responsive, more democratic housing service. This rather vague aspiration was dislodged by a new vocabulary – of the accountant rather than the radical local politician or progressive housing officer – emphasising performance appraisal, value for money, economy, efficiency and service effectiveness. The Audit Commission's report laid the ground for this change of emphasis, and the research evaluations of service effectiveness followed in its wake (Centre for Housing Research 1989; School for Advanced Urban Studies 1989).

In the first wave of initiatives, the aims of responsiveness, accessibility and convenience required no further justification or elaboration. They were simply accepted as important ingredients in improving local housing services. Cost implications were secondary, or even overlooked altogether. This position could not be sustained. The second wave of initiatives was set against the mixed fortunes of the early programmes. Certainly some ambitious schemes were downscaled or abandoned on cost grounds. Furthermore, the ever-tightening pressure on resources, the threat of stock transfer and the post-1989 regimes for capital and revenue finance meant that the proclaimed advantages of ideas like decentralisation had to be weighed in the balance against the expenditure implications. For many local authorities, the question was not 'will decentralisation improve our services?', but 'will it be worth the extra cost?'. This immediately raised the question of how 'effectiveness' might be defined. Rounded evaluations of managerial performance and effectiveness would be required to take account of the impact of initiatives like decentralisation.

It would be misleading to assume that all local authorities were in a headlong rush to decentralise their housing services during the 1980s. Survey research of decentralised services in the North of England, for example, uncovered crucial differences between smaller and larger local authorities in their approach to reorganisation (Windle *et al.* 1988). In smaller authorities, structural changes concerned lateral, rather than vertical, responsibilities and channels of communication in the housing department. These councils were not concerned with the devolution of tasks and responsibilities to neighbourhood offices and front-line staff. They were more involved in redefining the span of activities and control exercised by housing officers. In many cases, housing functions were still very fragmented between housing, finance, technical and environmental health departments. Organisational change had been based on the reallocation of functions to achieve the familiar aim of providing a more comprehensive housing service.

In larger housing authorities, a very different pattern emerged as the trend towards decentralisation became well established. A wide variety of organisational structures were adopted. In many cases, area, neighbourhood or project offices were grafted on to the central service in an incremental fashion. As a result, many authorities had a four-tier system of decentralisation. The Walsall model – a skeleton central service surrounded by satellite neighbourhood offices – represented a purer representation of the principles of decentralisation, but it was something of a rarity among local authorities which subsequently decentralised.

From the start, decentralisation embraced both managerial and political objectives, but in practice most local authorities clearly opted for 'consumerist' priorities rather than a 'collectivist' approach, highlighting greater democratisation (Hambleton and Hoggett 1987). Decentralisation proposals were generally framed by housing officers rather than councillors. However, it was often difficult to disentangle the process by which politically generated ideas became jointly developed over time to the point where officers viewed the overall strategy as managerially inspired. While a stronger role for tenant and staff involvement was envisaged by many decentralised authorities, this took second place to improving the public image, convenience and effectiveness of the housing service (Cole *et al.* 1988a).

To what extent did the widespread adoption of decentralisation initiatives mitigate the residualisation of the local authority housing services outlined earlier? In fact, it is difficult to gauge the impact precisely (or even imprecisely), partly due to the general lack of information and monitoring undertaken by local housing authorities. In many cases, the initial impulse behind decentralisation – to provide a more responsive service – soon came up against the barrier of cost. There were usually pressures on both capital spending – through building new local offices or converting accommodation – and revenue spending due to additional staffing, repair demands, computing and training requirements, staff regradings, and so on. Any systematic before–after analysis of the costs of decentralisation by local authorities was, however, very rare.

An assessment of decentralisation is therefore forced to rely on the more impressionistic evidence of the perceptions of key actors in the programmes. An extensive survey of chief housing officers in the North of England, for example, showed that decentralisation tended to reduce the average time to let properties and bring down the number of long-term voids. In more than one-third of decentralised housing services, a local management presence was held to reduce arrears and average repair times, minimise property 'refusals' by applicants and reduce the extent of vandalism on estates (Cole *et al.* 1988b).

There are several problems in interpreting such information. First, chief officers are hardly disinterested observers. The level of financial, personal and professional commitment to decentralisation may be such that chief officers will be loath to admit to difficulties or acknowledge problems. A second set of problems arises in attempting to establish a cause–effect relationship between decentralisation and changes in housing management performance, while controlling for the impact of other variables. Trends in rent arrears, for example, may be influenced by Housing Benefit changes, regardless of the organisational structure in place at the time. Third, any reliance on management indicators accentuates measurable aspects of service provision at the expense of less tangible elements.

If one is to assess the extent to which decentralisation revived the image and quality of service in council housing, it is necessary to refer to the different perceptions of chief officers, front-line staff, elected members and tenants. The different criteria used by these groups provide a more complex picture than the reliance on performance indicators by organisations bereft of systematic and continuous intelligence about the changing nature of the housing service. Any generalised statements about the effectiveness of decentralisation must therefore be clearly related to the interests of different groups involved in the process: officers, elected members and tenants themselves.

For officers, decentralisation tended to promote more generic forms of housing management, which was in itself something of a double-edged sword. It often seemed to increase job satisfaction – front-line staff in particular welcoming the opportunity to take on more varied tasks – but it also increased pressure due to increased demands and the wider span of responsibilities.

We noted in Chapter 5 that the level of councillor intervention in local authority housing management had been more pronounced than in other services. It is not surprising, therefore, to find councillor-led systems of decentralised housing services. Case-study analysis revealed interesting contrasts with officer-dominated schemes, suggesting that differing criteria have been used to assess the outcomes of decentralisation. Elected members focused on the quality of front-line provision, and staff–tenant interaction as the first point of contact in the localised structure. Officers, on the other hand, concentrated on measured management performance and viewed the system as developing outwards from a central hierarchy. The research found that councillors' judgements about the localised housing service were coloured less by statistics than by the complaints and comments of tenants at surgeries about the response and helpfulness of front-line staff in dealing with their problems (Arnold *et al.* 1989b).

The litmus test of organisational restructuring through decentralisation for local authorities was, however, its impact on consumers. How far could programmes for more responsive services win over new support from apparently dissatisfied customers? Could decentralisation turn the tide of disenchantment with state housing? Three factors have seemed particularly significant in influencing tenant perceptions of the housing service. First, the knowledge, approach and attitudes of neighbourhood-based staff were crucial. Tenants placed great emphasis on a friendly and sensitive response from staff, the opportunity to discuss problems in private and the need for action to be taken quickly (Arnold *et al.* 1989a). Research by INLOGOV, for example, found that 50 per cent of tenants rated as a priority 'staff who understood problems', 46 per cent mentioned 'staff who explained things well, and 43 per cent valued 'privacy when talking about personal matters' (Walsh and Spencer 1990). These research findings are perhaps unexceptionable, in that tenants are hardly likely to prefer a hostile or uncaring response from staff, but the priority given to the nature of officer attitudes is striking. Tenants have been far more concerned about the *process* of staff–tenant interaction than the organisational *structure* in which it has taken place. The greater accessibility afforded by decentralisation has been popular, but it has been the manner in which problems are dealt with which has been more significant for tenants. The research underlines the fact that managerial and consumer priorities for reforms to the council housing service are often quite different.

The second main influence on tenant views – the quality of the repairs service – carries echoes of the limitations of the narrow, fragmented base for housing management in local authorities which was discussed in Chapter 5. Tenants were often critical of the speed, quality and organisation of the repairs service, which was rarely decentralised alongside housing functions. Research in Newcastle, for example, found that tenants' responses were shaped by lack of liaison between Housing and Works Departments over repairs inspection, ordering, completion and monitoring and the subsequent division between management and technical functions (Arnold *et al.* 1989a).

The third influence on consumer opinions about decentralised services concerned wider environmental and community issues, extending well beyond mainline housing functions. In many localised services, Neighbourhood Housing Offices became a focus for more generalised concerns about council services. The provision of an estate base has tended to raise expectations for other services to be equally accessible – and continuous 'signposting' by housing officers to other departments often undermined attempts to achieve consumer responsiveness.

On the whole, research evidence has suggested that the strategy of decentralisation proved successful and challenged a priori assumptions about the inevitable shortcomings of local authority housing services. The experience lent support to claims that council housing was in principle capable of reform and revival. Its role had been perennially undermined by the subjugation of public provision to market principles and private-sector material and ideological interests over the years, as we have shown in earlier chapters. Yet, within these constraints, the qualitative aspects of the service were more amenable to change – and the network of local estate offices opened up since 1980 in many local authorities provided a beacon of hope. Decentralisation improved some of the most apparent weaknesses in local authority housing management, and kept alive principles of accessibility, participation and responsiveness.

ENHANCING THE QUALITY OF COUNCIL HOUSING

So how far is it possible to effect a transformation of state housing through internal reorganisation and reform in the tenure? One should not underestimate the limits, as well as the possibilities, of improvements. Decentralisation, for instance, was initially seized on as a relatively cost-free solution to perceived deficiencies in the housing service. It often proved to be anything but – a local presence raised expectations about what could be delivered – and the bill had to be paid eventually. With ceilings on capital investment, and growing external intervention in revenue subsidies, it was not even feasible for local authorities to negotiate freely with their tenants by balancing service improvements against rent increases. Rents were increasing in real terms in any case – even if the council stood still.

Increasingly intrusive financial controls over the operation of local authority housing services called into question the government's enthusiasm to impart the language of 'value for money' and 'effectiveness' as a measure for services in the public sector. The determinacy and applicability of these terms remains open to dispute. The research on housing management for the Department of the Environment, for example, related the concept of effectiveness to 'an understanding of the quality and success of service provision' and the relationship of 'costs to outcomes' according to 'tenant' and the 'government' (Centre for Housing Research 1989: 4). This definition was an unsatisfactory resolution of competing perspectives, and begged questions about how 'outcomes' could be measured or prioritised.

In spite of the government's confident assertions throughout the 1980s about the poor quality of local authority housing services, any such specification of quality is in fact fraught with difficulty. The perspectives of different actors in the process – senior officers, elected members, front-line staff, consumers – require sophisticated appraisal before firm judgements can be made. In practice, quite different criteria will be used by these parties to assess their experience of the service.

As we saw in the previous section, senior managers tend to gauge the quality of the service according to the selected indicators – especially rents, voids, repairs and lettings information. This provides a defined, quantitative and replicable source of material to monitor change – whether across the service as a whole, or with respect to certain functions. This managerial perspective was duly enshrined in government legislation in section 167 (i) of the Local Government and Housing Act 1989, which required all local housing authorities to publish the results of their performance to tenants in the form of prescribed indicators.

The list of indicators emphasised quantitative, rather than qualitative, measures. Most indicators related to input (such as staff ratios) and immediate output measures (such as the number of accepted homeless applicants in a year), expressing the criteria of 'economy' or 'efficiency'. Only a handful were outcome measures which analysed effectiveness in accordance with tenant satisfaction. It was not clear how useful such signals would be in gauging the standards of housing management during the 1990s.

There are both technical and conceptual difficulties involved in devising performance indicators. Analysis of rent arrears information, for example, needs to contend with the vagaries of delayed, and fluctuating, Housing Benefit payments which are beyond the immediate control of the housing department itself. Effectiveness is itself difficult to measure for public services. It is often wrongly expressed as the ratio of immediate output to input (capacity utilisation) – such as the level of vacancy rates in the housing stock. A more properly conceived measure of effectiveness is the relationship between output and outcome – that is, the capacity to provide a service alongside the impact of the service on users. Performance indicators are susceptible to wilful (or unconscious) misinterpretation – and their use was advocated less as a means of meeting the conditions of John Major's 'Citizens' Charter' initiative than of adding substance to criticisms about the inherently poor quality of council housing management. At worst, councils have been forced to provide half-digested statistics, collected for an unclear purpose, devoid of adequate interpretation and giving a misleading signal to those expected to benefit most from the exercise – its customers.

An emphasis on more easily measurable outcomes also formed part of a strategy to retain, or strengthen, central control in those authorities which had taken the step of decentralising. Comparisons could be made between the performance of different sub-areas, with area or neighbourhood managers under increasing pressure to compete with colleagues elsewhere to achieve 'good scores'. This emphasis itself began to skew the priorities for locally-based generic housing management – with priority given to void control work, for example – because this could be readily measured, as opposed to dealing successfully with racial harassment, which defies quantitative assessment.

In practice, the tenant response to local authority housing services has only been incorporated into an evaluation of quality in a casual way. The 'tenant view' is often culled from a one-off survey that may cover issues which have a very low salience for the respondents. The capacity for performance measures to incorporate conflicting or ambiguous tenant views is strictly limited.

As Chapter 5 indicated, independent research has suggested that tenants are in fact less concerned with comparative statistics than with their own recent experience of treatment by housing staff, or the outcome of their last repairs request. The attitude and response of front-line officers are crucial. Tenants do have clear opinions about whether 'their' service has improved or deteriorated over a given period. They are not too concerned about whether an adjacent neighbourhood is performing better or not. There is rarely a 'tenant view' on service quality. There are multiple and conflicting opinions, priorities and experiences – often dependent on the outcome of the most recent problem or issue. The short-term, contingent nature of staff–tenant interaction makes for a more open-ended and indeterminate appraisal of the performance of a local housing service than, say, quarterly void returns. But the quantitative measures are accorded a degree of authority as a more tangible sign of the quality of the service overall.

The increasing pressure on local authorities to improve on their (assumed) poor performance during the 1980s may have in fact provoked a risk that aspects of the housing service which were most important to tenants were neglected. A wide-ranging conceptual model of effectiveness needed to be adopted for such an assessment of housing management, readily incorporating tenant interests and perceptions. In practice, housing staff at the sharp end of the service were having to meet a demanding and conflicting set of expectations from central government, senior managers and consumers – requiring them to be responsive, efficient, caring, flexible, rigorous and amenable in turn. In the midst of this confusion, several local authorities began to rescue tenant views from impending obscurity as a way of promoting support for their services – and in this manner 'customer care' was born.

CARING FOR THE CUSTOMER?

Towards the end of the 1980s a growing number of local authorities initiated 'customer care' programmes for their housing service. The seminal work on customer care claimed that the essence of a successful business was a 'customer obsession' which 'characteristically occurred as a seemingly unjustifiable over-commitment to some form of quality, reliability or service' (Peters and Waterman 1982: 157). The basic idea was simple enough, although Peters and Waterman provided an extended elaboration of the theme: the customer should always be at the heart of business activities and not seen as an interruption to its affairs. Companies which directed expenditure on keeping their customers satisfied would achieve a degree of loyalty which would pay long-term dividends in profitability levels. Companies needed to listen to what both customers and employees were saying and then act upon it. The authors quote numerous examples of this orientation – from the apparent practice of the Walt Disney organisation, where every manager and executive spends one week a year selling popcorn and tickets, to IBM's practice of carrying out employee attitude surveys every three months (Peters and Waterman 1982: Ch. 6). (It was, after all, written ten years before the debacle of Euro-Disney and the mass redundancies announced by IBM.) The customer care ethic comprised active and intensive involvement from all staff, a 'people orientation' and continuous measurement and feedback.

So how did Walt Disney become a paradigm for the organisation of a council housing service in Britain apparently under crisis? There are several reasons, other than a mutual interest in fantasy and happy endings. As the early inflated promises of decentralisation were scaled down, local authorities began to accept that the simple replacement of one set of organisational structures by another did not of itself produce a better service. It was equally necessary to improve communication *processes* in the organisation, and especially between officers and tenants. Several councils were attempting to create a distinctive organisational culture and open style of management which could thrive in a centralised and de-centralised service.

The interest in the customer also accorded with the enthusiasm for tenant satisfaction studies, no matter how one-dimensional or imperfect a barometer they might be. As we saw in Chapter 6, the 1988 Housing Act produced a flurry of MORI opinion surveys undertaken by anxious local authority landlords. While survey results generally recorded a high level of support, in the face of competition tenants had to be cosseted to ensure brand loyalty. Customer care was also attractive in that it borrowed the language of the market place, offering an individualised, rather than collectivist, model of tenant participation. Consumer sovereignty held sway.

The wholesale adoption of American management methods by British local authorities does not have a happy history – as the career of corporate planning and management in the 1970s indicates (Dearlove 1979). However, a form of interpretation of the customer care approach was at hand, through the development of the Public Service Orientation (PSO) promoted by Michael Clarke and John Stewart. PSO smoothed the edges of corporate business-speak, so that the domesticated version of customer care became more palatable. Many of the potential shortcomings of decentralisation – low staff morale, poor communication, distant management – were addressed by customer care. Local authorities were encouraged to become closer to their public, devise rapid complaints procedures, value staff input and promote easy access to decision-takers. Clarke and Stewart summarised the need for change as follows:

> In the procedures of local authorities, the sense of purpose can be lost. In the agenda of the committee, the public can be forgotten. Many tiers in the hierarchy separate chief officer from field worker. The staff can be isolated in their role. The authority protects its boundaries and the departments and sections protect their boundaries. The enclosed local authority has to be challenged.
>
> (Stewart and Clarke 1987: 24)

The Public Service Orientation was an anglicised version of the Peters and Waterman philosophy – even the tone and syntax were similar. PSO, like customer care, seemed to demand short sentences and staccato observations – conveying a beguiling simplicity to organisations facing an increasingly uncertain, complex and threatening future. Possibly for this reason, the talisman of customer care proved irresistible across the retail and service sector in the 1980s, from British Telecom to British Home Stores, from breweries to banks. The message carried particular force, though, for local authority housing departments, confronted with the most fundamental changes since the inception of council housing a hundred years earlier.

The translation of the customer care idiom into practice by housing departments prompted a wide variety of measures – from the transcendental to the merely cosmetic. Initiatives comprised greater use of attitude surveys – of tenants and staff; empowerment programmes – developing local budgets, or setting up complaints and appeals procedures, to strengthen 'citizenship' rights; staff attitudes and demeanour – the 'have a nice day' syndrome from uniformed staff wearing ID badges (first names only); extensive staff training and consultation; improvements to publicity, reception areas, even tidier noticeboards; and the development of customer care codes and service contracts, whereby the council pledges itself to respond by a certain time, or in a certain manner.

While a degree of scepticism may be in order for some of the wilder rhetorical shores of customer care, genuine advances in the service ethic were made by several local authorities as a result. York City Council, for example, devised an interdepartmental system of survey/review/training feedback which wrought considerable changes in priorities and procedures. Welwyn and Hatfield District developed a detailed staff care code, to accompany the customer care code, which committed the authority to providing good working conditions, eliminating discrimination, encouraging promotion on merit, continuous training and listening to employees. While this constituted a moral, rather than legally binding, obligation, the practice at least acknowledged the fact that demoralised staff were unlikely to provide an efficient service, no matter how many performance indicators they were faced with.

Customer care in housing services itself may have been something of a fashion, and the more mechanistic versions failed to acknowledge the fact that the nature of what is consumed in social housing, and the relationship between provider and consumer, cannot be equated so easily with Marks & Spencer. However, customer care may yet prove to be the impetus for more significant and longer-term changes in the organisational culture of housing departments so that renewed support is gained for the service. With the introduction of the compulsory competitive tendering of housing management it will be instructive to assess the different outcomes between those councils which have taken organisational changes seriously and those content with merely cosmetic improvements.

However, even for Marks & Spencer the most sophisticated customer care strategy imaginable was no bulwark against falling retail sales in the context of severe economic recession. Likewise, the ethic in local authorities would not of itself stem the tide running against a properly resourced council housing service. In one analysis of customer care in public services, Harrow and Willcocks have made the obvious but pertinent point that

> whilst this may encourage improved communication and feedback, it cannot contribute much to solving services supply and resource problems, or staff shortages which may be behind the non-delivery or poor quality of service . . . a smiling doctor or nurse is not contributing much to effectiveness when telling a patient that he or she has to wait months for an operation.
>
> (Harrow and Willcocks 1990: 295)

Or, for that matter, a smiling housing officer dealing with a repairs request.

DEVISING A NATIONAL AGENDA

In this chapter we have deliberately selected examples of local authority initiatives aimed at restoring confidence in the provision of housing services in the midst of antagonistic central government policies. The

mixed fortunes of decentralisation and customer care programmes provided grounds, however, for cautious optimism – that council housing was
not yet dead and buried. But what kind of policies would be needed to
ensure that local authorities played a leading role in providing good quality
housing at a modest cost in the 1990s?

Some guiding principles behind such a 'rescue package' for council
housing are outlined below – not as an attempt to recreate the late 1940s,
but to preserve some enduring features of the tenure and locate councils as
one among several social housing agencies – offering a more flexible
pattern of provision which would be attuned to specific local requirements
and conditions in the housing stock.

The prospects for a vigorous promotion of 'social housing' objectives
are now hardly promising, even though the Conservative Governments'
promulgation of the twin virtues of owner-occupation and private renting
has proved vulnerable, when set against the background of structural
economic decline, increased mortgage costs, rising homelessness and the
reluctance of private landlords to invest in housing on a large scale.

Ironically, the intended 'last act' in the decimation of council housing –
the 1989 Housing and Local Government Act – could have become its
salvation. The legislation provided opportunities for central government to
control and increase capital and revenue expenditure more readily than
before, while balancing the differences between councils which arose due
to historical factors, the rate of Right to Buy, different rent-setting regimes
and levels of capital investment. There was greater scope for a central
government committed to public sector housing to enhance housing investment in the short term, by manipulating subsidy and capital spending rules.
Part of this strategy would have depended on parallel financial reforms in
other tenures, to create additional resources for socially directed
investment.

Other potential initiatives were made possible through changing the
internal composition of local authority housing expenditure. There was, for
example, an insistent campaign to lift the restrictions on the spending of the
capital receipts which have accrued from the sale of council houses – under
a phased programme to reduce the risk of overheating the construction
industry. A twelve-month relaxation of these spending restrictions was
eventually introduced by the Major Government at the end of 1992. However, a more developed housing strategy – rather than a panic measure
induced by the downturn in the construction sector – could have gone
further and introduced a system of pooling a proportion of all receipts and
redistributing them to local authorities, through a regional bidding process
and taking account of local housing needs. In releasing this investment,
encouragement could then have been given to schemes in housing stress

areas drawing in private financing, involving housing associations or experimenting with new forms of housing management.

Funding for revenue expenditure by local authorities immediately raises complex issues about the basis of rent setting, and comparability with subsidies and benefits in other tenures (for a review see Hills 1991). The basic principle of historic cost pricing has been integral to the development of council housing. It is now being cast aside in favour of a rather spurious notion of a 'market rent' (when the council itself is usually the main provider of rented housing in the market). Alternative proposals argued for rents to be set on the basis of a proportion of household income, incorporating a regional management and maintenance allowance, estimated depreciation costs and reflecting changing capital values. Local authorities would then have been able to set actual rents around this 'mean', striking a balance between local discretion and central control.

The Conservative White Paper on Housing in 1987 encouraged local authorities to take an enabling role in housing markets, though the precise nature of this function was left obscure. Perhaps it was merely designed to sweeten the pill of sharply reducing the council's role as direct provider of housing. Yet there was scope for a more interventionist strategic function for local authorities in housing markets than simply as a tepid 'enabler'. This would have required the development of opportunities for local authorities to deploy specialist housing expertise in the private sector: the provision of property, legal and estate agency services, repair and improvement for the private sector, mortgage rescue schemes, building for sale, alarm and warden services for elderly private tenants and owner occupiers, loans for property improvement, improvement of homes to mobility standard, and so on. The local authority could then have taken on a more genuinely comprehensive housing function – not as an alternative to landlordism, but as a complementary activity. Links could also have been forged with parallel strategies in urban renewal, economic development and employment regeneration.

In practice, of course, this has not happened: local authorities have been bypassed or ignored in new initiatives. The government has relied increasingly on its 'flexible friend' – the housing association movement – to fulfil this function: in mortgage rescue schemes, for example, or in myriad emergency homelessness initiatives. Yet there is growing evidence that the capacity of housing associations is being overstretched in order to meet the diverse and conflicting demands placed on them (Cope 1990).

We noted at the beginning of the chapter how a particularly distorted notion of 'choice' was applied to the rented housing sector during the 1980s. It hinged on providing an ever increasing variety of exit routes out of the public sector. It would not have been too difficult, in theory at least, to have extended this stunted version of consumer choice to all sectors of the rented market: by permitting transfers into, as well as out of, council landlordism. The comparative strengths and weaknesses of different sectors could then have been put to a genuine test, based less on statistical indicators and more on consumers' own sense of security and their aspirations, perceptions and experiences.

The positive steps taken by several local authorities to improve their housing service during the 1980s could therefore have prompted more fundamental reforms to council housing had they received greater sustenance and support from central government. Nationally, the Labour Party remained ambivalent about the contribution of local authorities in its housing strategy – mindful, no doubt, of the past failings of council housing and the voting power of owner-occupiers. Yet a Labour Government (or non-Conservative alliance) might have been able to stem the process of decline. It could even have given a positive lead, by identifying experimental initiatives which furthered the principles of accountability and participation, and prioritised training as a means of improving management quality, without a parallel obsession to eliminate local authorities as major landlords.

A stronger role for council housing in the early 1990s would not necessarily have required a massive increase in additional resources if judicious use was made of local authorities' unspent capital receipts. Yet the opportunity to effect such a revival in the fortunes of this sector probably passed with the result of the 1992 general election. The Conservatives' victory meant that even modest proposals to rescue council housing gave way to the more familiar and insistent policy of recent years – to eliminate this form of landlordism in the interests of 'choice' and 'diversification'. The introduction of compulsory competitive tendering of housing management became the latest example. The outstanding issue for debate was simply the character of the residual functions left with the local authority – providing hostels for the homeless, perhaps, while 'enabling' other landlords to take over, or manage, their stock.

CONCLUSION

The account in this chapter has challenged the view that local authorities have been uniformly poor landlords, offering an expensive and ineffective service, out of touch with tenants and unable to adapt to changing circumstances. Strategies such as decentralisation and customer care questioned assumptions about lack of responsiveness being an inevitable feature of council housing departments. They indicated possible ways in which service quality, relationships with tenants and standards of management could be enhanced. While the impact of such changes has been relatively modest, more positive support from central government could have resurrected a role of local authorities as both owners and managers of rented housing – even if these activities were in the future to be conducted at arm's length from other local government functions on a quasi-agency basis.

By undertaking reforms to the management, finance and control of public sector housing, genuine opportunities might have arisen for consumers to influence local housing strategies. These aims could have been pursued with tenants acting in partnership with local authorities and receiving endorsement from government policies devised to improve the quality of council housing rather than to bypass or destroy it. Local authorities would have remained as significant providers of rented property, drawing on their considerable resources in both management expertise and capital investment, acting in concert with other social housing agencies to provide a range of decent and affordable housing – which is precisely where the story of council housing in Britain began.

Such a scenario is now, of course, more distant than ever. The government's commitment to home ownership remains sacrosanct, and the management and ownership of rented housing will be passed to larger housing associations and private landlords. It remains to be seen whether this strategy will be successful in sustaining a vibrant rented sector. If it founders, it is likely that many households will still be forced to face up to the risks of owner-occupation at a very early stage in their housing careers. The case for structural change to the system of housing finance, management and development in all tenures remains a compelling one. However, the 1992 election victory of John Major confirmed the view that the *realpolitik* of housing policy points in a different direction to careful policy analysis. The need to mollify the owner-occupied majority, even through ineffective policy and financial instruments, will prevail, and thereby diminish opportunities to develop a more flexible and varied housing system, in which local authorities could have played a significant role. We return to these issues in our Conclusion.

Conclusion: a total eclipse?

The Conservative Governments after 1979 have worked towards a total and final eclipse of council housing as a major tenure in Britain. Fourteen years on, this project is continuing at a steady pace, with initiatives to privatise the housing stock through 'Rent to Mortgages' schemes and to implement compulsory competitive tendering of housing management services.

However, by the early 1990s, the Conservatives had achieved only a partial eclipse. The long-term drift towards residualisation of the public sector was certainly accelerated by Right to Buy sales and the broader sponsorship and subsidy of owner-occupation. A further contraction of council housing was achieved by the virtual cessation of new construction. The refurbishment of council stock was drawn increasingly under the direct control of central government by expanding the activities of Estate Action. A variety of measures have encouraged the transfer of the public stock to alternative landlords through Tenants' Choice, Voluntary Transfer and Housing Action Trusts. Incentives for any but the poor to remain council tenants were removed steadily, as universal investment subsidies were displaced by means-tested Housing Benefit. Council rents rose substantially towards market levels without a corresponding rise in investment in modernisation and maintenance of the stock. Management expenditure was limited by central government assumptions about service levels when setting subsidy. The legislative and financial framework was designed to ensure the uncompetitiveness and virtual disappearance of British council housing, even as a tenure for the poor.

It is possible to summarise the government's approach to ending council housing in terms of two basic strategies: to turn council tenants into owner-occupiers and to offer tenants increasing opportunities to transfer to other landlords. Since 1979, the government has lacked neither determination nor ingenuity in devising various means to 'push' tenants out of the public sector. The government has found it less straightforward to control 'pull' factors, by ensuring that the alternatives were duly inviting and accessible. The unexpected loyalty shown by tenants to council land-lords was in part a demonstration that the service provided by many local authorities was not as dismal as portrayed by central government; but it also stemmed from a hard-headed calculation that the apparent attractions of home ownership or non-municipal landlordism also carried risks and insecurities. This caution was borne out by the housing market conse-quences of the economic recession in the late 1980s and early 1990s.

The housing market boom of the mid-1980s was succeeded by a cyclical peak in income/house price ratios and rising interest rates, followed by record repossession levels, growing mortgage arrears, static or falling house prices, market stagnation, a dramatic contraction in private house-building, a new wave of bankruptcies in the construction industry and a rapid increase in the number of homeless households and those living on the streets. The government's tentative support to building societies and housing associations to develop 'mortgage rescue schemes' was hardly the outcome desired by the enthusiasts for owner-occupation in the Conserva-tive administration when embarking on their housing revolution.

Real doubts must surround the potential for a further substantial increase in owner-occupation, even if the recession eases. The 'economic miracle' of Thatcherism has now yielded to a general recognition of the persistence of the long-term relative weakness of the British economy. In this context, the increasingly expensive government commitment to subsidising owner-occupation, seen previously as inviolate, has become subject to a growing challenge. Quite apart from its inefficiency and inequity in failing to increase new house production or to provide support to those with the least means, the contribution of mortgage tax-relief in fuelling the upward spiral of house prices was increasingly recognised as having highly damaging consequences for the British macro-economy (Muellbauer 1990). The accumulation of housing wealth and related growth in private consumption of predominantly imported manufactures caused by 'equity leakage' was seen more readily as being bought at the cost of future employment. Any government would run significant political risks in belatedly extending its general principle of 'targeting' to mortgage tax-relief, or developing such supply-side measures as reforms to land-use planning controls which have hitherto had the general effect of protecting the interests and property values of middle-class households.

What does the future hold for home ownership in Britain? At the time of writing, the cyclical changes familiar to the development of owner-occupation since the war seem likely to contain more 'slump' than 'boom' in the future, as the economic upturn is further delayed. The prospects for economic integration with other EC countries are also less certain now than they were at the start of the decade. It is still quite likely that the vulnerabilities of the British housing system will be 'exported', and become played out on a larger European stage, as the growth of a second-hand owner-occupier market gathers pace elsewhere (Ball 1991).

It would seem extremely difficult to achieve the final elimination of council housing through the further extension of owner-occupation during the 1990s. The displacement of local authorities by alternative landlords is also proving far from straightforward. Deregulation and other liberalising measures in the private rented sector have failed to produce a large-scale upsurge in new lettings at rents affordable to low-income households or attractive to middle-income households who continue to turn to owner-occupation. The limited impact of the Business Expansion Scheme underlines the difficulties in achieving a full resuscitation of private renting. It is likely that the government will explore the prospects of devising further tax concessions for institutional landlords, but the prospects remain uncertain.

The search for private capital to supplement government resources for housing associations has also proved of limited success in compensating for the decline in council house building. Even if building output for owner-occupation recovered quickly from the slump, it has been estimated that a further 100,000 extra dwellings would be required in Britain each year until 2001 (Institute of Housing 1992b). With local authorities completing less than 10,000 dwellings annually, housing associations were scheduled by the government to double their output to 40,000 dwellings per annum; but even if this target were achieved, which is unlikely, it would still leave a major shortfall in new homes to meet estimated demand. The increased reliance of housing associations upon private funding has made the 'affordability' of rents a central, and problematic, issue and there is a continuing concern over the reluctance of major institutional investors to become involved in the finance of social housing.

When we began writing this book it seemed that, just as housing could be viewed as the sector to be 'first in' to the welfare state, albeit less wholeheartedly than other services, so it might be the 'first out', as Conservative policy cast an increasing shadow over council housing and every other tenure was burnished by government promotion and support. It has since become clear that owner-occupation, private renting, and housing associations each face barriers to their expansion, while the development of co-operatives in recent years remains small in absolute terms. In 1993, over one-fifth of British households still lived in the local authority sector. The final eclipse of council housing had not yet occurred.

In housing, of course, we have stressed the popularity of the first and biggest 'opt-out' of them all, the right to buy council houses. Also, we have underlined the relative strength of the ideology of private ownership in relation to housing. However, even in housing the general drift of

Conservative policy after 1979 has provoked not only a mounting economic 'rationality deficit' in housing, but also a related political challenge. Many tenants have mounted strong resistance to later variants of the housing 'opt-out' strategy. Even where stock transfers have taken place, tenants have often campaigned for, and achieved, concessions compelling their new landlords to accept modifications which bring the new tenancy arrangements into a greater conformity with tenants' previous experiences of public renting.

The greater pragmatism which characterised housing debates by the end of the 1980s was exemplified by the significantly different responses to the two inquiries chaired by the Duke of Edinburgh in 1985 and 1991 (Inquiry into British Housing 1985, 1991). While the first, with its call for major reforms in housing finance – including the replacement of mortgage interest tax relief by alternative subsidy arrangements – was dismissed immediately by government ministers, the second report attracted a less hostile official response. Through both reports the Inquiry favoured a 'pluralism of providers' of rented housing – with a growth in the involvement of housing associations, co-operatives and private landlords – but it identified also the remit of councils as being more than that of enablers in housing provision. The second Inquiry argued for an end to conflict between central and local government and for a continuing and substantial role for councils (albeit in a more 'free-standing' form removed from traditional public sector finance) as *providers* of housing.

LOOKING TO THE FUTURE

The Conservative Governments have reaped a considerable political reward since 1979 for ignoring the growing consensus among housing analysts, and focusing their efforts on supporting the mass of the population in their desire to remain home owners. The cost of this political project is, however, becoming increasingly difficult to bear, and it is likely that the government will seek new ways of reducing its financial commitment to owner-occupation without too much political pain. The view of the members of the Inquiry into British Housing, echoed elsewhere, was that government policy would be better directed to sustaining a lively rented sector, so that households were not forced to take on the vagaries of home ownership at a very early stage in their housing careers. The case for structural change to the housing finance system in all tenures in the British housing market is more compelling than ever, but electoral considerations will continue to inhibit any fundamental transformation.

The extent to which the privatisation of state housing has foreshadowed strategies towards state education and health services remains worthy of attention. The current Major administration continues to encourage 'opt-out' schools and hospitals operating as independent cost centres. The direct role of local government is being further eroded. The development of a two-tier system of public services – with those services dependent directly on central government given more support and funding than those remaining in the local authority sector – will continue. Yet this policy of creeping privatisation is likely to be stripped of the triumphalist rhetoric which accompanied the sale of council housing in the early 1980s; instead, the vocabulary will become imbued with a new terminology of citizenship, quality and responsiveness rather than the harsher tones of the free market first and last. The evidence of housing policies suggests that public sector agencies will prove initially resistant to strategies designed to undermine them, and that the financial inducements to shift consumer preferences towards private provision will have to be considerable. Yet the foundations for parallel policy changes in other sectors of the welfare state have now been laid; for example, in the development of 'quasi-market' regimes in health and education which mirror the current structure and funding of the social housing sector (Le Grand 1990; Satsangi 1992).

Some other books on British housing, written from the perspectives of both the Left and Right, have ended with bold and detailed blueprints for the future. These can be vehicles for the construction of some exhilarating, innovative and ideologically consistent scenarios. However, read again in later years, they often resemble beached whales, stranded by subsequent shifts in economic and political tides or the failure of long-running currents to change. We hope to avoid this pitfall, but we cannot resist tempting fate by sketching some likely future trends in housing policy during the 1990s.

This conclusion is being written one year on from the Conservatives' election victory in 1992. While we hesitate to anticipate the form and impact of new housing legislation, it is reasonable to assume that council housing will decline even more rapidly. The financial regime for local authority housing departments consolidated in 1989 will start to bite, so that the transfer of stock to alternative landlords or to Housing Action Trusts – under DoE guidelines – will be seen by an increasing number of councils as the only means of meeting local housing needs. This strategy is likely to have a greater impact than any 'Rent to Mortgage' schemes proposed by the government, if the experience of pilot schemes in Scotland, Wales and Basildon is any guide. However, the limitations on the scale of transfers will also be set by the capacity of other agencies, notably housing associations, to respond.

Our conclusion is that the hastening of British council housing into oblivion rests more on ideological zealotry than on a rational and balanced analysis of the tenure's past performance and future potential. In previous chapters we have described council housing's significant shortcomings: the failure to empower users through effective participation in the design process or in management; paternalism, remoteness and (in some cases) inefficiency; and the inability or unwillingness of local authorities to give significant redress to racial and gender inequalities and discrimination. Problems of producer power and bureaucratic rigidity have indeed been critical problems in a public housing service which the Left in Britain was slow to identify, let alone confront. However, many of the weaknesses of council housing can be traced to its origins and development in a society in which the power and ideology of private property and other capitalist interests have exercised a powerful constraining force on the quality, cost and efficiency of the service which could be offered. The shifting patterns of the British class structure have left their mark on public housing, particularly in the pressures caused by the associated effects of economic restructuring and the residualisation of council housing. Similarly, local authority housing management has been undertaken in a wider and more profound context of racism and sexism which could not be confronted simply within 'housing policy' alone. The participation of tenants in housing affairs has been limited, but this is congruent with a general British political system and cultural tradition in which participation and a truly active citizenship have confronted long-standing and continuing obstacles.

More positively, we have been able to point to the very real successes of council housing which challenge the 'institutional truths' and conventional wisdoms of an indelibly marred and necessarily second-rate tenure. Some past design failures and architectural indulgences have undoubtedly served to undermine the legitimacy of public housing, by establishing a dominant image of the sector in the vandalised tower block. However, we have seen that most council housing has been successful and popular, offering standards and amenities which the private sector could not match. The Conservatives in the 1980s simply reaped the political dividend from this long-term national investment in good housing through their Right to Buy strategy. In a similar vein, there is considerable evidence of efficient and responsive management practice which compares with anything which can be offered currently by alternative landlords. Survey evidence, more qualitative social research and the actions of many tenants all serve to question the view that local authority housing is an overwhelmingly unpopular form of housing consumption. While many tenants are highly critical, many more express satisfaction with their housing circumstances, certainly in relation to likely alternatives.

Finally, the historic-cost basis of local authority rents has been a crucial factor in permitting affordable rents in the tenure. This aspect is now being jettisoned in favour of support for capital-value and market rents. The detailed practices of past municipal rent-fixing are certainly a subject for critical scrutiny, but the historic-cost principle, and the related issue of public land acquisition, have been neglected dimensions in debates about the viability of the social housing sector. Indeed, in this respect, council housing has been too competitive, compared with other modes of provision, rather than not competitive enough.

Chapter 8 examined recent developments in the administration of local authority housing services which have brought significant improvements for many tenants. Other changes would require broader social and political change. Real progress in tenant participation, for example, must be based upon constitutional and educational reforms – and not just public relations campaigns – sustaining an 'active citizenship' which means more than offering alternatives to those with the private resources required to make real 'choices'. Greater housing access and choice for women, black people, one-parent households, the disabled, the elderly, the young, the single, lesbians and gay people, and others who do not 'fit' the present housing system, is dependent significantly upon wider change. A genuinely comprehensive housing programme would also need to tackle issues of housing quality and supply, and to look beyond the question of tenure which has so dominated government policy since the war.

In the past, council housing has not been a tenure noted for its democracy, efficiency, participation and equity. The potential for owner-occupation, alternative landlords or housing co-operatives to meet such objectives more effectively is, however, open to question. Progress could be achieved by working with the strengths of public sector provision, rather than by sweeping denunciations of its principles and value. It is still possible that disparate economic forces in Britain and Europe during the 1990s will compel changes in housing tenure, leading to a better balance between owning and renting in local housing markets, more attuned to households' changing life-style requirements for accommodation. Yet this is less likely to occur as a result of conscious government policy than through the continuing pressures on owner-occupation at the margins. More diverse forms of ownership and management – involving councils, housing associations and co-operatives – may also emerge in the next ten years, and this may perhaps broaden housing opportunities. This would be far better achieved through authentic partnerships between a range of housing agencies rather than through shotgun weddings of unwilling suitors.

As housing policy unfolds in the 1990s, council tenants will be faced with further experiments with their lives, through ever more elaborate schemes to dispose of the housing stock. It is ironic that this is taking place at the very time when local authorities have been working with their tenants to improve the quality of the service, against the odds. These initiatives have contained set-backs, delays and conflicts, in the nature of democratic management seeking to break with prevailing practice and to confront deeply-rooted structures. However, such activity, combining central government support with local imagination, had offered the brightest hope of better future housing services for those households marginalised by the relentless and misguided pursuit of market miracles in housing policy since 1979. But if council housing is indeed eclipsed in the next few years, how much longer will it be before the sun sets on the rest of the British welfare state?

Bibliography

Abel-Smith, B. and Titmuss, K. (eds) (1987) *The Philosophy of Welfare*, London: Allen & Unwin.

Adam Smith Institute (1983) *Omega Report: Local Government Policy*, London: Adam Smith Institute.

Addison, P. (1977) *The Road to 1945: British Politics and the Second World War*, London: Quartet Books.

Anderson, D. (1981) *Breaking the Spell of the Welfare State*, London: Social Affairs Unit.

Anderson, D. and Marsland, D. (eds) (1983) *Home Truths*, London: Social Affairs Unit.

Anderson, R., Bulos, M. and Walker, S. (1985) *Tower Blocks*, London: Polytechnic of the South Bank/Institute of Housing.

Andrews, C.L. (1979) *Tenants and Town Hall*, London: HMSO.

Arendt, H. (1961) *Between Past and Future*, London: Faber.

Arnold, P., Cole, I. and Windle, K. (1989a) *Decentralisation in Newcastle: The Tenant Perspective*, Housing Decentralisation Research Project Research Working Paper 7, School of Urban and Regional Studies, Sheffield: Sheffield City Polytechnic.

Arnold, P., Cole, I. and Windle, K. (1989b) *Decentralisation in Leeds: The Role of Local Councillors*, Housing Decentralisation Research Project Research Working Paper 8, School of Urban and Regional Studies, Sheffield: Sheffield City Polytechnic.

Association of Metropolitan Authorities (1985) *Defects in Housing, Part 3: Repair and Modernisation of Traditional Built Dwellings*, London: AMA.

Audit Commission (1986) *Managing the Crisis in Council Housing*, London: HMSO.

Ball, M. (1978) 'British housing policy and the housebuilding industry', *Capital and Class* 4: 78–99.

—— (1983) *Housing Policy and Economic Power*, London: Methuen.

—— (1991) 'Housing markets and financial liberalisation in Europe', Abstract for presentation to Housing Studies Association Conference, *Housing and Europe*, University of Oxford.

Barlow, J. (1987) 'The housing crisis and its local dimensions', *Housing Studies* 2, 1: 28–41.

Bassett, K. (1984) 'Labour, socialism and local democracy' in M. Boddy and C. Fudge (eds) *Local Socialism?*, London: Macmillan.

Bennett, F. (1987) 'What future for Social Security?' in A. Walker and C. Walker, (eds) *The Growing Divide: A Social Audit 1979–87*, London: Child Poverty Action Group.

Bentham, G. (1986) 'Socio-tenurial polarisation in the United Kingdom 1953–83: income evidence', *Urban Studies* 23, 2: 157–62.

Birchall, J. (1988) *Building Communities the Co-operative Way*, London: Routledge & Kegan Paul.

Black, J. and Stafford, D.C. (1988) *Housing Policy and Finance*, London: Routledge & Kegan Paul.

Booker, C. (1979) 'City of Towers': contribution to *Where We Live Now*, series broadcast on BBC2.

Bosanquet, N. (1983) *After The New Right*, London: Heinemann Educational.

—— (1987) 'Interim report: housing' in C. Jowell, C. Airey and L. Brook (eds) *British Social Attitudes: 1986 Report*, London: Social and Community Planning Research.

Bowley, M. (1945) *Housing and the State, 1919–1944*, London: Allen & Unwin.

Boys, J. (1989) 'From Alcatraz to the OK Corral: images of class and gender' in J. Attfield and P. Kirkham (eds) *A View from the Interior: Feminism, Women and Design*, London: The Women's Press.

British Market Research Bureau (1989) *Housing Tenure*, London: Building Societies Association.

Brittan, S. (1977) 'The economic tensions of British democracy' in E. Tyrrell (ed.) *The Future That Doesn't Work*, London: Doubleday.

—— (1983) *The Role and Limits of Government: Essays in Political Economy*, London: Temple Smith.

Broady, M. (1968) *Planning for People: Essays in the Social Context of Planning*, London: National Council of Social Service.

Brown, C. (1984) *Black and White Britain: the Third PSI Survey*, London: Heinemann.

Bulos, M. and Walker, S. (1988) 'A call for intensive management: the UK experience' in N. Teymur, T. Markus and T. Woolley (eds) *Rehumanising Housing*, London: Butterworth.

Burnett, J. (1986) *A Social History of Housing, 1815–1985* 2nd edn, London: Methuen.

Byrne, D. and Damer, S. (1980) 'The state, the balance of class forces and early working class housing legislation' in Political Economy of Housing Workshop, *Housing Construction and the State*, London: Political Economy of Housing Workshop.

Cantle, E. (1986) 'The deterioration of public housing' in P. Malpass (ed.) *The Housing Crisis*, London: Croom Helm.

Castells, M. (1977) *The Urban Question: a Marxist Approach*, London: Edward Arnold.

—— (1978) *City, Class and Power*, London: Macmillan.

—— (1983) *The City and the Grassroots*, London: Edward Arnold.

Central Housing Advisory Committee (1944) *Design of Dwellings* (Dudley Report), London: HMSO.

—— (1969) *Council Housing: Purposes, Procedures and Priorities*, London: HMSO.

Centre for Housing Research (1989) *The Nature and Effectiveness of Housing Management in England*, A Report to the Department of the Environment, University of Glasgow, London: HMSO.

Champion, A.G., Green, A.E. and Owen, D.W. (1986) 'Housing, labour mobility and unemployment', Paper to ESRC/Rowntree Housing Studies Group Conference *Housing and Labour Markets*, University of Newcastle-upon-Tyne, Mimeo.

Cherry, G. (1988) *Cities and Plans: the Shaping of Urban Britain in the Nineteenth and Twentieth Centuries*, London: Edward Arnold.

Cicourel, A. (1964) *Method and Measurement in Sociology*, New York: Free Press of Glencoe.

City University (1977) *Housing Training*, Education and Training for Housing Work Project, London: City University.

Clapham, D. (1989a) 'Goodbye council housing?', *Housing Review* 38, 4: 100-2.

—— (1989b) *Goodbye Council Housing?*, London: Unwin Hyman.

Clapham, D., Kemp, P. and Smith, S.J. (1990) *Housing and Social Policy*, London: Macmillan Education.

Clapham, D. and MacLennan, D. (1983) 'Residualisation of public housing – a non-issue', *Housing Review* 32: 1, 9–10.

Clarke, J. (1979) 'Capital and culture: the post-war working class revisited' in J. Clarke, C. Critcher and P. Johnson (eds) *Working Class Culture: Studies in History and Theory*, London: Hutchinson.

Clarke, J., Cochrane, A. and Smart, C. (1987) *Ideologies of Welfare: From Dreams to Disillusion*, London: Hutchinson.

Clarke, J., Critcher, C. and Johnson, R. (1979) *Working Class Culture: Studies in History and Theory*, London: Hutchinson in association with the Centre for Contemporary Cultural Studies, University of Birmingham.

Coates, K. and Silburn, R. (1980) *Beyond the Bulldozer*, Nottingham: Department of Adult Education, University of Nottingham.

Cockburn, C. (1977) *The Local State*, London: Pluto Press.

Cole, I., Arnold, P. and Windle, K. (1988a) *Decentralisation – The Views of Elected Members*, Housing Decentralisation Research Project Research Working Paper 4, Department of Urban and Regional Studies, Sheffield: Sheffield City Polytechnic.

Cole, I., Arnold P. and Windle, K. (1988b) *The Impact of Decentralisation*, Housing Decentralisation Research Project Research Working Paper 5, Department of Urban and Regional Studies, Sheffield: Sheffield City Polytechnic.

—— (1991) 'Decentralised housing services – back to the future?' in D. Donnison and D. MacLennan (eds) *The Housing Service of the Future*, Essex: Longman/Institute of Housing.

Cole, I. and Wheeler, R. (1986) *New Directions in Housing Policy – The Challenge for Building Societies*, London: Chartered Building Societies Institute.

Coleman, A. (1985) *Utopia on Trial: Vision and Reality in Planned Housing*, London: Hilary Shipman.

Coles, A. (1989) 'Satisfying Preference', *Housing Review* 38: 4.

Community Development Project (1976) *Whatever Happened to Council Housing?* London: CDP Information and Intelligence Unit.

Conservative Party (1992) *The Best Future for Britain: Conservative Manifesto 1992*, London: Conservative Central Office.

Conservative Political Centre (1950) *Home Ownership*, London: Conservative Political Centre.

Cooke, P. (1983) *Theories of Planning and Spatial Development*, London: Hutchinson.

Cooney, E. (1974) 'High flats in local authority housing in England and Wales since 1945' in A. Sutcliffe (ed.) *Multi-Storey Living: the British Working Class Experience*, London; Croom Helm.

Cooper, S. (1985) *Public Housing and Private Property*, London: Gower.

Cope, H. (1990) *Housing Associations: Policy and Practice*, London: Macmillan.

Cousins, C. (1987) *Controlling Social Welfare*, Sussex: Wheatsheaf Books.

Cowling, M. and Smith S. (1984) 'Home ownership, socialism and realistic socialist policy', *Critical Social Policy* 9: 64–8.

Craig, F.W. (1970) *British General Election Manifestos 1918–1966*, Chichester: Political References Publications.

Crook, A. and Kemp, P. (1991) 'The impact of the Business Expansion Scheme on the provision of rented housing', *Housing Research Findings No. 29*, York: Joseph Rowntree Foundation.

Crosland, A. (1971) quoted in the *Guardian*, 15 June 1971.

Crossman, R.H.S. (1975) *The Diaries of a Cabinet Minister* vol. 1, London: Hamish Hamilton and Jonathan Cape.

Cullingworth, J. (1966) *Housing and Local Government*, London: Allen & Unwin.

Damer, S. (1980) 'State, class and housing: Glasgow 1885–1919' in J. Melling (ed.) *Housing, Social Policy and the State*, London: Croom Helm.

Daunton, M. (1983) *House and Home in the Victorian City: Working Class Housing 1850-1914*, London: Edward Arnold.

—— (1984) Introduction to M. Daunton (ed.) *Councillors and Tenants: Local Authority Housing in English Cities 1919–39*, Leicester: Leicester University Press.

Deakin, N. (1987) *The Politics of Welfare*, London: Methuen.

Dearlove, J. (1979) *The Reorganisation of British Local Government*, London: Cambridge University Press.

Dearlove, J. and Saunders, P. (1984) *Introduction to British Politics*, Cambridge: Polity Press.

Dennis, N. (1970) *People and Planning*, London: Faber.

—— (1971) *Public Participation and Planners' Blight*, London: Faber.

Department of the Environment (DoE) (1977a) *Housing Policy: A Consultative Document*, Cmnd 6851, London: HMSO.

—— (1977b) *Housing Policy Technical Volume 1*, London: HMSO.

—— (1980) *Development Control: Policy and Practice*, Circular 22/80, London: HMSO.

—— (1981a) *Local Authority Project Control: New Procedures*, Circular 9/81, London: HMSO.

—— (1981b) *An Investigation of Difficult to Let Housing* vols 1–3, London: HMSO.

—— (1982) *Press Notice: Improving Problem Council Estates* 11 May 1992, London: HMSO.

—— (1989) *The Nature and Effectiveness of Housing Management in England*, a report to the Department of the Environment by the Centre for Housing Research, University of Glasgow, London: HMSO.

Dibblin, J. (1989) 'Homefront', *Roof* 14, 3: 44.

Dickens, P. (1981) 'A case study of reformist state intervention: the introduction of rent control policies in Britain, 1915' in A. Blowers, C. Brook, P. Dunleavy and L. McDowell (eds) *Urban Change and Conflict: an Interdisciplinary Reader*, London: Harper & Row in association with the Open University Press.

Dickens, P. (1990) *Urban Sociology: Society, Locality and Human Nature*, Hemel Hempstead: Harvester Wheatsheaf.

Dickens, P., Duncan, S., Goodwin, M. and Gray, F. (1985) *Housing, States and Localities*, London: Methuen.

Donnelly, D. (1980) 'Are we satisfied with "housing satisfaction"?', *Built Environment* 6: 29–34.

Donnison, D. and Ungerson, C. (1982) *Housing Policy*, Harmondsworth: Penguin Books.

Dresser, M. (1984) 'Housing policy in Bristol, 1919–30' in M. Daunton (ed.) *Councillors and Tenants: Local Authority Housing in English Cities, 1919–39*, Leicester: Leicester University Press.

Duncan, J. (1981) *Housing and Identity: Cross-Cultural Perspectives*, London: Croom Helm.

Duncan, S. and Goodwin, M. (1988) *The Local State and Uneven Development*, Cambridge: Polity Press.

Duncan, S. and Greaves, K. (1989) 'Better the devil you know?', *Housing* 25, 5: 20-3.

Dunleavy, P. (1977) 'Protest and quiescence in urban politics: a critique of pluralist and structuralist Marxist views', *International Journal of Urban and Regional Research* 1: 193–218; reprinted in A. Blowers *et al.* (eds) *Urban Change and Conflict*, London: Harper & Row, 1982.

—— (1979) 'The urban bases of political alignment', *British Journal of Political Science* 9: 409–43.

—— (1980) *Urban Political Analysis*, London: Macmillan.

—— (1981a) *The Politics of Mass Housing in Britain 1945–75: a Study of Corporate Power and Professional Influence in the Welfare State*, Oxford: Clarendon Press.

—— (1981b) 'Professions and policy change: notes towards a model of ideological corporatism', *Public Administration Bulletin* August: 3–16.

—— (1982) 'Public housing', Unit 26, D202, *Urban Change and Conflict*, Open University, Milton Keynes: Open University Press.

—— (1986) 'The growth of sectoral cleavages and the stabilization of state expenditures', *Society and Space* 4: 129–44.

Dyos, H. (n.d.) 'The slum observed' in *The Origins of the Social Services*, London: New Society.

Edgell, S. and Duke, V. (1983) 'Gender and social policy: the impact of public expenditure cuts and the reaction to them', *Journal of Social Policy* 12, 3: 357–78.

Edwards, R. (1986) *No Say? No Way! – a Review of the Tenants' Participation Advisory Service, 1980-86*, Edinburgh: Scottish Council for Voluntary Organisations.

Elliott, P. (1972) *The Sociology of the Professions*, London: Macmillan.

Elliott, P. and McCrone, D. (1982) *The City: Patterns of Domination and Conflict*, London: Macmillan.

Emms, P. (1990) *Social Housing: a European Dilemma?* Bristol: School for Advanced Urban Studies, University of Bristol.

Englander, D. (1983) *Landlord and Tenant in Urban Britain, 1838–1918*, Oxford: Clarendon Press.

Finnigan, R. (1984) 'Council housing in Leeds, 1919–39: social policy and urban change' in M. Daunton (ed.) *Councillors and Tenants: Local Authority Housing in English Cities, 1919–39*, Leicester: Leicester University Press.

Flynn, R. (1988) 'Political acquiescence, privatisation and residualisation in British housing policy', *Journal of Social Policy* 17: 289–312.

Foot, M. (1975) *Aneurin Bevan 1945–60*, St. Albans: Paladin.

Forrest, R. (1982) 'The social implications of council house sales' in J. English (ed.) *The Future of Council Housing*, London: Croom Helm.

Forrest, R. and Murie, A. (1983) 'Residualisation and council housing: aspects of the changing social relations of housing tenure', *Journal of Social Policy* 12: 453–68.

—— (1986) 'Marginalisation and subsidised individualism: the sale of council houses in the restructuring of the British welfare state', *International Journal of Urban and Regional Research* 10: 46–65.

—— (1988) *Selling the Welfare State: the Privatisation of Public Housing*, London: Routledge.

—— (1990a) 'A dissatisfied state? consumer preferences and council housing in Britain', *Urban Studies* 27, 5: 617–35.

—— (1990b) 'Profits of doom', *Roof* 15, 5: 38–41.

Forrest, R., Murie, A. and Williams, P. (1990) *Home Ownership: Differentiation and Fragmentation*, London: Hyman.

Franklin, A. (1990) 'Ethnography and housing studies', *Housing Studies* 5, 2: 92–111.

Freidson, E. (1970) *Profession of Medicine*, New York: Dodd, Meade & Co.

Fudge, C. (1984) 'Decentralisation: socialism goes local?' in M. Boddy and C. Fudge (eds) *Local Socialism?*, London: Macmillan.

Furbey, R. (1974) 'National and local in social class relations: some evidence from three Scottish cities', *Social and Economic Administration* 8, 3: 192–219.

Furbey, R. and Goodchild, B. (1986a) 'Method and methodology in housing user research', *Housing Studies* 1, 3: 166–81.

—— (1986b) *Housing in Use: Standards in the Public Sector*, Sheffield: Pavic Publications, Sheffield City Polytechnic.

Galbraith, J.K. (1989) 'In pursuit of the simple truth', *Guardian*, 28 July: 23.

Gallagher, P. (1982) 'The ideology of housing management' in J. English (ed.) *The Future of Council Housing*, London: Croom Helm.

Gallup Omnibus Report (1988) *Council Tenants*, London: Social Surveys (Gallup Poll) Limited.

Gamble, A. (1974) *The Conservative Nation*, London: Routledge & Kegan Paul.

—— (1985) *Britain in Decline*, 2nd edn, London: Macmillan.

—— (1986) 'The political economy of freedom' in R. Levitas (ed.) *The Ideology of the New Right*, Cambridge: Polity Press.

—— (1988) *The Free Economy and the Strong State: The Politics of Thatcherism*, London: Macmillan.

Gauldie, E. (1974) *Cruel Habitations*, London: Allen & Unwin.

George, V. and Wilding, P. (1985) *Ideology and Social Welfare*, 2nd edn, London: Routledge & Kegan Paul.

Giddens, A. (1973) *The Class Structure of the Advanced Societies*, London: Hutchinson.

Ginsburg, N. (1979) *Class, Capital and Social Policy*, London: Macmillan.

Glass, R. (1989) *Cliches of Urban Doom and Other Essays*, Oxford: Basil Blackwell.

Goldthorpe, J. and Lockwood, D. (1968–9) *The Affluent Worker*, (3 vols), Cambridge: Cambridge University Press.

Goodchild, B. (1991) 'Postmodernism and housing: a guide to design theory', *Housing Studies* 6, 2: 130–44.

Goodchild, B. and Furbey, R. (1986) 'Standards in housing design: a review of the main changes since the Parker Morris report', *Land Development Studies* 3: 79–99.

Gough, I. (1979) *The Political Economy of the Welfare State*, London: Macmillan.

Gould, F. and Roweth, B. (1980) 'Public spending and social policy', *Journal of Social Policy* 9, 3: 337–57.

Gray, M. (1968) *The Cost of Council Housing*, London: Institute of Economic Affairs.

Gurney, C. (1990) *The Meaning of the Home in the Decade of Owner-Occupation*, Working Paper No. 88, Bristol: School for Advanced Urban Studies.

Gyford, J. (1985) *The Politics of Local Socialism*, London: Allen & Unwin.

Gyford, J., Leach, S. and Game, C. (1989) *The Changing Politics of Local Government*, London: Unwin Hyman.

Hague, C. (1990) 'The development and politics of tenant participation in British council housing', *Housing Studies* 6, 1: 44–56.

Hambleton, R. and Hoggett, P. (eds) (1984) *The Politics of Decentralisation*, Working Paper No. 46, Bristol: School of Advanced Urban Studies

—— (1987) 'Beyond bureaucratic paternalism' in P. Hoggett and R. Hambleton *Decentralisation and Democracy: Localising Public Services*, Occasional Paper 28, Bristol: School for Advanced Urban Studies.

Hamnett, C. (1984) 'Housing the two nations: socio-tenurial polarisation in England and Wales 1960–81', *Urban Studies* 21, 3: 389–405.

Hamnett, C. and Randolph, B. (1988) *Cities, Housing and Profits: Flat Break-Up and the Decline of Private Renting*, London: Hutchinson.

Hampton, W. (1987) *Local Government and Urban Politics*, New York: Longman.

Harloe, M. (1978) 'The Green Paper on housing policy' in M. Brown and S. Baldwin (eds) *The Year Book of Social Policy in Britain 1977*, London: Routledge & Kegan Paul.

Harris, D. (1987) *Justifying State Welfare: The New Right Versus the Old Left*, Oxford: Blackwell.

Harris, R. and Seldon, A. (1987) *Welfare Without the State: A Quarter Century of Suppressed Public Choice*, London: Institute of Economic Affairs.

Harrow, J. and Willcocks, L. (1990) 'Public service management: activities, initiatives and limits to learning', *Journal of Management Studies* 27: 280–304.

Hartley, O. (1973) 'Local inquiries and council house rents in Scotland 1958–71', *Policy and Politics* 2, 1: 63–78.

Harvey, D. (1973) *Social Justice and the City*, London: Edward Arnold.

—— (1982) *The Limits to Capital*, Oxford: Basil Blackwell.

Heald, D. (1983) *Public Expenditure*, Oxford: Martin Robertson.

Henderson, J. and Karn, V. (1984) 'Race, class and the allocation of public housing in Britain', *Urban Studies* 21: 115–28.

—— (1987) *Race, Class and State Housing: Inequality and the Allocation of Public Housing*, Aldershot: Gower.

Henney, A. (1985) *Trust the Tenant: Devolving Municipal Housing*, Centre for Policy Studies Policy Study no. 68, London: Centre for Policy Studies.

Hills, J. (1987) 'What happened to spending on the welfare state?' in A. Walker and C. Walker (eds) *The Growing Divide: A Social Audit 1979–1987*, London: Child Poverty Action Group.

—— (1990) *The State of Welfare: The Welfare State in Britain since 1974*, Oxford: Oxford University Press.

Hills, J. (1991) *Unravelling Housing Finance: Subsidies, Benefits and Taxation*, Oxford: Oxford University Press.

Hills, J., Berthoud, R. and Kemp, P. (1990) *The Future of Housing Subsidies*, London: Policy Studies Institute.

HMSO (1971) *Fair Deal for Housing*, Cmnd 4728, London: HMSO.

—— (1979) *The Government's Expenditure Plans 1980-81* Cmnd 7746, London: HMSO.

—— (1987) *Housing: The Government's Proposals*, Cmnd 214, London: HMSO.

Hobsbawm, E. (1969) *Industry and Empire*, London: Penguin Books edn.

Holmans, A. (1987) *Housing Policy in Britain: a History*, London: Croom Helm.

Hoppe, M. (1983) 'Direct labour organisations' in D. Anderson and D. Marsland (eds) *Home Truths*, London: Social Affairs Unit.

Houlihan, B. (1983) 'The professionalisation of housing policy-making: the impact of Housing Investment Programmes and professionals', *Public Administration Bulletin* 41.

Howard, E. (1902) *Garden Cities of Tomorrow*, London: Faber, 1965 edn.

Hughes, G.A. and McCormick, B. (1981) 'Do council housing policies reduce migration?' *Economic Journal* 91: 919-37.

Inquiry into British Housing (1985) *Report*, London: National Federation of Housing Associations.

—— (1986) *Supplement*, London: National Federation of Housing Associations.

—— (1990) *Information Notes*, York: Joseph Rowntree Foundation.

—— (1991) *Second Report*, York: Joseph Rowntree Foundation.

Institute of Economic Affairs (IEA) (1961) *Radical Reaction: Essays in Competition and Affluence*, London: Hutchinson.

Institute of Housing (1992a) *Annual Report, 1991/2*, London: Institute of Housing.

—— (1992b) *A Radical Consensus*, London: Institute of Housing.

Institute of Housing/Royal Institute of British Architects (RIBA) (1984) *Homes for the Future*, London: IoH/RIBA.

Institute of Housing/Tenants' Participation Advisory Service (TPAS) (1989) *Tenant Participation in Housing Management*, London: Institute of Housing/TPAS.

Jacobs, S. (1985) 'Race, empire and the welfare state: council housing and racism', *Critical Social Policy* 5: 6-28.

Jamous, H. and Peloille, B. (1970) 'Changes in the French university system' in J.A. Jackson (ed.) *Professions and Professionalisation*, Cambridge: Cambridge University Press.

Jessop, B., Bonnett, K., Bromley, S. and Ling, T. (1988) *Thatcherism: A Tale of Two Nations*, Oxford: Polity Press.

Johnson, J.H., Salt, J. and Wood, P.A. (1974) *Housing and the Migration of Labour in England and Wales*, Farnborough: Saxon House.

Jowell, R., Witherspoon, T. and Brock, R. (1986) *British Social Attitudes: Third Report*, Social and Community Planning Research, London: Gower.

Karn, V. (1977) 'The newest profession', *Roof* November: 177-9.

Kavanagh, D., (1987) *Thatcherism and British Politics: The End of Consensus?*, Oxford: Oxford University Press.

Kemeny, J. (1988) 'Defining housing reality: ideological hegemony and power in housing research', *Housing Studies* 3, 4: 205-18.

Kemp, P. (1987) 'Some aspects of housing consumption in late nineteenth century England and Wales', *Housing Studies* 2, 1: 3-16.

Kemp, P. and Williams, P. (1987) 'Housing management; a contested history?', Paper presented at the British Sociological Association Study Group, Sociology and the Environment.

Kirby, K., Finch, H. and Wood, D. (1987) *The Organisation of Housing Management in English Local Authorities*, London: Department of the Environment.

Kleinman, M. (1991) *Housing and Urban Policies in Europe: Towards A New Consensus*, Paper to Housing Studies Association Conference, York, England, Mimeo.

Laffin, M. (1986) *Professionalism and Policy: the Role of the Professions in the Central-Local Government Relationship*, Aldershot: Gower.

Lambert, J., Paris, C. and Blackaby, B. (1978) *Housing Policy and the State*, London: Macmillan.

Lansley, S. (1979) *Housing and Public Policy*, London: Croom Helm.

Lee, P. and Raban, C. (1988) *Welfare Theory and Social Policy: Reform or Revolution*, London: Sage Publications.

Leeds City Council (1948) *Housing Annual Report 1947–48*, Leeds: Leeds City Council.

Le Grand, J. (1982) *The Strategy of Equality: Redistribution and the Social Services*, London: Allen & Unwin.

—— (1990) *Quasi Markets and Social Policy*, Bristol: School for Advanced Urban Studies.

Le Grand, J. and Goodwin, R.E. (eds) (1987) *Not Only the Poor: The Middle Classes and the Welfare State*, London: Allen & Unwin.

Le Grand, J. and Robinson, R. (eds) (1984) *Privatisation and the Welfare State*, London: Allen & Unwin.

Levitas, R. (ed) (1986) *The Ideology of the New Right*, Cambridge: Polity Press.

Levitt, M.S. and Joyce, M.A.S. (1987) *The Growth and Efficiency of Public Spending*, Cambridge: Cambridge University Press.

Lewis, J. and Foord, J. (1984) 'New towns and new gender relations in old industrial regions: women's employment in Peterlee and East Kilbride', *Built Environment* 10, 1: 42–52.

Lipman, A. and Harris, H. (1980a) 'Social symbolism and space usage in daily life', *Sociological Review* 28, 2: 415–28.

—— (1980b) 'Environmental psychology – sterile research enterprise', *Built Environment* 6: 68–74.

—— (1988) 'Dystopian aesthetics – a refusal from "nowhere"' in N. Teymur, T. Markus and T. Woolley (eds) *Rehumanising Housing*, London: Butterworth.

Local Government Board (1918) *Report of the Committee appointed to consider questions of building construction in connection with the provision of dwellings for the working class, etc.*, Cmnd. 9191 (The Tudor Walters Report).

Lowe, S. (1986) *Urban Social Movements: the City After Castells*, London: Macmillan.

Lowe, S. and Hughes, D. (eds) (1991) *A New Century of Social Housing*, Leicester: Leicester University Press.

Lukes, S. (1974) *Power: a Radical View*, London: Macmillan.

McCarthy, M. (ed.) (1989) *The New Politics of Welfare: An Agenda for the 1990s?*, London: Macmillan.

McCrory, M. (1990) *Loaded Dice: the Struggle for Control Over Housing Investment and the Image of Council Housing in Leicester*, unpublished dissertation submitted for the Postgraduate Diploma in Housing Administration, Sheffield City Polytechnic.

MacDonald, A. (1986) *The Weller Way*, London: Faber & Faber.

Macmillan, H. (1969) *Tides of Fortune 1945–1955*, London: Macmillan.

Macpherson, C.B. (1978) *Property: Mainstream and Critical Positions*, Oxford: Blackwell.

Madigan, R. (1988) 'A new generation of home owners?', discussion paper, Centre for Housing Research, University of Glasgow.

Mainwaring, R. (1987) *The Walsall Experience – A Study of the Decentralisation of Walsall's Housing Services*, Estate Action/Department of the Environment, London: HMSO.

Malpass, P. (1975) 'Professionalism and the role of the architect in local authority housing', *RIBA Journal* June: 6–29.

—— (1988) 'Utopia in context: class and the restructuring of the housing market in the twentieth century' in N. Teymur, T. Markus and T. Woolley (eds), *Rehumanising Housing*, London: Butterworth.

—— (1990) *Reshaping Housing Policy: Subsidies, Rents and Residualisation*, London: Routledge.

—— (1993) 'Housing policy and the housing system since 1979' in P. Malpass and R. Means (eds) *Implementing Housing Policy*, London: Open University Press.

Malpass, P and Murie, A. (1982) *Housing Policy and Practice*, 1st edn, London: Macmillan.

—— (1987) *Housing Policy and Practice*, 2nd edn, London: Macmillan.

—— (1990) *Housing Policy and Practice*, 3rd edn, London: Macmillan.

Marquand, D. (1988) 'The paradoxes of Thatcherism' in Skidelsky, R. (ed.) *Thatcherism*, Oxford: Blackwell, pp. 159–72.

Marsh, C. (1982) *The Survey Method: the Contribution of Surveys to Sociological Explanation*, London: Allen & Unwin.

Marsh, D. and Rhodes, R.A.W. (1992) *Implementing Thatcherite Policies: Audit of an Era*, Buckingham: Open University Press.

Marwick, A. (1990) *British Society Since 1945*, 2nd edn, Harmondsworth: Penguin.

Massey, D. (1984) *Spatial Divisions of Labour*, London: Macmillan.

Matrix (1984) *Making Space: Women and the Man-Made Environment*, London: Pluto Press.

Melling, J. (1980) Introduction to J. Melling (ed.) *Housing, Social Policy and the State*, London: Croom Helm.

Mellor, J.R. (1977) *Urban Sociology in an Urbanised Society*, London: Routledge & Kegan Paul.

Merrett, S. (1979) *State Housing in Britain*, London: Routledge & Kegan Paul.

Merrett, S. with Gray, F. (1982) *Owner-Occupation in Britain*, London: Routledge & Kegan Paul.

Minford, P. (1984) 'State expenditure: a study in waste', *Economic Affairs* April–June.

Minford, P., Peel, M. and Ashton, P. (1987) *The Housing Morass*, Hobart Paper 25, London: Institute of Economic Affairs.

Ministry of Housing and Local Government (MHLG) (1954) *Housing: Slum Clearance*, Circular 30/54, London: HMSO.

—— (1961) *Homes for Today and Tomorrow* (the Parker Morris Report), London: HMSO.

—— (1965a) *Report of the Committee on Housing in Greater London* (The Milner Holland Report), Cmnd 2605, London: HMSO.

—— (1965b) *The Housing Programme 1965 to 1970*, Cmnd 2838, London: HMSO.

Mishra, R. (1984) *The Welfare State in Crisis: Social Thought and Social Change*, Brighton, Sussex: Wheatsheaf.

Moorhouse, B., Wilson, M. and Chamberlain, C. (1972) 'Rent strikes – direct action and the working class', *The Socialist Register:* 133–56.

MORI (1986) *Attitudes to Local Authorities and their Services*, research study conducted for the Audit Commission, May 1986.

Morris, J. and Winn, M. (1990) *Housing and Social Inequality*, London: Hilary Shipman.

Muellbauer, J. (1990) *The Great British Housing Disaster and Economic Policy*, Institute of Public Policy Research Economic Report Number 5, London: Institute of Public Policy Research.

Murie, A. (1983) *Housing Inequality and Deprivation*, London: Heinemann Educational.

National Consumer Council (1976) *Tenancy Agreements*, London: National Consumer Council.

—— (1983) *Measuring the Performance of Local Authorities in England and Wales – Some Consumer Principles*, London: National Consumer Council.

National Federation of Housing Associations (NFHA) (1992) *Core Quarterly Bulletin No. 9*, London: National Federation of Housing Associations.

Newton, J. (1991) *All in One Place: The British Housing Story 1970–1990*, London: Catholic Housing Aid Society.

Niskanen, W. (1973) *Bureaucracy: Servant or Master? Lessons from America*, London: Institute of Economic Affairs.

Offer, A. (1981) *Property and Politics 1870-1914: Landownership, Law, Ideology and Urban Development in England*, Cambridge: Cambridge University Press.

OPCS (1983) *Recently Moving Households: A Follow-up to the 1978 National Dwelling and Housing Survey*, London: HMSO.

Orwell, G. (1937) *The Road to Wigan Pier*, London: Penguin Books edn.

—— (1970) *Collected Essays, Journalism and Letters of George Orwell*, vol. 2, Harmondsworth: Penguin Books edn.

Pahl, R. (1970) *Patterns of Urban Life*, London: Longman.

—— (1975) *Whose City?*, 2nd edn, London: Penguin Books.

Papadakis, E. and Taylor-Gooby, P. (1987) *The Private Provision of Public Welfare: State, Market and Community*, London: Wheatsheaf.

Parker, R.A. (1971) *The Housing Finance Act and Council Tenants*, London: Child Poverty Action Group.

Parker, T. (1983) *The People of Providence: a Housing Estate and Some of its Inhabitants*, London: Hutchinson.

Patten, J. (1987) 'Housing – room for a new view', *Guardian* 30 January 1987.

Pawley, M. (1971) *Architecture Versus Housing*, London: Studio Vista.

—— (1986) 'The incredible shrinking home', *New Society* 77, 1230: 12–15.

Pelling, H. (1984) *The Labour Governments 1945–51*, London: Macmillan.

Pennance, F.G. (1969) *Housing Market: Analysis and Policy*, London: Institute of Economic Affairs.

Peters, T. and Waterman, R. (1982) *In Search of Excellence*, New York: Harper & Row.

Phillips, D. (1985) *What Price Equality?*, London: Greater London Council.

Piachaud, D. (1987) 'The growth of poverty' in A. Walker and C. Walker (eds) *The Growing Divide: A Social Audit 1979–87*, London: Child Poverty Action Group.

Pickup, L. (1984) 'Women's gender-role and its influence on travel behaviour', *Built Environment* 10, 1: 60–8.

252   *Bibliography*

Pickup, L. (1988) 'Hard to get around: a study of women's travel mobility' in J. Little, L. Peake and P. Richardson (eds) *Women in Cities: Gender and the Urban Environment*, London: Macmillan.

Pickvance, C. (1976) 'On the study of urban social movements' in C. Pickvance (ed.) *Urban Sociology: Critical Essays*, London: Tavistock.

—— (1977) 'From "social base" to "social force": some analytical issues in the study of urban protest' in M. Harloe (ed.) *Captive Cities*, London: John Wiley.

—— (1982) 'The state and collective consumption', Unit 24, D202, *Urban Change and Conflict*, Open University, Milton Keynes: the Open University Press.

Pierson, C. (1991) *Beyond the Welfare State?* Cambridge: Polity Press.

Power, A. (1982) *Priority Estates Project 1982: Improving Problem Council Estates*, London: Department of the Environment.

—— (1987) *Property Before People: The Management of Twentieth Century Housing*, London: Allen & Unwin.

Prentice, R. (1983) 'Who is hurt by "cuts" in public expenditure' in D. Anderson and D. Marsland (eds) *Home Truths*, London: Social Affairs Unit.

Quirk, B. (1982) 'Local authority housing: the consumer's view', *Housing Review* November–December: 199–201.

Rapoport, A. (1977) *Human Aspects of Urban Form*, Oxford: Pergamon Press.

—— (1982) *The Meaning of the Built Environment*, London: Sage Publications.

Ravetz, A. (1974) 'From working class tenement to modern flat: local authorities and multi-storey housing between the wars' in A. Sutcliffe (ed.) *Multi-Storey Living: the British Working Class Experience*, London: Croom Helm.

—— (1980) *Remaking Cities: Contradictions of the Recent Urban Environment*, London: Croom Helm.

—— (1989) 'A view from the interior' in J. Attfield and P. Kirkham (eds), *A View from the Interior: Feminism, Women and Design*, London: The Women's Press.

Reade, E. (1982) 'Residential decay, household movement and class structure', *Policy and Politics* 10: 27–45.

Rees, A.M. (ed.) (1985) *T.H. Marshall's Social Policy in the Twentieth Century*, London: Hutchinson.

Rees, G. and Lambert, J. (1985) *Cities in Crisis: the Political Economy of Urban Development in Post-War Britain*, London: Edward Arnold.

Reeve, A. (1986) *Property*, London: Macmillan.

Richardson, H.W. (1967) *Economic Recovery in Britain, 1932–39*, London: Weidenfeld & Nicolson.

Richardson, H.W. and Aldcroft, D.H. (1968) *Building in the British Economy Between the Wars*, University of Glasgow Social and Economic Studies, London: Allen & Unwin.

Riddell, P. (1983) *The Thatcher Government*, Oxford: Martin Robertson.

Robbins, M. (1977) *Liberty and Equality*, IEA Occasional Paper No. 52, London: Institute of Economic Affairs.

Robinson, I. (1983) 'Subsidising stigma: social consequences of council housing policies' in D. Anderson and D. Marsland (eds) *Home Truths*, London: Social Affairs Unit.

Robinson, R. (1986) 'Restructuring the welfare state: an analysis of public expenditure 1979/80-1984/85', *Journal of Social Policy* 15: 1–21.

Robinson, V. (1980) 'Asians and council housing', *Urban Studies* 17: 323–31.

Ross, S. (1985) *Discrimination By Design*, unpublished dissertation for the degree of

BA Housing Studies, School of Urban and Regional Studies, Sheffield City Polytechnic.

Royal Institute of British Architects (RIBA) (1989) *Housing in Crisis: a Policy Statement*, London: Royal Institute of British Architects.

Royal Institution of Chartered Surveyors (RICS) (1987) *Housing – The Next Decade*, London: Royal Institution of Chartered Surveyors.

—— (1991) *Housing the Nation: Choice, Access and Priorities*, London: Royal Institution of Chartered Surveyors.

Ryan, A. (1984) *Property and Political Theory*, Oxford: Blackwell.

Ryder, R. (1984) 'Council house building in County Durham, 1900-39: the local implementation of national policy' in M. Daunton (ed.) *Councillors and Tenants: Local Authority Housing in English Cities, 1919–39*, Leicester: Leicester University Press.

Sarre, P., Phillips, D. and Skellington, R. (1989) *Ethnic Minority Housing: Explanations and Policies*, Aldershot: Avebury Gower.

Satsangi, M. (1992) 'Markets and quasi-markets in British public service: does the customer gain?', Paper to Housing Studies Association Conference, *Management and Change in Social Housing*, University of York, Mimeo.

Saunders, P. (1979) *Urban Politics: a Sociological Interpretation*, London: Hutchinson.

—— (1981) *Social Theory and the Urban Question*, 1st edn, London: Hutchinson.

—— (1984a) 'Beyond housing classes: the sociological significance of private property rights in means of consumption', *International Journal of Urban and Regional Research* 8, 2: 202–25.

—— (1984b) 'Rethinking local politics' in M. Boddy and C. Fudge (eds) *Local Socialism?*, London: Macmillan.

—— (1986) *Social Theory and the Urban Question*, 2nd edn, London: Hutchinson.

—— (1990) *A Nation of Home Owners*, London: Unwin Hyman.

School for Advanced Urban Studies (1989) *The Effectiveness of Housing Management in Wales*, Bristol: School for Advanced Urban Studies/Welsh Office.

Seabrook, J. (1971) *City Close-Up*, Harmondsworth: Penguin Books.

—— (1984) *The Idea of Neighbourhood*, London: Pluto Press.

Seldon, A. (1981) *Wither the Welfare State*, London: Institute of Economic Affairs.

Sennett, R. (1970) *The Uses of Disorder: Personal Identity and City Life*, New York: Vintage.

Sennett, R. and Cobb, J. (1976) *The Hidden Injuries of Class*, Cambridge; Cambridge University Press.

Short, J.R. (1982) *Housing in Britain – The Post-War Experience*, London: Methuen.

Shorter, E. (1977) *The Making of the Modern Family*, London: Fontana Books edn.

Singer, H. (1941) 'An index of urban land rents and house rents in England and Wales, 1845–1913', *Econometrica*, vol. 9.

Skidelsky, R. (ed.) (1988) *Thatcherism*, Oxford: Basil Blackwell.

Skinner, D. and Langdon, J. (1974) *The Clay Cross Story*, Nottingham: Spokesman.

Sklair, L. (1975) 'The struggle against the Housing Finance Act' in R. Miliband and J. Saville (eds) *The Socialist Register*, London: Merlin.

Stewart, J. and Clarke, M. (1987) 'P.S.O. – developing the approach', *Local Government Policy Making* 13,4: 23–42.

Stoker, G. (1987) 'Decentralisation and the restructuring of local government in Britain', *Local Government Policy Making* 14,2: 3–11.

—— (1988) *The Politics of Local Government*, London: Macmillan.

Swenarton, M. (1981) *Homes Fit For Heroes: the Politics and Architecture of Early State Housing in Britain*, London: Heinemann.

Tarn, J. (1973) *Five per Cent Philanthropy*, Cambridge: Cambridge University Press.

Taylor-Gooby, P. (1985) *Public Opinion, Ideology and State Welfare*, London: Routledge & Kegan Paul.

—— (1988) 'The future of the British welfare state: public attitudes, citizenship and social policy under the Conservative Governments of the 1980s', *European Sociological Review* 4: 1–19.

—— (1991) *Social Change, Social Welfare and Social Science*, London: Harvester/Wheatsheaf.

Thane, P. (1982) *The Foundations of the Welfare State*, London: Longman.

Titmuss, R. (1968) *Commitment to Welfare*, London: Allen & Unwin.

—— (1974) *Social Policy*, London: Allen & Unwin.

Urban Housing Renewal Unit (1986) *First Annual Report*, London: Department of the Environment.

Urry, J. (1981) 'Localities, regions and social class', *International Journal of Urban and Regional Research* 5, 4: 455–74.

Walker, A. and Walker, C. (eds) (1987) *The Growing Divide: A Social Audit 1979–1987*, London: Child Poverty Action Group.

Walsh, K. and Spencer, K. (1990) *The Quality of Service in Housing Management*, Birmingham: Institute of Local Government Studies.

Ward, C. (1974) *Tenants Take Over*, London: Architectural Press.

—— (1985) *When We Build Again*, London: Pluto Press.

Watson, S. with Austerberry, H. (1986) *Housing and Homelessness: a Feminist Perspective*, London: Routledge & Kegan Paul.

Wellman, D. (1977) *Portrait of White Racism*, Cambridge: Cambridge University Press.

Whitehead, C. (1984) 'Privatisation and housing' in J. Le Grand and R. Robinson (eds) *Privatisation and the Welfare State*, London: Allen & Unwin.

Wicks, M. (1987) *A Future for All. Do We Need a Welfare State?* Harmondsworth: Penguin Press.

Wilding, P. (1972) 'Towards Exchequer subsidies for housing, 1906–1914', *Social and Economic Administration* 6, 1: 3–18.

—— (1982) *Professional Power and Social Welfare*, London: Routledge & Kegan Paul.

Williams, N.J., Sewell, J. and Twine, F. (1986) 'Council house sales and residualisation', *Journal of Social Policy* 15, 3: 273–92.

Williams, P. (1982) 'Restructuring urban managerialism: towards a political economy of urban allocation', *Environment and Planning: A* 14.

Willmott, P. and Murie, A. (1988) *Polarisation and Social Housing*, London: Policy Studies Institute.

Willmott, P. and Young, M. (1960) *Family and Class in a London Suburb*, London: Routledge & Kegan Paul.

Windle, K., Cole, I. and Arnold, P. (1988) *Organising Housing Services on a Small Scale*, Housing Decentralisation Research Project Research Working Paper 1, Department of Urban and Regional Studies, Sheffield: Sheffield City Polytechnic.

Wolmar, C. (1991) 'Tenants' movement', *Roof* 6, 6: 13–15.

Woodward, R. (1991) 'Mobilising opposition: the campaign against Housing Action Trusts in Tower Hamlets', *Housing Studies* 6, 1: 44–56.

Index

268 *Index*